EASTON AREA PUBLIC LIB.
3 1901 00136 598 2

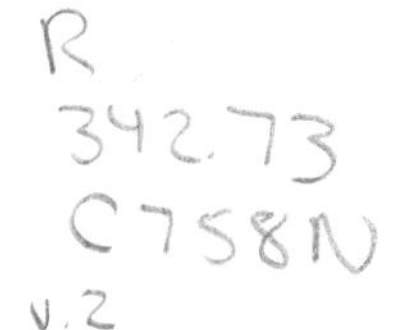

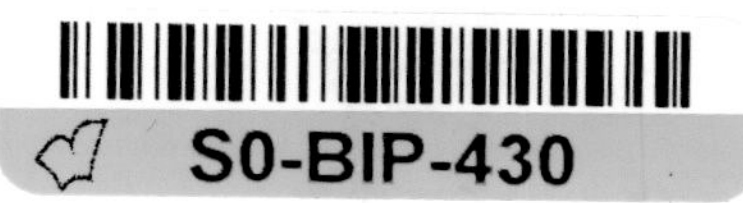
S0-BIP-430

The Constitution *and* Its Amendments

Editorial Board

Editorial and Production Staff

MACMILLAN REFERENCE

Elly Dickason, *Publisher*

THE CONSTITUTION *and* ITS AMENDMENTS

Volume 2

Roger K. Newman
Editor in Chief

MACMILLAN REFERENCE USA
NEW YORK

Macmillan Reference USA
1633 Broadway
New York, NY 10019

Library of Congress Catalog Card Number: 98-8570

Printed in the United States of America

Printing Number
3 4 5 6 7 8 9 10

Library of Congress Cataloging-in-Publication Data
The constitution and its amendments/ Roger K. Newman, editor in chief.

p. cm.

Includes index.

ISBN 0-02-864858-7 (set : alk. paper).—ISBN 0-02-864854-4 (Vol.1 : alk. paper). ISBN 0-02-864855-2 (Vol. 2 : alk. paper)

1. Constitutional amendments–United States–History.

I. Newman, Roger K.

KF4557. C66 1998

342.73'03–98-8570 CIP dc21

This paper meets the requirements of ANSI-NISO Z39.48-1992 (Permanence of Paper).

Contents

Volume 1

Volume 2

Volume 3

Article II (Continued)

The Cabinet

Forrest McDonald

ARTICLE II, SECTION 2, OF THE CONSTITUTION STATES:

The President . . . may require the opinion, in writing, of the principal officers in each of the executive departments upon any subject relating to the duties of their respective offices. . . .

He shall have the power, by and with the advice and consent of the Senate, to . . . appoint . . . all other officers of the United States whose appointments are not herein otherwise provided for. . . .

cabinet a body of advisers, made up of the heads of various governmental departments

Article II, Section 2 of the Constitution contains two provisions that made possible the development of the president's **cabinet**. However, their language (which is given above) does not specifically authorize a cabinet. The first provision gives the president the power to appoint officials, including the heads of the executive departments, with the Senate's approval. The other provision gives the president the power to require, in writing, the opinions of those officials. Although some Framers of the Constitution strongly favored establishing the president's cabinet, most of them believed such a body would make it difficult to learn who was responsible in case of wrongdoing in the government.

George Washington with cabinet members Henry Knox, Alexander Hamilton, Thomas Jefferson, and Edmund Randolph.

The Early Years

In his first two years in office, starting in 1789, President George Washington regularly asked for written opinions from his cabinet. Its officials included Secretary of State Thomas Jefferson, Secretary of the Treasury Alexander Hamilton, Secretary of War John Knox, and Attorney General Edmund Randolph. However, President Washington believed that he did not have the power, under the Constitution, to have them meet with him as advisers. Yet, depending on written opinions from these officials did not work well. These department heads also found that writing reports took up too much time. Besides, President Washington felt that their ideas and opinions were expressed best in talking to him. He even turned to the Supreme Court and members of the Senate to give him advice, but this effort was not successful.

In 1791, the first step was taken toward using the heads of the executive departments as an advisory body. Washington left the capital for a few months. He asked his department heads to meet with Vice President John Adams to help decide minor matters while he was gone. He also asked the group to call him back if serious problems arose that required his personal attention.

Two years later, in 1793, when a crisis developed in America's relations with France, Washington began to ask the department heads to meet with him on a regular basis. Because of the bitter disagreements between Jefferson and Hamilton, these meetings often were stormy. But American presidents have held meetings with their cabinets ever since.

This informal meeting of President George Bush's cabinet suggests its modest role. Only one cabinet member, Secretary of State James Baker (on Bush's right), was a key Presidential adviser.

Development of the Cabinet

President John Adams, Washington's successor in 1797, kept most of Washington's cabinet, except Jefferson and Hamilton, who had resigned. For a while, Adams seemed to allow the members of the cabinet to run the federal government. Then in 1800, after becoming convinced that they were disloyal, Adams fired them. However, he all but ignored the men he chose to replace these officials.

The Constitution does not empower the president to remove the cabinet officials he appoints. Even so, it was generally accepted that the president was entitled to do this if he wished. Only once, under the 1867 Tenure of Office Act, has Congress required the Senate's approval of the president's removing his cabinet appointees—and that act was **repealed** in 1887.

repeal revoke or cancel

The idea of a "Kitchen Cabinet" started when President Andrew Jackson met with a group of friends and advisers in the White House kitchen. Later administrations confirmed that the official cabinet lacked real power. Under President Clinton, for example, the cabinet all but disappeared as an advisory body. Clinton held just six formal cabinet meetings during his first year in office. He all but abandoned formal cabinet meetings entirely by 1995. Meetings of department heads and the president's senior staff continued to be held every few weeks. However, President Clinton did not attend, and the White House chief of staff presided instead. When Clinton wanted advice, he turned to advisers outside his cabinet.

Presidents and Their Cabinets

Presidents have dealt with their cabinets in various ways. Jefferson often treated his cabinet as if it were a small committee, made up of Secretary of State James Madison, Secretary of the Treasury Albert Gallatin, and himself. Andrew Jackson tended to bypass the cabinet. Instead, Jackson relied on a "Kitchen Cabinet" made up of his personal friends, not the heads of the executive departments. Most active, strong-willed presidents, such as Abraham Lincoln, Theodore Roosevelt, Woodrow Wilson, and Franklin Roosevelt (who called his private advisers a "brain trust"), followed Jackson's example. Less activist presidents have depended much more on their cabinet.

Under no president has the cabinet acted as an executive council with its own powers. The president, not the cabinet, makes all final executive decisions. According to a famous story, Lincoln asked his cabinet members to vote on an issue he himself opposed. Every member of the cabinet

In 1965, economist and civil rights activist Robert C. Weaver was named Secretary of Housing and Urban Development in the Johnson administration. He was the first African-American cabinet member.

voted "aye" (yes). Then Lincoln firmly declared: "There are seven 'ayes' and one 'nay' (no). The 'nays' have it."

Despite its limited power, until the 1920s the cabinet exercised enough power that each executive department worked out its budget with Congress and was responsible to Congress for its spending. As a result, until then the nation's government operated without a federal budget. In practice, the executive branch was administered largely independently of the president.

During the nineteenth century, all members of the cabinet were white male Americans, and most of them were Protestants. Early in the twentieth century, however, several Catholics and Jews were appointed to the president's cabinet. In 1933, President Franklin Roosevelt selected the first woman cabinet member, Secretary of Labor Frances Perkins. In 1965, under President Lyndon Johnson, Robert Weaver was named Secretary of Housing and Urban Development, becoming the first African-American cabinet member. The appointment of women and minorities to cabinet posts has since become routine.

The Cabinet Increases in Size

The number of cabinet positions grew as new executive departments were established to meet the nation's changing needs. In 1798, the Department of the Navy was created as a separate department from the Department of War. (Both departments became part of the Department of Defense in 1947.) The Department of the Interior was established in 1849; the Department of Agriculture, in 1889. The nation became more industrialized through the latter 1800s, and Congress created the Department of Commerce and Labor in 1903. This executive department became two separate departments in 1913. The Department of Health, Education and Welfare was set up by Congress in 1953. In 1979, it was divided into the Department of Health and Human Services, and the Department of Education. The Department of Housing and Urban Development was created in 1965. The Department of Transportation was established in 1966, the Department of Energy in 1977, and the Department of Veterans Affairs in 1988. The cabinet lost one member, the Postmaster General, when the United States Postal Service was made a private organization in 1970.

The Cabinet at the End of the Twentieth Century

Since World War II, the cabinet's role has declined in importance. Many executive departments have developed close ties with the industries and groups they were set up to regulate, as well as with related congressional committees. The work of department heads has become very specialized. As a result, they rarely have the broad knowledge and viewpoint needed to contribute ideas to general discussions of policy. It is not surprising that presidents increasingly depend on their White House staff and agencies in the Executive Office of the President, especially the National Economic Council, the Office of Management and Budget, and the National Security Council.

The Pardon Power

David Gray Adler

militia a part-time army made up of ordinary citizens

impeachment method by which the House of Representatives may charge the nation's highest-ranking officials, including the president, with wrongdoing; following impeachment, if the officials are found guilty of the charges, the Senate then may try them and remove them from office

ARTICLE II, SECTION 2, CLAUSE 1, OF THE CONSTITUTION STATES

The President shall be Commander in Chief of the Army and Navy of the United States, and of the ***Militia*** *of the several States, when called into actual Service of the United States; he may require the Opinion, in writing, of the principal Officer in each of the executive Departments, upon any subject relating to the Duties of their respective Offices, and he shall have Power to Grant Reprieves and Pardons for Offenses against the United States, except in Cases of* ***Impeachment****.*

The authority to issue pardons is the broadest and most sensitive of the president's powers. The pardon power is the authority to prevent the punishment of a person who has committed an offense against the United States. A presidential pardon may be granted before or after the person's trial. Because a presidential pardon may be granted for almost any offense against the United States, except in cases of impeachment, the pardon power is practically unlimited in its scope. The exception of impeachment bars the president from pardoning a person who is the subject of an impeachment inquiry. Without the ban, a president might destroy the impeachment power of Congress, which the Framers believed might be necessary to protect the nation from a tyrannical chief executive.

The Views of the Framers

The pardon power always has carried with it a great potential for abuse. The Framers were keenly aware of the arbitrary ways that England's monarchs used this power. Indeed, the roots of the pardon power go back to one of the royal privileges of English kings. Despite this background, the Framers decided to give the president a broad pardon power to be used as seemed necessary to correct miscarriages of justice and to restore tranquility after a rebellion. Creating the pardon power showed that the Framers recognized the possibility of judicial errors and the need to restore justice in such cases.

Although the Framers understood the pardon power as a final source of justice, they faced the problem of where this power should be placed in government. While they feared a powerful executive, they nevertheless saw the benefits of giving this power to the president. Pardons in cases of rebellion would have to be timely, the Framers reasoned, or the opportunity to end the violence by granting them might quickly pass. If a pardon gave the rebels an opportunity to put down their weapons and rejoin society without fear of punishment, the whole nation would benefit. Since Congress was not in session throughout the year, this meant that the president would be granted the authority.

This decision was not an easy one to make. What would happen if the president abused the power by pardoning his friends and supporters for his own reasons? Worse still, what would happen if the president were involved in some act of treason? Might the president then pardon the people he was connected with in order to protect himself?

Alexander Hamilton explained the Framers' reasoning in *The Federalist*, No. 74. He argued that the president was unlikely to abuse the pardon power, because the people would be carefully examining how the president was using it. Moreover, if the president were involved in any act of treason, he could be impeached and prosecuted. Knowing that Congress's power of impeachment would curb any presidential effort to shield himself and his friends and supporters in any act of treason satisfied the Framers. They would have been further encouraged had they known that a future Supreme Court would rule that presidential abuse of the pardon power is subject to judicial review.

treason the offense of attempting to overthrow the government

prosecute to begin and carry on a lawsuit; bring legal action against

Pardons in American History

Presidents have granted pardons for various offenses since the earliest days of the Republic. George Washington in 1795 pardoned those who had taken part in the Whiskey Rebellion. Presidential pardons have since been given to pirates who assisted the United States in military actions, persons who took part in rebellions, deserters in wartime, federal officials, and polygamists, among others. Occasional pardons, such as those of Jefferson Davis and Confederate soldiers and President Richard Nixon, have stirred up intense controversy and heightened public interest in the power. Yet in practice, a great many pardons have been granted with little publicity to federal prisoners who are old and near death.

On January 21, 1977, one day after being inaugurated, President Jimmy Carter pardoned nearly all Vietnam-era draft evaders. This "full, complete and unconditional pardon" applied to all persons whether or not they had been formally convicted. The only exceptions were military deserters and persons who had violated the draft laws through force or violence. Americans who had left the country to avoid the draft and had become citizens of another country were permitted to return and reapply for citizenship without threat of prosecution. Overall, about ten thousand persons were pardoned.

The Pardon of President Nixon

The most controversial presidential pardon was the one President Gerald Ford granted to Richard Nixon on September 8, 1974, for offenses against the United States. Americans had not expected this bombshell, and Ford may have paid a high price for his action: public opinion polls seemed to suggest that it cost him the 1976 presidential election. So it is clear that public opinion, too, exercises an important check on the pardon power. The Nixon pardon renewed discussion of a proposed constitutional amendment to permit Congress to veto a pardon to prevent an abuse of power. But, as in the case of a similar proposal made at the Constitutional Convention of 1787, this idea did not get much support. The pardon power thus remains the broadest of the presidential powers and perhaps the one most subject to abuse.

veto refuse to sign a bill into law

ARTICLE II—The Executive Branch

A political cartoon satirizes the presidential pardon granted to Richard M. Nixon by Gerald Ford after the Watergate scandal. While other Watergate conspirators are shown serving their sentence, former President Nixon is seen enjoying a luxurious lifestyle.

The Treaty Power

Jane E. Stromseth

ARTICLE II, SECTION 2, CLAUSE 2, OF THE CONSTITUTION STATES

He [the president] shall have Power, by and with the Advice and Consent of the Senate, to make ***Treaties****, provided two-thirds of the Senators present concur . . .*

treaty binding international agreement

The ability to make treaties with foreign countries is a vital power of the national government. The Constitution grants this power to the president and the Senate. The Framers wanted to ensure that treaties made by the president and approved by the Senate would be honored by all the states of the Union. So they provided in Article VI, Section 2, that **ratified** treaties, like the Constitution and federal laws, are "the **supreme** law of the land."

ratify to formally approve a document, thereby making it legal

supreme having the highest authority

The Framers and the Treaty Power

The Framers decided to give the power to make treaties to the president and the Senate for many reasons. The **Articles of Confederation** had granted Congress the treaty power if nine of the thirteen states agreed. In the Constitution, the Framers chose the president to make treaties because they believed that a single person could act more quickly and effectively in conducting relations with other nations and so gain their respect. Also, as the one individual elected by all the voters of the United States, the president would represent the interests of the entire country.

Articles of Confederation the first constitution of the thirteen original United States; in effect 1781–1789

The Framers gave the Senate a role in the treaty power in order to take into account the concerns of the different states that the senators represented. By requiring that two-thirds of the senators present agree to a treaty, the Constitution ensured that such commitments would not be made lightly but would have broad national support. The Senate's approval also acted as a check on the president, so that one lone executive could not make the nation's treaty commitments.

Some Framers wanted to include the House of Representatives in the treaty-making process. They felt that this was especially necessary in treaties dealing with trade because Congress as a whole had the authority to regulate commerce with other countries. But in the end the Framers excluded the House from treaty-making because they feared that its size and the turnover of its members every two years would make it difficult for it to act in secrecy or to gain the necessary expertise in foreign affairs. They decided that the president and the Senate together would be the nation's most effective treaty makers.

The Treaty Process

Making, enacting and enforcing treaties involves all three branches of government.

The president's role. The president's power to make treaties includes deciding which treaties to **negotiate**, appointing and instructing the negotiators, and reviewing proposed treaties and deciding whether to submit them to the Senate for approval. The Framers probably expected that

negotiate to deal or bargain with another, as in the preparation of a treaty or contract

Soviet President Leonid Brezhnev and U.S. President Jimmy Carter sign the strategic arms limitation treaty (SALT II), Vienna, Austria, June 18, 1979.

the Senate would give its advice throughout the negotiating process. But presidents quickly found that this idea was not workable. Instead, presidents have consulted with Senate leaders or with members of the Senate Foreign Relations Committee when negotiating treaties.

Treaties in the Senate. The whole Senate is consulted after a treaty has been negotiated, and it has to decide whether to consent to it. The Senate has the power to approve or reject a treaty. It can also withhold its approval while the president negotiates certain changes that the Senate requests. The Senate has rejected few treaties outright, but starting in the mid-1970s, it approved many treaties subject to reservations and understandings. Once the Senate approves a treaty, the president makes the final decision whether to ratify it.

Treaties in the courts. A ratified treaty is a legal obligation between nations. As the "supreme law of the land," it may be enforced in U.S. courts. "Self-executing" treaties create these obligations on their own. Other treaties, which are not self-executing, promise to pass laws to achieve the treaties' goals. Once these laws are passed, they too become enforceable in U.S. courts.

Treaties in American History

Throughout the nation's history, presidents have made treaties with other nations on a great variety of subjects, including security alliances, control of conventional and nuclear weapons, trade, investment, the law of the sea, and human rights. Article II of the Constitution puts no limit on the subject matter or type of treaty the president may make with the Senate's consent.

statute a law enacted by the legislative branch of governmen

Like federal statutes, treaties must not violate the Constitution, including the Bill of Rights. As Supreme Court Justice Hugo Black wrote

in *Reid* v. *Covert* (1957), "[t]he prohibitions of the Constitution were designed to apply to all branches of the National Government and they cannot be nullified by the Executive or by the Executive and the Senate combined." Supporters of states' rights have at times raised concerns that treaties, and laws made to carry them out, may violate the reserved powers of the states under the Tenth Amendment. But the Supreme Court rejected such claims in *Missouri* v. *Holland* (1920), saying that the Constitution gives the treaty power to the national government and that Congress does not violate the Tenth Amendment when it passes a law necessary and proper to implement a valid treaty.

The Versailles Treaty of 1919, named after the city outside Paris, was the main document that ended World War I. It called for the creation of the League of Nations, forced Germany to pay compensation to victorious nations, placed limits on German armed forces, and made many territorial changes. President Woodrow Wilson was the leading American negotiator and sponsor. He signed the treaty, calling the territorial boundaries "the heart of the covenant" while isolationists attacked them. While battling for Senate ratification, Wilson suffered a stroke and never recovered. The Senate refused to ratify the treaty.

Other Forms of International Agreements

Since the Constitution took effect, presidents have made hundreds of treaties with the Senate's consent. But agreements with other countries can also be made in other ways. Most international agreements made by the United States since World War II have not been treaties. Instead, they have been congressional-executive agreements. These agreements are negotiated by the president and approved by a simple majority in both the Senate and the House of Representatives. In the years after World War II, officials and scholars have debated whether congressional-executive agreements are interchangeable with treaties, since the Constitution does not expressly provide for them.

Modern Treaties

In the last decades of the twentieth century, the president, Congress, and the courts generally regarded congressional-executive agreements as comparable to treaties in their legal validity and, therefore, as "the supreme law of the land." These agreements have become favored for settling trade issues, perhaps recognizing, as some Framers did, that Congress's power to regulate foreign commerce gives the House of Representatives a central role in trade matters.

Most agreements affecting national security, such as alliances with other nations and those involving arms control, are still generally concluded as treaties. Examples include the North Atlantic Treaty Organization (NATO), made in 1949, the United Nations Charter (1945), and numerous nuclear weapons control treaties.

authority the power to grant legal allowance

International agreements can also be concluded by the president acting alone under the chief executive's constitutional authority. The courts have upheld the validity of these "sole executive agreements," although the extent of the president's authority has not been defined. Executive agreements have been used in settling legal claims with other nations.

In determining what form an international agreement should take, the president considers a variety of factors, including the views of members of Congress and past practices. The president must keep Congress informed of the international commitments of the United States whatever their form—even oral promises. A law called the Case Act requires the president to report all international agreements to Congress in writing within sixty days after they take effect.

Although less than 10 percent of the international agreements entered into by the United States since 1939 have been treaties approved by two-thirds of the senators voting on them, the treaty power remains an important national power. It has been critical in advancing key American interests and foreign-policy goals.

Appointments

William Lasser

treaty binding international agreement

nominate to propose that a person be appointed to an office

vest to grant with particular authority, property, and rights

ARTICLE II, SECTION 2, CLAUSE 2, OF THE CONSTITUTION STATES

He [the president] shall have Power, by and with the Advice and Consent of the Senate, to make ***Treaties,*** *provided two-thirds of the Senators present concur; and he shall* ***nominate,*** *and by and with the Advice and Consent of the Senate, shall appoint Ambassadors, other public Ministers and Consuls, Judges of the Supreme Court, and all other Officers of the United States, whose Appointments are not herein otherwise provided for, and which shall be established by Law; but the Congress may by Law* ***vest*** *the Appointment of such inferior Officers, as they think proper, in the President alone, in the Courts of Law, or in the Heads of Departments.*

The Constitution gives the president the authority to appoint ambassadors, Supreme Court justices, and all other officers of the United States, with the approval of the Senate. Congress, however, may vest the power to appoint officers of lesser standing in the president alone, in the heads of departments, or in the courts of law. Excluding military officers and certain other routine appointments, approximately 1,500 positions in the national government must be confirmed by the Senate. The Constitution also gives the president the authority to "fill up all vacancies that may happen during the recess of the Senate."

confirm to approve formally

What the Framers Wanted

The Constitutional Convention's decision to divide the responsibility for the appointment of federal officials between the president and the Senate was a compromise. Many delegates, including several leading Federalists, wanted to follow the British practice of leaving the power of appointment to the executive branch alone. Other delegates, including several leading Anti-Federalists, feared the expansion of executive power and sought to give this power to Congress or to the Senate. For some months it appeared that the Anti-Federalists would prevail. But at the last minute the delegates decided to divide the power between the president and the Senate.

compromise an agreement or settlement reached when each side gives up some demands or yields on others

Federalist advocating a strong central government of separate states and the adoption of the U.S. Constitution

Anti-Federalist member of the group opposing the adoption of the U.S. Constitution; favored states' rights and argued successfully for the Bill of Rights

The wording of the Constitution allows the president to "nominate" officers, and to appoint them after receiving the "advice and consent" of the Senate. But the Constitution has never been interpreted to require the president to seek the Senate's "advice." According to long-standing

nominee a person who has been proposed for an office

practice that dates back to the administration of President George Washington, presidential **nominees** need only be approved by the Senate after they are nominated. Senate confirmation of nominees requires only a majority vote, not the two-thirds vote needed for treaty approval.

The Role of the Senate

In actual practice, the Senate's role is somewhat more complicated than the words of the Constitution might suggest. For certain positions, including lower court judges, the Senate expects the president to consult in advance with senators from the states affected by the appointment, or at least with those senators of the president's own party. This practice is known as "senatorial courtesy." If the president fails to follow it, the Senate may refuse to confirm the nominee out of respect for the senators snubbed by the president. Moreover, Senate committees routinely investigate the backgrounds of nominees, hold confirmation hearings, and recommend for or against confirmation to the full Senate.

authority the power to grant legal allowance

A Senate committee may refuse to conduct a confirmation hearing and thus doom a nominee, thereby giving tremendous **authority** to the committee chair, who is usually responsible for scheduling such hearings. In 1997, for example, the refusal of Senator Jesse Helms, chairman of the Senate Foreign Relations Committee, to hold a hearing on the nomination of William Weld to be ambassador to Mexico forced Weld to withdraw.

From the very beginning, the Senate reserved for itself the power to reject presidential nominees for office not only for reasons of their fitness or competence, but also because of their political views. In 1795 the Senate rejected the appointment of John Rutledge to be Chief Justice largely because he had opposed Jay's Treaty, which attempted to restore normal trade relations with Great Britain.

When Justice Thurgood Marshall, the first African American to serve on the Supreme Court, retired in 1991, President George Bush nominated Clarence Thomas, a little-known conservative federal judge and an African American, to replace him. The Senate was ready to vote on Thomas's nomination when the press revealed that Anita Hill, a law professor, had accused him of sexually harassing her when she worked for him in federal agencies years before. Thomas categorically denied Hill's calmly presented charges before the Senate Judiciary Committee. A huge television audience watched as unprecedented evening sessions were held. It was high drama, emotionally charged. The Senate confirmed Thomas by a margin of 52 to 48, the closest Supreme Court confirmation vote in modern times.

In general, the Senate rarely turns down presidential nominees appointed to the executive branch and lower federal courts. In a typical year, the Senate confirms over 97 percent of all such appointments, while most of the others are either withdrawn by the president or simply not acted upon. At times in the past, Senate confirmation of even major appointments was almost certain. Between 1961 and 1966, the Senate rejected or forced the withdrawal of only two nominees. But in the 1980s and 1990s the Senate became more aggressive, largely because different political parties typically controlled the White House and the Senate. During the Clinton administration in the 1990s, a combination of White House foot-dragging and inaction or opposition by Congress brought the appointments process to a near-standstill.

Supreme Court Nominations

In the case of the Supreme Court, the Senate has been more inclined to oppose nominations. By the end of the twentieth century, the Senate had rejected, or forced the president to withdraw, at least twenty-eight nomi-

nees. Five of these rejections occurred in the twentieth century: John J. Parker in 1930, Abe Fortas in 1968, Clement F. Haynsworth in 1969, G. Harrold Carswell in 1970, and Robert H. Bork in 1987. Other Supreme Court nominees, including Clarence Thomas in 1991, survived bitterly fought attempts to block their appointments.

Constitutional Issues

Over the years, the Supreme Court has faced a number of thorny issues arising from the appointments clause. Two of the most important involve the meaning of the terms "officers of the United States" and "inferior officers."

The Supreme Court has ruled that any official "exercising significant authority pursuant to the laws of the United States" is an officer of the United States and must be appointed according to the procedures outlined in the Constitution. Thus, the term "officers of the United States" includes high-ranking federal officials but excludes those whose functions are merely routine or advisory, or who do not exercise independent power. In the same way, Congress may not vest independent executive authority in an official who is not appointed in the manner set forth in the appointments clause. The appointments clause does not apply to the large number of federal workers who are considered nonpolitical **civil service** employees.

civil service administrative staff of the government; employment granted on the basis of a competitive examination

The line separating "principal" officers—whose appointment requires Senate confirmation—from "inferior" officers—who may be appointed by the president alone, by the heads of departments, or by the courts of law—is "far from clear," as the Supreme Court has admitted. The Court has cited as one characteristic of an inferior officer that he or she can be removed by a higher official of the executive branch and is authorized to carry out only specific, limited duties. Thus, in *Morrison* v. *Olson* (1988), the Court held that the federal courts could appoint an independent counsel. Since the attorney general could initiate the removal of the independent counsel and since the counsel was charged with the duty of investigating and **prosecuting** only specific crimes **allegedly** carried out by top-ranking White House officials, the independent counsel was an "inferior officer" and thus could be appointed by federal courts.

prosecute to begin and carry on a lawsuit; bring legal action against

allegedly asserted to be true without or before proving

The Removal Power

The authority to remove a federal officer is not part of the appointments power. The president has the general authority to dismiss any federal officer who has strictly executive duties, and thus who can be considered as directly serving under him. But in the case of federal officers who have significant independent legislative or **judicial** authority and serve for fixed terms of office, Congress may limit the president's removal power. In those cases, Congress may allow dismissal for only specific reasons, such as an inability or failure to perform the duties of the office.

judicial having to do with judgments in courts of justice or with the administration of justice

The Supreme Court upheld this principle in *United States* v. *Humphrey's Executor* (1935), when it ruled that the president could not remove a commissioner of the Federal Trade Commission (FTC) for his own reasons. This case distinguished the FTC example from an earlier Court ruling in *Myers* v. *United States* (1926), which held that the president has the authority to dismiss a postmaster for any reason.

Congress may remove officers of the United States only by the impeachment process, which requires the House of Representatives to charge an official with wrongdoing, followed by a trial and conviction by the Senate. In *Bowsher* v. *Synar* (1986), the Supreme Court ruled that Congress could not vest executive authority in an official who was removable by a joint resolution of Congress. Such an official, the Court ruled, was by definition an officer of the legislative branch.

Recess Appointments

recess appointment temporary appointment to office that expires at the end of the next session of Congress

adjournment suspension of a session until a future time

The president's power to make **recess appointments** extends to both the executive and judicial branches. The wording of the Constitution seems to limit recess appointments to those vacancies that actually occur during a congressional recess. Yet long-standing practice allows the president to make recess appointments for positions that occurred while Congress was in session but that remain unfilled after Congress has recessed. A recess, for these purposes, means the times between actual sessions of Congress and does not cover merely temporary **adjournments** or vacations.

Recess appointments to executive positions raise no constitutional difficulties. In contrast, judicial recess appointments may cause problems, because federal judges are usually appointed to serve "during good behavior"—meaning that they serve for life, unless they resign or are impeached by Congress. Lifetime appointment provides judges with a necessary degree of judicial independence from executive or legislative pressure. But a recess appointment to the federal courts is subject to Senate confirmation, and the recess appointee can be removed from office if the Senate fails to take any action. The question arises: Does the Constitution permit such an individual, who might be subject to undue influence, to carry out the duties of a federal judge?

In 1986, the Supreme Court refused to consider a challenge to a lower court ruling that recess appointments of federal judges are constitutional. The lower court's opinion laid great stress on the long-standing tradition of recess appointments to the courts, pointing out that Chief Justice Earl Warren, Justice William Brennan and Justice Potter Stewart, among others, were recess appointees. Yet in 1960 the Senate had passed a nonbinding resolution suggesting that recess appointments of federal judges should be avoided.

ARTICLE I—The Impeachment Power; ARTICLE II—Enforcing the Laws; Removal of Officers

Enforcing the Laws

Martin S. Flaherty

adjournment suspension of a session until a future time

vest to grant with particular authority, property, and rights

ARTICLE II, SECTION 3, OF THE CONSTITUTION STATES

He [the president] shall, from time to time, give to the Congress information of the State of the Union, and recommend to their Consideration such Measures as he shall judge necessary and expedient; he may, on extraordinary occasions, convene both Houses, or either of them, and in Case of Disagreement between them, with respect to the Time of ***Adjournment****, he may adjourn them to such Time as he shall think proper; he shall receive Ambassadors and other public Ministers; he shall take care that the Laws be faithfully executed, and shall Commission all the Officers of the United States.*

Not long after the Revolution, Americans began to think of government as exercising three now familiar powers. For them, government action often began with legislative power—the power to make laws or rules that applied to all citizens. Government involvement in people's lives often led to the use of judicial power—the power of the courts to settle disputes between the government and individuals, or between individuals, that involved violating laws. It was thought that yet another group of government officials would need to enforce laws by bringing those suspected lawbreakers before the courts, by collecting taxes and spending revenues, and by running government institutions established by specific laws. The Framers referred to this power to enforce laws as the executive power.

Separation of Powers

The Constitution reflects this understanding of governmental authority by assigning each of these three principal powers to three distinct branches of government. This division of powers, known as "the separation of powers," seeks to enable government to carry out its duties more efficiently while at the same time preventing any one branch from becoming too powerful.

Constitutional definitions. Article I states, "All legislative powers herein granted shall be vested in a Congress of the United States." Article III states, "The judicial power of the United States, shall be vested in one Supreme Court, and in such inferior courts as the Congress may from time to time ordain and establish." Between these two articles, Article II directs that "The executive power shall be vested in a president of the United States of America." With this provision, the Constitution grants the main law enforcement responsibilities of the federal government to the president.

Origins of the concept. The Framers drew the concept of the separation of powers from the ideas of political thinkers like Niccolo Machiavelli, John Locke, and David Hume. Even more directly, it was based on the experiences of the Framers' generation itself. American colonists viewed the different branches of government in the unwritten British Constitution as representing different social classes rather than dealing with different types of authority. American patriots entered the

The first presidential inauguration (April, 30 1789). President George Washington is sworn into the office that the new constitution just created.

Articles of Confederation the first constitution of the thirteen original United States; in effect 1781–1789

Tory any American who supported the efforts of the British crown against colonial independence during the American revolution

veto refuse to sign a bill into law

treaty binding international agreement

electoral college a body of people chosen by the voters in each state to elect the president and vice president of the United States

Anti-Federalist member of the group opposing the adoption of the U.S. Constitution; favored states' rights and argued successfully for the Bill of Rights

Revolution deeply suspicious of executive power. They resented the British monarch's officials in the colonies, the royal governors, for abusing their law enforcement powers. By 1776, the colonists had come to reject King George III himself for failing to protect their liberties against the acts of the British Parliament.

The Growth of Executive Branch Authority

After winning their independence, Americans were free to implement their distrust of executive authority. This distrust was clear in the first state constitutions. In Virginia, for example, the legislature not only selected the governor but also controlled his salary. Pennsylvania outdid Virginia by abolishing the post of governor altogether and replacing it with a twelve-man supreme executive council.

Articles of Confederation. The new national government made a similar effort to limit executive authority. The Articles of Confederation, the nation's first constitution, had not even provided for an executive branch. Instead, it left federal law enforcement to congressional committees. But soon the problems of such a weak executive branch became clear. At best, state governments feebly carried out national policies. Worse, perhaps, many state laws targeted unpopular groups like **Tories** and creditors, and undermined traditional rights such as trial by jury.

Strengthening the executive. These problems led to calls for reform and for strengthening the executive authority. The Framers kept the idea of the separation of powers in mind when they decided to set up a strong executive branch. Article II created a "unitary executive," placing the executive power in the hands of one individual, the president, rather than in a committee. It then directed that "he shall take care that the laws be faithfully executed." Other provisions in the Constitution gave the president the power to **veto** laws, to appoint judges of the Supreme Court, to make **treaties**, and to act as commander-in-chief of the armed forces. Article II also provided that the president would be indirectly elected by the people through an **electoral college** rather than by the legislature, the way most state governors had been elected in the past.

This shift toward strengthening executive power was so striking that it cannot be explained solely as an an attempt to repair the weaknesses of the Articles of Confederation and the state constitutions. One important reason for such a striking change was that everyone expected that George Washington, the most admired and trusted American of his time, would be chosen president. Even so, **Anti-Federalists** regarded the proposal for a stronger executive branch as little more than a return to the tyranny they had suffered under the British monarch; they had fought the Revolution to end it.

Limits of the constitutional provisions. The Constitution left much to be worked out in practice. As in many other areas, that document provided only broad, general directions regarding executive power in general and law enforcement in particular. But it turned out that Americans often found it hard to agree about the meaning of these general understandings. As James Madison wrote in *The Federalist*, No. 37, "Experience has instructed us that no skill in the science of government has yet been able to discriminate and define, with sufficient certainty, its three great provinces—the legislative, the executive, and the judicial." The Framers expected that over time the three branches would resolve important questions, including issues relating to how laws would be implemented. Although two centuries of practice have in fact settled many matters, a surprising number of issues are still being debated. Yet it is clear that as federal law enforcement responsibilities have increased, the executive branch has become significantly stronger.

Enforcing the Laws in the Nineteenth Century

For much of the nation's early history, the government took little responsibility for enforcing federal laws. Congress did not pass many laws during the first half of the nineteenth century, and when it did, it usually left enforcement to state and local officials. A handful of strong presidents, such as George Washington, Thomas Jefferson, and Andrew Jackson, made the most of executive power. But the legislative branch generally dominated, just as the Framers had expected.

The role of the executive branch began to change as a result of the Civil War. During the years of Reconstruction, the federal government followed a policy of massive intervention in matters that state and local governments had handled in the past. In its efforts to give power to newly freed African Americans, Congress enacted landmark civil rights laws and set up executive agencies to enforce them, including the Freedmen's Bureau and the Justice Department. But Reconstruction policies failed to shift authority to the president or even to cause a lasting expansion of federal power. President Andrew Johnson opposed the Radical Republicans' Reconstruction plan and became the only chief executive ever to be impeached. Moreover, Reconstruction itself ended just over a decade after the end of the Civil War.

impeach to set up a formal hearing on charges of high crimes and misdemeanors

Enforcing the Laws in the Twentieth Century

A more significant and lasting change in federal law enforcement came in the twentieth century, particularly during the administration of President Franklin D. Roosevelt. A response to the Great Depression, the New Deal called for federal involvement in social, economic and local affairs on an unprecedented scale. Roosevelt's policies speeded up a trend that had started early in the century during the administrations of Presidents Woodrow Wilson and Theodore Roosevelt. Those presidents increased the federal government's authority through reform legislation enacted in Congress.

Even more important, federal power grew because Congress established many new government agencies, such as the Securities and Exchange Commission, the Federal Aviation Administration, and the National Labor Relations Board, among others. Many of these agencies were granted legislative and judicial power to enforce the laws. Despite

An aide rattles off a list of acronyms of various federal agencies to a Washington politician.

"H.U.D. called the F.A.A. The F.A.A. called the S.E.C. The S.E.C. called G.S.A. G.S.A. called O.M.B. O.M.B. called Y-O-U."

federal bureaucracy the large, complex administrative structure in the executive branch

this trend, many people regarded the federal bureaucracy that developed as just an expansion of the executive branch. But others considered it to be more like a fourth branch of government.

Some people feared that *Myers* v. *United States* (1926) would destroy the **civil service** system. Yet the decision had little effect. *Humphrey's Executor* v. *United States* (1935) had much more impact. But that impact was much more political than legal. In its decision in *Humphrey*, the Supreme Court implied that President Franklin D. Roosevelt had violated the Constitution by removing from office William E. Humphrey, a conservative member of the Federal Trade Commission. This ruling infuriated President Roosevelt, who determined to find a way to curb the Court. As much as any other single decision, *Humphrey* led President Roosevelt to propose his ill-fated Court-packing plan in 1937.

civil service administrative staff of the government; employment granted on the basis of a competitive examination

The Supreme Court's Rulings

Many of the battles between the president and Congress in the last half of the twentieth century involved the question of who would control the huge bureaucracy implementing the countless federal programs and policies. The Supreme Court has settled some of these controversies. In *INS* v. *Chadha* (1985), for example, the Supreme Court invalidated the legislative veto, which Congress had used to control the decisions of federal agencies.

Removing officers. The Court's decisions have been less clear in determining who decides when federal officials enforcing laws may be fired from their jobs. In *Myers* v. *United States* (1926), the justices ruled that Congress could not limit the president's power to remove executive officials such as postmasters. In a partial reversal, *Humphrey's Executor* v. *United States* (1935), established that Congress could restrict the president's power to remove officials in independent agencies. *Morrison* v. *Olson* (1988) later expanded this principle to include certain executive officials, such as an independent prosecutor investigating a government scandal, as long as the restrictions on the president's overall power appeared slight.

Conflicting decisions. The Supreme Court's lack of direction on this issue is part of a larger, ongoing debate. Advocates of presidential authority argue that the president alone should control how laws are enforced and who should enforce them. Opponents contend that, at the very least, Congress may place some limits on the president's power in this area. The Court's conflicting decisions suggest that this debate will probably last as long as the Constitution itself.

see also

ARTICLE I—Congress; ARTICLE II—Removal of Officers; ARTICLE III—The Judiciary

Removal of Officers

Steven Calabresi

impeachment method by which the House of Representatives may charge the nation's highest-ranking officials, including the president, with wrongdoing; following impeachment, if the officials are found guilty of the charges, the Senate then may try them and remove them from office

treason the offense of attempting to overthrow the government

high crimes and misdemeanors any or all of the following types of conduct: (1) a serious offense against the federal government, (2) criminal misconduct for which an official can be indicted, tried, and convicted, or (3) misconduct that violates a criminal law, constitutes a serious offense against the federal government, and relates to the performance of his or her duties

President Woodrow Wilson delivering a speech (1912). Wilson backed the creation of the Federal Trade Commission, and the act proposing its founding breezed through Congress in September 1914.

ARTICLE II, SECTION 4, OF THE CONSTITUTION STATES

The President, Vice President, and all civil Officers of the United States, shall be removed from Office on ***Impeachment*** *for, and Conviction of,* ***Treason****, Bribery, or other* ***High Crimes and Misdemeanors.***

The power to remove or fire federal officials is for the most part not spelled out in the Constitution. Although Congress has the power to impeach and remove executive officers and judges and also to expel one of their own members, no clause of the Constitution clearly gives the president the power to fire cabinet secretaries or other officials serving in the executive branch.

The Issues at Hand

From 1789 on, there has been a broad consensus that the president does have the power to fire most, if not all, executive officials in policy-making jobs for any reason whatsoever.

Broad presidential power. Advocates of a broad presidential removal power think that the president needs such power to control the executive branch of the government and to implement his electoral mandate from the voters.

Independent regulatory agencies. Skeptics argue that Congress should be allowed to set up independent agencies or offices within the government to make policy or enforce laws when a conflict of interest exists for the president.

Examples of independent agencies are the Federal Trade Commission (FTC) and judicially appointed independent counsels that investigate wrongdoing in the executive branch. Typically, independence is secured by a provision of the law that allows the president to fire the independent officer only "for cause" instead of "at will." This means that the officer must be guilty of misconduct before he can be dismissed.

A fourth branch of government. At the end of the twentieth century, a significant number of independent regulatory agencies exist within the federal government including the Federal Reserve Board and the Federal Communications Commission (FCC), as well as many court-appointed independent counsels. Critics describe these entities as comprising a headless fourth branch of government that is responsible and accountable to no one.

There has been much debate throughout America's history over whether Congress can constitutionally limit the president's removal power by setting up independent entities (units) within the executive branch. The debate has focused on:

1. the meaning of the Constitution;
2. the practice over the last two hundred years;
3. Supreme Court opinions; and
4. public policy arguments.

Textual and Originalist Arguments

Advocates of a broad presidential removal power note that the Framers made a deliberate decision to create a single executive branch headed by one person who would be fully accountable to the voters. They argue that the Framers set up three, not four, branches of government and gave the president full executive power to execute the laws. The First Congress, in a famous series of votes known as the Decision of 1789, interpreted these constitutional provisions as giving the president broad removal power. All the early presidents exercised that power by at least occasionally firing subordinate officials.

Critics concede these points but note that the first few Congresses reduced presidential powers of control by setting up the Treasury Department, the Postal Service, the U.S. Attorney's offices, and the Bank of the United States. In addition, they note that the first six presidents seldom used their removal power.

Two Centuries of Practices

proponent advocate

Proponents of a broad presidential removal power note that for two centuries, presidents have had the power to fire all cabinet secretaries or subordinate policy-making officials. They note also that independent entities have been the exception rather than the rule. They point out that this removal power was justified in two major struggles during the nineteenth century. The first was when President Andrew Jackson prevailed in firing his treasury secretary during his successful struggle to destroy the Bank of the United States. The second was when the Senate, by one vote, refused to convict President Andrew Johnson on a bill of impeachment for firing his secretary of war in violation of the Tenure of Office Act of 1868. That Act, which sought to impose broad limits on presidential removal power, was ultimately repealed in 1887.

civil service administrative staff of the government; employment granted on the basis of a competitive examination

Critics point out that Presidents Jackson and Johnson faced major political opposition for asserting broad presidential removal power. The opposition included Daniel Webster, Henry Clay, and, in Johnson's case, the leaders of the Reconstruction Congress. They note that civil service laws were adopted and upheld as constitutional during the nineteenth century, limiting the president's power to remove personnel that did not make policy and thus ending the Jacksonian spoils system. Finally, they note that many independent agencies were created since the 1880s, beginning with the Interstate Commerce Commission (ICC) and continuing down through the New Deal era. They argue that it is far too late to claim that these agencies, which comprise an important part of the administrative state, are unconstitutional.

> "The spoils system, that practice which turns public offices, high and low, from public trusts into objects of prey and booty for the victorious party, may without extravagance of language be called one of the greatest criminals in our history, if not the greatest. In the whole catalogue of our ills there is none more dangerous to the vitality of our free institutions."
>
> —Carl Schurz (1829–1906), U.S. Senator

Precedent

The Supreme Court has reached conflicting decisions in cases testing the constitutionality of statutes limiting presidential removal power. In *Myers v. United States* (1926), Chief Justice William Howard Taft, the only former president ever to serve on the Supreme Court, wrote a sweeping

and well-researched landmark decision upholding a broad presidential power of removal. Nine years later, in *Humphrey's Executor* v. *United States* (1935), the Court significantly limited the reach of *Myers*. It upheld the creation of an independent Federal Trade Commission because that Commission performed partial legislative and partial judicial functions.

precedent established ruling understanding, or practice of the law

Subsequent decisions reaffirmed this **precedent** of allowing for agency independence where the character of the office seemed to warrant it. Then, in the 1980s, the Reagan administration openly challenged the constitutionality of the independent agencies. The Supreme Court issued two strong separation of powers opinions—*INS* v. *Chadha* and *Bowsher* v. *Synar*—that again seemed to question the constitutionality of congressional limits on removal power. The Reagan administration challenge collapsed in *Morrison* v. *Olson* when the Supreme Court upheld the constitutionality of the law creating independent counsels. Only Justice Antonin Scalia dissented. Subsequent decisions, however, seemed to reaffirm presidential removal power in other contexts, and both the *Morrison* decision and the Independent Counsel law itself have come under sustained criticism.

The act of March 1, 1792 assumed that George Washington became president on March 4, 1789, when the Constitution went into effect, even though he did not take the oath until April 30, 1789. The Chief Justice of the United States usually administers the oath of office, but any judicial officer may do so. Calvin Coolidge's father, a justice of the peace, administered the oath to his son upon Warren Harding's death in 1923. When John Kennedy was assassinated in Dallas in 1963, Lyndon Johnson asked Attorney General Robert Kennedy who could swear him in as president. Kennedy told Johnson that any judicial officer could. So Federal Judge Sarah Hughes of Dallas, who had been appointed at Johnson's urging, did so. The Johnson—Robert Kennedy discussion was not necessary since Johnson had become president upon his predecessor's death. As Martin Van Buren wrote after leaving the presidency, "The Presidency under our system, like the king in a monarchy, never dies."

Policy Arguments

Finally, those in favor of a broad presidential removal power have argued that such a power is vital to ensure energy and accountability in the executive branch. They believe that a headless fourth branch of government is likely to fall under the influence of special interest groups, the congressional committee structure, or the press. Such an outcome would weaken the president who is, along with the vice president, one of only two officials elected by the whole nation and who, therefore, has the whole country's interests at heart. Allowing Congress to carve up the one executive branch created by the Framers into independent entities is a prescription for interest-group capture and **paralysis**. It also permits finger-pointing and mutual accusations as different executive entities seek to avoid responsibility for policy failures and take credit for policy successes.

paralysis loss of ability to move or function

ARTICLE II—Enforcing the Laws; The Executive Branch

Advocates of independent agencies point to the success of an independent Federal Reserve Board in preventing inflation of the money supply in the late twentieth century. They also cite the success of the Independent Counsel law in uncovering executive branch wrongdoing in a post-Watergate political culture. Some defend the independent regulatory agencies like the FTC, FCC, and the ICC, which was abolished in 1995, while other people agree that they have not worked well. The key position of the defenders of agency independence is that Congress should have the option to create such entities when it needs to.

Supporters of broad presidential removal power reply that a constitutional question of this importance should not be left to an institution as self-interested as the Congress. They note that Congress is a rival of the president, and that Congress has consistently abused **statutes** like the Independent Counsel law for its own **partisan** gain.

statute a law enacted by the legislative branch of government

partisan a member of a group or participant in an event

Article III

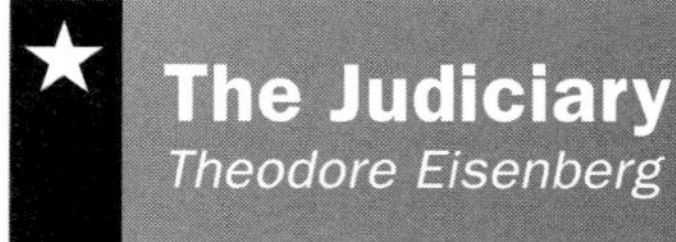

The Judiciary

Theodore Eisenberg

judicial having to do with judgments in courts of justice or with the administration of justice

vest to grant with particular authority, property, and rights

supreme having the highest authority

treaty binding international agreement

authority the power to grant legal allowance to

jurisdiction the territory or area within which authority may be exercised

original jurisdiction the first courts to hear the case

appellate jurisdiction authority to hear appeals from lower courts that have tried these cases

impeachment method by which the House of Representatives may charge the nation's highest-ranking officials, including the president, with wrongdoing; following impeachment, if the officials are found guilty of the charges, the Senate may try them and remove them from office

treason the offense of attempting to overthrow the government

ARTICLE III OF THE CONSTITUTION STATES

Section 1. *The **judicial** Power of the United States, shall be **vested** in one **supreme** Court, and in such inferior courts as the Congress may from time to time ordain and establish. The Judges, both of the supreme and inferior Courts, shall hold their Offices during good Behaviour, and shall, at stated Times, receive for their Services, a Compensation, which shall not be diminished during their Continuance in Office.*

Section 2. *The judicial Power shall extend to all Cases, in Law and Equity, arising under this Constitution, the Laws of the United States, and **Treaties** made, or which shall be made, under their **Authority**;—to all Cases affecting Ambassadors, other public Ministers and Consuls;—to all Cases of admiralty and maritime **Jurisdiction**;—to Controversies to which the United States shall be a Party;—to Controversies between two or more States;—between a State and Citizens of another State;—between Citizens of different States;—between Citizens of the same State claiming Lands under Grants of different States, and between a State, or the Citizens thereof, and foreign States, Citizens or Subjects.*

*In all Cases affecting Ambassadors, other public Ministers and Consuls, and those in which a State shall be Party, the supreme Court shall have all **original Jurisdiction**. In all other Cases before mentioned, the supreme Court shall have **appellate Jurisdiction**, both as to Law and Fact, with such Exceptions, and under such Regulations as the Congress shall make.*

*The Trial of all Crimes, except in Cases of **Impeachment**, shall be by jury; and such Trial shall be held in the State where the said Crimes shall have been committed; but when not committed within any State, the Trial shall be at such Place or Places as the Congress may by Law have directed.*

Section 3. ***Treason** against the United States, shall consist only in levying War against them, or in adhering to their Enemies, giving them Aid and Comfort. No Person shall be convicted of Treason unless on the Testimony of two Witnesses to the same overt Act, or on Confession in open Court.*

The Congress shall have Power to declare the Punishment of Treason, but no Attainder of Treason shall work Corruption of Blood, or Forfeiture except during the Life of the Person attained.

The Seal of the United States Supreme Court.

Article III of the Constitution establishes and regulates the judiciary, the third branch of the federal government. A key provision of the Article centers on the Supreme Court, which is to exercise the "judicial power of the United States." It also grants Congress the power to create "such inferior courts as the Congress may from time to time ordain and establish," although it does not expressly require that such courts be set up. Congress has, of course, created such a system of federal courts.

Congress passed the Judiciary Act of 1789 to carry out the Constitution's command that there be a Supreme Court. Although the Constitution establishes a "supreme" federal court, it also limits the authority of federal courts to hear cases. This limitation is part of the constitutional system of limits on power on each branch of government. Courts may consider only cases in which they have jurisdiction.

The authority of courts to hear cases can be limited in different ways. Some courts have original jurisdiction. Usually courts with original jurisdiction are trial courts. Other courts have appellate jurisdiction. Appellate courts decide whether the lower courts decided a case correctly.

The Supreme Court

Article III limits the Supreme Court's original jurisdiction to cases in which a state is a party and to cases involving ambassadors, public ministers, or consuls. Congress also has required that lower courts usually hear the cases before they can be appealed to the Supreme Court.

All of the Supreme Court's other jurisdiction is appellate. This is by far the largest part of its authority. The Court hears cases coming from both state and federal courts. Its review of state court decisions is limited to cases involving federal laws, including the Constitution. Even this limited power of review is extremely important. By centralizing the review of federal law in one supreme court, Congress helped establish and protect the power of the federal government. Without such a court, the

An overworked Supreme Court is depicted in this 1885 cartoon.

final interpretation of federal law would be left to the highest court of each state or to several federal appellate courts. No one could be sure that these various courts would interpret federal laws the same way.

Article III authorizes Congress to make exceptions to the Supreme Court's appellate jurisdiction. But Congress's power to make such exceptions is the subject of debate. If Congress were to make very broad exceptions, this could undermine the Supreme Court's role as a unifying national court and enforcer of constitutional rights.

NO FREE GOVERNMENT CAN SURVIVE THAT IS NOT BASED ON THE SUPREMACY OF LAW
Inscription on the Justice Department Building, Washington, D.C.

The Lower Federal Courts

When Congress established the Supreme Court, it also carried out its power to establish federal courts "inferior" to the Supreme Court. The Judiciary Act of 1789 created federal trial courts throughout the United States. It divided the country into districts that usually follow state lines. As states were added and the nation's population grew, more districts were created. By the late twentieth century, there were over ninety federal district courts.

Thirteen United States Courts of Appeals have been created. Twelve of these courts hear appeals from federal district courts in specific geographic areas. Eleven of these twelve courts are responsible for federal cases in the states, and one is responsible for federal cases in the District of Columbia. The thirteenth court of appeals, the United States Court of Appeals for the Federal Circuit, is more specialized. Its responsibility is not based on specific geographic areas. Rather, it hears cases on appeal from specialized federal courts and hears many cases involving patents and trademarks. The circuit courts also may hear appeals from rulings of agencies in the federal government. Appeals from circuit courts may go to the Supreme Court, which itself decides which cases to consider. It declines to hear most of the cases brought before it. Therefore, a circuit court is usually the final court to decide a case that has been appealed from a federal court.

A police officer takes an oath before testifying against a teen defendant in traffic court.

Subject Matter Jurisdiction of Federal Courts

Article III of the Constitution also specifies the issues that federal courts may decide, thereby limiting their subject matter jurisdiction. Of course, no courts can decide all kinds of cases. For example, a traffic court may not decide a serious criminal matter, such as a murder case. Thus, the limits on the subject matter jurisdiction of federal courts help define the boundary between the federal government and state governments.

Area of the law involved. Article III, Section 2, covers two kinds of subject matter jurisdiction. The first kind allows federal courts to decide cases based on the area of law involved in the case. The judicial power extends to all cases "arising under" the Constitution and the laws of the United States. Thus, a case arises under the Constitution or U.S. laws when the Constitution or laws provide the legal grounds on which the case is brought to court. A discrimination case alleging violations of civil rights statutes "arises under" the laws of the United States. But a divorce

case based on state divorce law does not "arise under" federal law. It arises under state divorce law, and nothing in Article III authorizes Congress to allow such cases to be heard by federal courts.

Since Article III grants the federal courts power to decide cases arising under the Constitution or the laws of the United States, Congress may authorize federal courts to hear any case brought on the basis of federal law. Congress also may authorize them to hear "all cases of admiralty and maritime jurisdiction." These cases usually involve accidents on the seas or the ownership of vessels and ships.

The parties involved. The second kind of subject matter jurisdiction covered in Article III, Section 2, relates to who the parties in the case are. For example, Article III authorizes Congress to allow federal courts to hear "all cases affecting ambassadors," regardless of the area of law involved in the case. It also authorizes Congress to allow federal courts to hear "controversies to which the United States shall be a party." Thus, whenever the United States sues someone or is sued by someone, Congress may authorize federal courts to hear the case, regardless of the area of law involved.

Cases between citizens of different states. Article III also authorizes federal courts to hear cases between citizens of different states. This authority is called diversity jurisdiction. Congress's purpose in authorizing diversity jurisdiction was to provide a neutral court to hear a case. Thus, diversity jurisdiction illustrates one major theme of Article III. The Framers wanted the federal courts to serve as a kind of umpire in cases where local interests might unfairly dominate such cases in state courts. If a citizen of one state sued a citizen of another state in the first citizen's home state, the Framers feared that this state court would be biased against the out-of-state citizen. By allowing a federal court to hear the case, they provided a more neutral court. Similar considerations caused the Framers to provide federal court jurisdiction over controversies between states, between a state and a citizen of another state, and between states, or their citizens, and foreign states or citizens.

diversity jurisdiction the authority to hear cases between citizens of diverse states no matter what area of the law is involved

Congress's other powers. Although Article III authorizes Congress to allow federal courts to decide many kinds of cases, Congress is not required to use all of its authority in deciding what cases it allows those courts to hear. Thus, it is important to distinguish between the kinds of cases Article III authorizes Congress to allow federal courts to decide and the kinds of cases that Congress has decided to allow federal courts to decide.

Congress had compelling reasons for its decision to allow federal courts to decide different classes of cases. In the Judiciary Act of 1789, Congress gave the district and circuit courts original jurisdiction over cases involving commerce on the seas, sometimes called maritime commerce. In the era before trains, cars, and planes, maritime commerce was very important to the United States. The first Congress believed the country needed a consistent body of maritime law and that a system of national courts was the best way to achieve that goal.

Sailing ships in eighteenth-century New York harbor. Federal courts received jurisdiction over maritime issues from the first Congress.

Provisions of the Judiciary Act. The Act also gave federal courts authority to hear cases based on who the parties to the case are. Since the

Judiciary Act gave federal courts authority to hear diversity jurisdiction cases, federal courts have regularly decided cases involving only questions of state law. But Congress has never given federal courts all the diversity jurisdiction that Article III authorizes it to confer. Congress has limited such jurisdiction to cases involving more than certain dollar amounts in order to avoid clogging the federal courts and to reserve them for more important cases. Thus, small diversity cases are never heard in federal court.

The Judiciary Act of 1789 did not authorize federal trial courts to hear all cases involving federal law. Not until 1875 did Congress authorize federal trial courts to hear cases involving all federal legal questions, that is, all cases "arising under" the Constitution and federal laws, as stated in Article III. Even then, Congress limited the jurisdiction of federal courts to decide cases arising under federal laws to claims that exceeded a certain dollar amount. Cases involving less than that amount had to be brought in state courts even though these cases arose under federal law. This dollar limit was finally removed in 1980, ensuring that a federal district court will now hear all such cases. Before 1875, most cases with federal claims had to be brought first in state courts. A review of federal claims in the case by a federal court could be obtained only by appeal to the Supreme Court. Many cases involving federal law claims are brought in state court.

The Constitution provides that federal judges "shall hold their Offices during good Behaviour . . . ." At the Constitutional Convention, John Dickinson of Delaware moved to insert after these words the words "provided that they may be removed by the Executive on the application by the Senate and the House of Representatives." Gouverneur Morris of Pennsylvania and Edmund Randolph of Virginia opposed the motion. Of the eight states on the roll call and voting, only Connecticut voted in the affirmative. An independent judiciary was therefore provided for, and one of the colonists' grievances against King George III was corrected. As the Declaration of Independence stated, "He has made Judges dependent on his Will alone, for the tenure of their offices, and the amount and payment of their salaries." The Constitution extends "judicial power" to "cases" and controversies." In the Constitutional Convention, Charles Pinckney of South Carolina proposed that "each branch of the Legislature, as well as the Supreme Executive, shall have authority to require the opinions of the Supreme Judicial Court upon important questions of law and upon solemn occasions." Some states have similar provisions in their constitutions, which enable the legislature or governor to get an advisory opinion from the courts on the constitutionality of legislation before it becomes law. But Pinckney's proposal was not adopted. In 1793, however, the Supreme Court respectfully declined to give their opinions on President George Washington's questions arising under certain treaties. The Court has consistently followed this early precedent.

Federal Judges

The Judiciary Act of 1789 also provided for judges in the circuit courts and district courts. The Supreme Court was to consist of a chief justice and five associate justices. Congress later increased the number of associate justices to eight.

Life tenure. A distinctive feature of Article III, which created the judicial branch, was its grant of life tenure to federal judges. Article III, Section 1, states that federal judges "shall hold their offices during good behaviour" and that the compensation paid them "shall not be diminished [decreased] during their continuance in office." The term "good behavior" here does not mean well behaved, as it usually does in referring to people's conduct. It means that federal judges can be removed from office only through impeachment by Congress. They cannot be removed simply because people disagree with their decisions. Moreover, federal judges not only are appointed for life, but Congress cannot reduce their salaries.

The status of federal judges is different from that of most state judges, who are not appointed for life and who are elected for a term of years or appointed by the governor for a certain number of years. This difference in status is a principal reason that federal judges are more independent than state judges. Since federal judges are not elected, they can make their decisions more free of political pressures than can most state judges. Federal judges do not have to worry about losing their jobs if politicians or the public disagree with their decisions.

The reason for a special status. This independence is important when federal judges must rule in cases involving difficult issues such as,

In a 1998 interview, U.S. Attorney General Griffin Bell was quoted as saying:

"If we (federal judges) had to run for election in the South of the 1960s we would have had a new set of judges every year."

for example, rulings handed down against school segregation. In contrast, state judges who hand down unpopular decisions sometimes lose their jobs. In California, Tennessee, and other states, judges have been removed from office or lost elections when their decisions in death penalty cases went against strong public opinion.

Because federal judges do not have to run for office, they do not need to worry about raising money for elections. Some critics believe that some state judges compromise their independence since they must win election to their office and may be sensitive, as a result, to political pressures. These state judges also often must raise funds from the parties and the lawyers who appear before them in court. There are also critics who believe that the independence of the federal judiciary creates real problems. Since federal judges do not fear removal or face election, they do not respond to the public will. Moreover, these critics argue, judges also take on cases that the courts should avoid.

Federal Courts Not Established Under Article III

Congress has created several courts that are not specifically provided for in Article III, and where judges do not have life tenure. These courts include local courts for the District of Columbia, Puerto Rico, and the territories. They also include bankruptcy courts, the Tax Court, the Claims Court, and the Court of International Trade.

The Contempt Power

contempt of court disobedience of a court's order or interference with the court's operation

Not all the powers exercised by federal courts are mentioned in Article III. One such power is of **contempt of court**. For example, a party who disrupts court proceedings by shouting may be held in contempt of court. The punishment for contempt of court can be jail or a fine. The power to punish contempt of court is an unusual power, not only because it is not mentioned in Article III or anywhere else in the Constitution, but also because it imposes criminal penalties without the procedural protections usually found in criminal proceedings.

Courts have long exercised contempt powers and believe them necessary. If only the usual protections of criminal proceedings applied whenever a person disobeyed a court's order, courts might not be able to function.

Political Questions

political question a decision that the courts determine is entirely within the power of the political branches of government, Congress and the president, to make if they choose to do so

The courts do not hear all cases that Article III and federal law authorize. The most important exceptions are cases that involve **political questions**. Courts have refused to accept jurisdiction in such cases.

For example, the requirement in Article IV, Section 4, that the federal government must guarantee every state a republican form of government has been held to be a political question. The Supreme Court has ruled that only the political branches of government can define what a republican form of government is. The Court also has refused to review

other political questions, such as contested elections, whether state governments are legitimate, and certain presidential actions. However, the Supreme Court has not clearly stated how questions proper for judicial review are to be separated from those that are political questions better left to the other two branches of government. Nevertheless, the political question doctrine enables federal courts to avoid disputes that could force confrontations with the Congress and the president.

ARTICLE I— Congressional Investigations; ARTICLE III—Establishment of Judicial Review: *Marbury* v. *Madison*; Origins of Judicial Review; ARTICLE IV—Republican Form of Government

Origins of Judicial Review

Charles Hobson

statute a law enacted by the legislative branch of government

judicial review a court's authority to evaluate laws for their constitutionality

enumerated powers the powers listed in a constitution; these powers also are sometimes called the *expressed* powers

popular sovereignty government created by and subject to the will of the people

In the American system of government, the judiciary has responsibility for enforcing the Constitution. When judges are faced with a conflict between the Constitution and an ordinary law, they must uphold the Constitution as the superior law and declare the state or federal statute void. This practice is called judicial review. It is the basis for the extraordinary power of the Supreme Court in American life.

Neither Article III of the Constitution nor any other provision clearly confers the power of judicial review. Yet the Constitution is a plan of limited government. It grants defined and enumerated powers to Congress, and it places expressed limitations and prohibitions on state governments. Would the Constitution be effective if its limits and prohibitions could not be enforced?

The Framers and Judicial Review

Although the nature of limited constitutional government seems to imply judicial review, the Framers of the Constitution did not have a fully developed theory or rationale for this practice. There was no agreement among Americans in 1787 that courts should be able to overturn laws passed by popularly elected legislatures. Many Americans believed that such power in the hands of judges with life tenure was contrary to the basic principles of democracy. They asked whether, in a government based on the consent of the people, the judiciary should be allowed to deny the validity of the laws passed by the people's chosen representatives.

After the Constitution was adopted, Americans gradually came to support the idea that, in certain instances, courts could strike down laws that were contrary to the Constitution. Political and legal theorists set forth a doctrine of judicial review that Chief Justice John Marshall drew upon in the case of *Marbury* v. *Madison* (1803). This was the first case in which the Supreme Court overruled a law of Congress because it conflicted with the Constitution.

The theory of judicial review is made up of several closely related ideas, including fundamental law, written constitutions, popular sovereignty, and the separation of powers. None of these ideas, alone, can explain or justify the development of judicial review, yet they all made important contributions.

Fundamental Law

When the Constitution was written, Americans firmly believed in the idea that bills passed by legislatures should follow some "higher," or fundamental, law. This higher law was given different names, such as divine law, natural law, or the basic principles of reason and justice. Before the Revolution, Americans had regarded the unwritten British constitution as fundamental law, and they often appealed to its principles to justify their protests against Parliament's attempts to control the colonies. But unwritten fundamental law was not the kind of law that judges could easily enforce. It was too general and abstract, and it lacked the concrete and specific nature of written documents that judges were used to dealing with in interpreting the law.

The North Carolina State seal. The state constitutions, written and enacted by state legislatures, were not based on the direct expression of the people, and were considered flawed for that reason.

Written Constitutions

The Declaration of Independence provided a model that helped Americans create a more definite fundamental law. Written state constitutions and declarations of rights were used in establishing the new state governments. Such written constitutions marked a significant stage in the development of judicial review. In 1787, James Iredell, a future Supreme Court justice, described the constitution of North Carolina as not "a mere imaginary thing, about which ten thousand different opinions may be formed, but a written document to which all may have recourse, and to which, therefore, the judges cannot willfully blind themselves." However, these first American state constitutions came to be considered defective because state legislatures wrote and passed them, and they were not based directly on the will of the sovereign (or ruling) people.

Popular Sovereignty

ratify to formally approve a document, thereby making it legal

supreme having the highest authority

With the Constitution of 1787, Americans made their most important contribution to political and constitutional theory: people meeting in conventions to frame and ratify written fundamental law. This was a deliberate departure from regular government practices of the past. Thus, Americans reshaped the idea of popular sovereignty, or rule by the people, from an ideal theory into a concrete reality. Through conventions, the people became the supreme lawmaking authority of the nation.

A constitution established in this way was more than just a plan of government. It was a law imposed upon government and to be obeyed by government in the same way that citizens obeyed ordinary laws. But the fact that the constitution was a "fundamental law" and a "written" document does not fully explain the development of judicial review. Americans quickly came to regard a constitution as a law that courts must apply like any other law.

The Framers were familiar with the idea that one part of the government had the power to decide that another part violated the "higher law." Under British rule, the Privacy Council, a group that advised the monarch, could **veto** laws passed by colonial legislatures if they violated British laws. After the Revolution, some state courts declared unconstitutional laws passed by their own legislatures. The Supremacy Clause in Article VI of the Constitution **implied** such review by federal courts over state actions. Ratification conventions in eight states explicitly accepted this power, and between 1789 and 1803 courts in ten states held that state laws violated state constitutions. Section 25 of the Judiciary Act of 1789, which created the national judiciary, granted the federal government the power to reverse state laws and constitutions that conflicted with the "Constitution, treaty, statute, or commission of the United States." All of this was done without specifically providing for judicial review.

veto refuse to sign a bill into law

implied assumed or suggested without being specifically stated

Separation of Powers

In the years leading to the Revolution, Americans believed that colonial legislatures were the true embodiment of the public will and that the chief threat to their liberty lay in oppression by the executive power. They had experienced the harsh rule of royal governors during the colonial period. As a result, the first state constitutions placed nearly all important powers of government in the legislatures. However, in the decade after independence was declared, Americans discovered that unchecked rule by popularly elected assemblies often was as arbitrary, oppressive, and unjust as government by royal governors. Americans gained a new understanding of the role that the executive and judicial branches could play in preventing or limiting the abuses of the legislative branch. They developed a more modern view of "separation of powers" to mean that government should be divided into legislative, executive, and judicial departments, each acting as a "check and balance" against the others. This arrangement of powers, Americans now understood, best secures the rights and liberty of the people.

Emergence of the Judiciary

The judiciary perhaps benefited the most from Americans' new thinking about fundamental law, written constitutions, and separation of powers. The idea of a supreme fundamental law as the original and deliberate act of the people made it possible to devise a theory of judicial review that fit well with popular sovereignty. Upholding the Constitution against an ordinary statute, Americans now believed, preserved and enforced this most perfect and permanent expression of the people's will. In a similar way, the changed view of separation of powers led to an expanded idea about judicial power that enabled the Supreme Court to apply and interpret the Constitution as law in deciding cases that came before it.

John Marshall, who would become chief justice of the Supreme Court, foresaw this expanded role for the judiciary in a speech he made supporting the Constitution in 1788. Marshall declared that if Congress should "make a law not warranted by any of the powers enumerated, it would be considered by the judges as an **infringement** of the Constitution which they are to guard." The fullest early argument in favor of judicial review was made by Alexander Hamilton in ***The Federalist***, No. 78. "The interpretation of the laws," said Hamilton, "is the proper and peculiar province of the courts. A constitution is, in fact, and must be regarded by the judges as a fundamental law," and if there was "an irreconcilable variance" between the constitution and a legislative statute, the constitution must be upheld as the law of "superior obligation and validity." Such a conclusion did not imply "a superiority of the judicial to the legislative power," but only "that the power of the people is superior to both." This passage from *The Federalist* in 1788, written fifteen years before *Marbury* v. *Madison,* remains the most powerful explanation and persuasive defense of the doctrine of judicial review.

infringement a violation or trespass on another person's rights

The Federalist set of 85 essays published 1787–1788 that analyzed the Constitution and urged its adoption; essays were written by John Jay, Alexander Hamilton, and James Madison

ARTICLE III—Establishment of Judicial Review: *Marbury* v. *Madison*

★ Establishment of Judicial Review: *Marbury* v. *Madison*

Roger K. Newman

judicial review a court's authority to evaluate laws for their constitutionality

Marbury v. *Madison* stands as the foremost precedent for judicial review. For the first time the Supreme Court held unconstitutional an act of Congress, establishing the doctrine that the Court has the final word among the branches of the federal government in determining what is legal under the Constitution.

By 1803 no one doubted that an unconstitutional act of government was null and void, but who was to judge? What the *Marbury* case settled was the Court's ultimate authority over Congress and the President. The significance of the case in its time derived from its political context and from the fact that the Court appeared to interfere successfully with the executive branch.

"Midnight Judges"

Federalist advocating a strong central government of separate states and the adoption of the U.S. Constitution

The Federalists lost the election of 1800, but on March 2, 1801, before leaving office, they created several new judicial posts. Among these were justice of the peace for the District of Columbia, whose duties included the trial of petty offenses and conducting marriage ceremonies. On March 3, the last day of his administration, President John Adams nominated forty-two persons, all fellow Federalists, to these positions, each one for a term of five years. The Senate confirmed the appointments that day, and the judicial commissions were signed and the official seal attached.

But in the rush of leaving office, John Marshall, who was serving as secretary of state, even though he had been confirmed as chief justice of the United States, failed to deliver seventeen of the commissions for the "midnight judges." "The extreme hurry of time" prevented him from sending them out, Marshall said later.

Jefferson Holds His Ground

nullities having no legal force; invalid

Thomas Jefferson, the new president, offered to allow some of the commissions to be delivered. But he refused to permit delivery of four of them. "The nominations crowded in by Mr. Adams after he knew he was not appointing for himself I treat as mere nullities," Jefferson wrote. One of those commissions was for William Marbury.

original jurisdiction the first courts to hear the case

writ of mandamus a court order directing an official to perform a ministerial duty, which the official has no choice but to do

Marbury sued to claim his post. He took his case directly to the Supreme Court, invoking the Court's original jurisdiction under Section 13 of the Judiciary Act of 1789. Marbury asked that the Court issue a writ of mandamus to the Jefferson administration, ordering it to deliver the commission. In December of 1801, the Court issued an order commanding James Madison, the new secretary of state, to show cause why the writ should not be issued.

A Charged Political Atmosphere

Congress, which was under the control of the Jeffersonian Republicans (the forerunner of the present Democratic party), soon changed the date

repeal revoke or cancel

of the Supreme Court's terms. This delayed the Court's hearing Marbury's case until February of 1803. During that time, Congress repealed the Federalist-sponsored Judiciary Act of 1801, and judges appointed under its provisions were dismissed. Both Congress and Republican-controlled state legislatures brought impeachment against Federalist judges. (All federal judges at this time had been appointed by the Federalists since the Federalist party had been the only one in power.)

The whole political atmosphere was charged. A week before the Court heard Marbury's case, Jefferson ordered the House of Representatives to impeach a federal judge. Plans were being made to impeach Supreme Court Justice Samuel Chase, who openly used his position on the bench to support the Federalist cause. (Chase was impeached in the House of Representatives, but acquitted in the Senate.) Jefferson's desire to replace Marshall with Spencer Roane of Virginia, a staunch advocate of states' rights, was also widely known. Before the *Marbury* case came down, a Republican newspaper wrote: "The attempt of the Supreme Court . . . by a mandamus, to control the executive functions, is a new experiment. It seems to be no less than a commencement of war."

Marshall's Alternatives

Chief Justice John Marshall presided over the Court when it heard the case. Under modern standards, he should have refused to participate since he had been so deeply involved in such a partisan way. But he wrote the Court's opinion, and he faced a difficult situation.

If the Court ordered the Jefferson administration (in the person of Madison, who became the named defendant in the case) to deliver the commission, the administration would likely ignore the order. The Court would not be able to enforce its decision and its prestige, already low, might suffer a fatal blow. On the other hand, if the Court said that Madison was within his rights in refusing to deliver the commission, the judiciary would be admitting to a subordinate position to the executive. This would have violated the Federalist principle that the Republican administration was responsible under the law.

John Marshall (1755–1835) was born in Virginia and fought in the American Revolution. He was a delegate to the Virginia assembly where he defended the new U.S. Constitution. After being a special envoy to France in 1797–98, Marshall served in Congress in 1799–1800 and then was secretary of state under President John Adams. Adams appointed him as chief justice in 1801. In cases such as *Marbury* v. *Madison, Dartmouth College* v. *Woodward, McCullough* v. *Maryland* and *Gibbons* v. *Ogden,* Marshall formulated basic principles of constitutional law. He served from 1801 to 1835, writing the Court's most important opinions. In the process Marshall established its prestige and independence. The Great Chief Justice, as he was called, viewed the Constitution as a national document: the states could not interfere with rights based on the Constitution. In *Marbury,* above all, Marshall seized the moment. By making judicial review an ongoing part of American government, he changed the course of American history.

Marshall Establishes Judicial Review

In his opinion Marshall asked three questions: Did Marbury have a right to the commission? If he had the right and this had been violated, did the laws grant him a remedy? If they did, was the remedy a writ of mandamus issued by the Supreme Court?

Marshall declared that Marbury was entitled to his commission, but that the Supreme Court did not have the power, based on its original jurisdiction, to issue the writ of mandamus, which would compel Madison to deliver it. He ruled unconstitutional Section 13 of the Judiciary Act of 1789, which had given the Court the power to do exactly what Marbury asked. In the Judiciary Act, Congress had given Marbury the right to bring his case directly to the Court. By doing this, Congress had changed the Constitution. Congress does not have the right to do so, Marshall ruled.

The Constitution Is Supreme

repugnant offensive or repulsive

"A law repugnant to the Constitution is void," Chief Justice Marshall wrote, and "courts as well as other departments [of government], are bound by that instrument." The Constitution is supreme. The people of the nation had adopted the Constitution as the supreme law of the land and consented to be governed by its rules. These rules include important limitations upon the powers of Congress. When the Congress violated those limitations, it violated the will of the people. Any act of Congress which conflicts with the Constitution is therefore null and void. If the Supreme Court could not strike down such acts, there would be no effective way to enforce the constitutional limits on the powers of Congress. Its powers would be unlimited, and there would no longer be a constitutional government.

Supreme Court Chief Justice John Marshall.

The Supreme Court should not enforce an unconstitutional law, Marshall wrote. But why should the Court's interpretation of the Constitution be preferred to that of Congress and the president? Here he reasoned: The Constitution is law; judges, not legislators or executives, interpret law; therefore, judges should interpret the Constitution. "If two laws conflict with each other, the courts must decide on the operation of each," he concluded.

Chief Justice Marshall also declared that the Court could not properly do this without violating its constitutional nature as an appellate court. That is, instead of considering cases of this sort in the first instance (original jurisdiction), the Court could only decide them after lower courts had first ruled. The Constitution clearly limits the cases which can go directly to the Supreme Court without having been heard first in the lower court. Marbury's case did not fit within these limits.

Having It Both Ways

vest to grant with particular authority, property, and rights

jurisdiction the territory or area within which authority may be exercised

paradox seemingly contradictory statement that may nonetheless be true

Marshall denied Marbury's petition after arguing for it at great length. In doing so, he managed both to have his cake and eat it. He angered Jefferson (who was his distant cousin) when he said that withholding Marbury's commission was not only illegal but violated "a vested legal right" even though the result of the case was to give Jefferson the immediate political result he desired—no appointments for Marbury and his friends. The immediate practical result of the decision was to reduce slightly the Court's jurisdiction. But in the process Marshall established the principle that the Court may declare acts of Congress unconstitutional.

Many people had anticipated this result, but Marshall made it in a manner that prevented any challenge to the principle. Jefferson could have protested that the voters have no check upon judges, who are appointed for life rather than elected. But Jefferson had achieved his immediate political goal and did not issue such a challenge. A paradox was established: the Court, which is not accountable to the people through elections, poses as the champion of their liberties and the keeper of the Constitution's meaning.

What *Marbury* Means

Over time, *Marbury* came to stand for the monumental principle that the Supreme Court may bind the coordinate branches of the national government to its rulings on what is the supreme law of the land. It is the ultimate interpreter of the Constitution. That principle stands out from *Marbury*. All else from the case, which preoccupied national attention in 1803, disappeared in our constitutional law.

National judicial review could have also disappeared if the impeachment of Justice Chase had succeeded. Indeed, John Marshall feared that he might be the victim of impeachment himself. *Marbury* remained as a precedent, never to be disturbed, and its influence soon spread into the states. Judicial review of local legislation by state courts was established under local constitutions, usually with far less support in state constitutions than the national constitution afforded judicial review of acts of Congress.

After *Marbury*, the Supreme Court did not again hold unconstitutional an act of Congress until 1857, when it decided *Dred Scott* v. *Sandford*. Fifty years after that, in 1907, long before he became Chief Justice, Charles Evan Hughes said, "We are under a Constitution, but the Constitution is what the judges say it is." That is because John Marshall in *Marbury* v. *Madison* established national judicial review as a permanent feature of the American system of government.

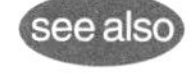

INTRODUCTION—Constitutional Concepts; Constitutional Origins; ARTICLE III—Impact of Judicial Review: *Dred Scott* v. *Sandford*; Judicial Review in the Nineteenth Century; The Judiciary; Origins of Judicial Review

★ Judicial Review in the Nineteenth Century

Howard Gillman

In 1803 in *Marbury* v. *Madison*, the Supreme Court asserted for itself the power of judicial review. The justices claimed the authority to declare acts of Congress unconstitutional. This claim was without precedent, and it made the judicial branch an equal branch of government, with power to keep a careful watch on the legislative and executive branches. The Supreme Court ensured that the other branches of the federal government must operate within the scope of their powers. But the justices did not effectively challenge the acts of Congress and the president until many years later.

judicial review a court's authority to evaluate laws for their constitutionality

precedent established ruling, understanding, or practice of the law

Nonjusticiable Disputes

Chief Justice John Marshall declared in *Marbury* that the Court would review the constitutionality of government acts as part of its general responsibility to settle legal cases and disputes. This meant if a dispute that involved the meaning of the Constitution did not lead to a lawsuit that came within the Court's jurisdiction, the dispute did not have justiciability. In that instance the justices have no authority to rule in the case. So the power of judicial review includes only cases that involve a valid legal dispute. It does not give the Supreme Court authority to hand down merely advisory opinions not based on actual cases about the meaning of the Constitution.

jurisdiction the territory or area within which authority may be exercised

justiciability the principle that courts can only resolve disputes that are brought as lawsuits in a court

President Thomas Jefferson discusses the Louisiana territory with explorer Merriwether Lewis. Jefferson bypassed Congress in his negotiations with France.

Historical Overview

Some justices had begun to assert the principle of justiciability at the end of the eighteenth century.

Washington's request. In Hayburn's Case (1792) and in Chief Justice John Jay's ruling on President George Washington's request for guidelines from the Supreme Court to help prepare his Neutrality Proclamation of 1793, the Court declined to give an advisory opinion. As a result, the Court did not become involved in or rule on many important constitutional controversies during the early nineteenth century.

Jefferson's concerns. President Thomas Jefferson had serious doubts about whether Article II allowed the president to bypass Congress and negotiate the deal with France that resulted in the Louisiana Purchase of 1803. Yet, since no one challenged the president's action in federal court or brought a lawsuit claiming Jefferson had violated his legal rights, this important and controversial assertion of presidential power was not subject to judicial review.

Congress's policies go undisputed. In 1815, when Congress decided to provide federal funds to build roads and canals as transportation needed for "internal improvements," many Americans, including President James Madison, who favored the measure, were worried. They feared that the national legislature had exceeded its authority under Article I, Section 8, of the Constitution. But, once again, this policy was never disputed in a lawsuit brought before the Supreme Court.

The political questions doctrine. In *Luther* v. *Borden* (1849), the Supreme Court expanded upon the principle of what cases it would not hear. The justices set forth the idea known as the political questions doctrine. Under this doctrine, certain disputes that were brought before the Court "belonged to the political power and not to the judicial." This meant that in those cases Congress or the president had the power to resolve the dispute, and the Supreme Court would not hear such cases. The Court made it clear that it would not involve itself in every constitutional dispute.

political question a decision that the courts determine is entirely within the power of the political branches of government, Congress and the president, to make if they choose to do so

Weakness of Early Supreme Courts

One of the major reasons that the Supreme Court in the early nineteenth century avoided becoming involved in constitutional disputes was that it still had little authority in the federal government. Even though *Marbury* v. *Madison* was a strong statement about the Court's power in the political system, the Court itself was not yet able to force the legislative and executive branches to accept its decisions. Alexander Hamilton had predicted this possibility in *The Federalist*, No. 78, when he wrote that the judicial branch of the national government was the "least dangerous branch" because it had the fewest sources of political power.

The Federalist set of 85 essays published 1787–1788 that analyzed the Constitution and urged its adoption; essays were written by John Jay, Alexander Hamilton, and James Madison

This meant that the Supreme Court, before the Civil War, still was often forced to find a way to assert its power without forcing the other branches of government to comply with its decisions. In a special way, *Marbury* was an effective decision because it produced an effective result. Chief Justice John Marshall had declared that the Court had no

jurisdiction in that case in order to avoid a dangerous possibility, namely, that President Jefferson would ignore the Court if it ruled that the judicial appointment must be withheld from William Marbury.

The Court used a similar tactic in *Cohens* v. *Virginia* (1821). In that case, Chief Justice Marshall wanted to establish the principle that the Supreme Court had the power to review interpretations of federal laws by state courts. At the same time, he wanted to avoid a conflict with Virginia's Supreme Court. The Cohens brothers had been selling tickets for the federal government lottery in Virginia, a state that considered the lottery illegal. Marshall's solution was to assert the authority of the court to rule on the legality of the Cohens's actions and then agree with the state court's interpretation of the federal law. The Court upheld the conviction of the Cohens brothers.

American financier Nicholas Biddle (1786–1844) served as president of the Bank of the United States from 1822 until 1839, when its charter expired.

The Supreme Court Supports National Power

In the early nineteenth century, the Supreme Court was more effective when its rulings supported national power than when it tried to limit that power. *McCulloch* v. *Maryland* (1819) was perhaps the most important decision the Court handed down during the nineteenth century. In *McCulloch*, the justices upheld Congress's power to charter the Second Bank of the United States, even though authority to set up a national bank is not mentioned in the powers granted to Congress in Article I, Section 8. The Court made its ruling only after general agreement had been reached in the national government that the Bank was needed. That agreement now was supported by leaders like James Madison who had argued that the Bank was unconstitutional back in the 1790s.

One of the outcomes of the Court's support of national power was that its rulings often asserted the national interest over that of the states. The Court felt more confident asserting its power in this area because the justices knew that they could count on support from the other branches of the national government. Before the Civil War, nearly all the Court's decisions that struck down laws as unconstitutional involved state laws that were not in keeping with federal policy. The Supreme Court provided essential protections for property owners against actions by the states, and thus favored the national interests that were building a strong commercial Republic.

Federal-state relations. Even in the field of federal-state relations, the Supreme Court usually moved cautiously in the years before the Civil War. When Andrew Jackson became president in 1828, the national government began to move away from strong, centralized federal authority. The Supreme Court, which now was headed by Chief Justice Roger Taney, who had been appointed by Jackson, followed this shift in power. The Court now allowed the states more opportunities to promote economic development and to regulate the economy. It did so in rulings in such cases as *Charles River Bridge* v. *Warren Bridge* (1837), *Mayor of New York* v. *Miln* (1837), and *Cooley* v. *Board of Wardens* (1852).

The Court and slavery. The Supreme Court also moved with great caution on the extremely controversial issue of slavery. For some time, the

justices tried to follow the lead of the national parties on this issue, striking a compromise whenever possible. In *Prigg* v. *Pennsylvania* (1842), the Court declared that the northern states were not required to assist the federal government in returning fugitive slaves to their owners. Then, in *Strader* v. *Graham* (1851), the Court ruled that the southern states had the authority to decide who was to be considered a slave.

Slavery was the issue that led the Court for the first time to check the powers of Congress on a major question of national policy. The results of this ruling, *Dred Scott* v. *Sandford* (1857), were disastrous for the Court. It ended any doubt that the Supreme Court's real authority was linked to promoting national power, not to limiting it. The justices ruled that Congress had no power to prohibit slavery in the territories. The firestorm of protest that swept across the northern states showed that the Court's ruling had only fanned the flames of this divisive issue. Chief Justice Taney then attempted to follow up this use of judicial review of Congress's power by declaring unconstitutional some of President Abraham Lincoln's actions at the start of the Civil War. But Lincoln ignored his decision in *Ex parte Merryman* (1861). The Court's long struggle to gain respect and power in the nation's political system seemed lost. Constitutional politics had moved from the courtroom to the battlefield.

Judicial Review Becomes a Major Force

The Supreme Court regained its authority only after the power of the national government itself was restored after the Civil War. The Civil War Amendments to the Constitution, especially the Fourteenth Amendment, dramatically increased the constitutional restrictions the federal government placed on the states. Moreover, it became clear that the Supreme Court would have the job of interpreting these restrictions and enforcing them. In addition, Congress also wanted to make sure that the states followed the policies set up by the federal government. As a result, the lawmakers in Congress expanded the jurisdiction of federal courts over matters that before this had been reserved to the states.

The *Civil Rights Cases*. At first, it was assumed that federal courts would use their power to promote the Republican party's post-Civil War agenda of protecting the rights of the newly freed slaves. But the agreement among Republican leaders about this policy collapsed in the disputed presidential election of 1876. To settle the election, Republicans and Democrats negotiated the Compromise of 1877. Under this compromise, the Republicans agreed to end Reconstruction in the South in exchange for Democratic support in securing the presidency for the Republican candidate, Rutherford B. Hayes. Once again, the Supreme Court followed the trend of national policies by declaring, in the *Civil Rights Cases* (1883), that the Civil Rights Acts of 1875 were unconstitutional.

***Plessy* v. *Ferguson*.** A few years later, the Court accepted the policies of the southern states that established a system of strict racial segregation in that region. In *Plessy* v. *Ferguson* (1896), the justices ruled that segregation of the races did not violate "the equal protection of the laws." The

> In *Worchester* v. *Georgia* in 1832, the Supreme Court ruled that states could not pass laws affecting federally recognized Indian nations. Worchester, a citizen of Vermont, was a missionary who had entered the Cherokee Nation with President Andrew Jackson's authorization but without the permission that Georgia required by law. The Court declared the law unconstitutional. Yet Jackson now opposed the ruling and sided with Georgia, likely because he did not wish to drive Georgia into the camp favoring the nullification of tariffs led by South Carolina. Chief Justice Marshall strongly implied in his opinion that it was the President's duty to honor and back the Cherokee Nation's rights under federal law. After the Court's decision, Jackson said, "John Marshall has made his decision—now let him enforce it!"

Court also transformed key provisions of the Fourteenth Amendment into protections for corporations and businesses seeking to reduce the authority of the federal government to regulate the nation's economy in the public interest. By the end of the nineteenth century, the Supreme Court had established principles that became known as "laissez-faire constitutionalism" because its rulings severely limited the government's power to regulate the national economy.

laissez-faire (French, "let do") a policy of making as little interference with freedom of choice and action as possible

Limiting the national government's authority. Once the Court began to take the side of powerful interests and corporations, it felt able to hand down rulings that checked and limited the authority of the national government. The Court's power of judicial review, which it had declared in principle at the beginning of the nineteenth century, finally was carried out in a series of cases in 1895. In *U.S.* v. *E.C. Knight,* the justices ruled that Congress had no authority to regulate businesses engaged in manufacturing. In *Pollock* v. *Farmers' Loan and Trust Company*, the Court held that Congress had no power to pass an income tax law. As a result of these and later decisions, the Supreme Court was at the center of a growing national debate. People argued about the ability of federal and state governments to meet the new and very difficult challenges brought by the rapid industrialization of the United States.

By the end of the nineteenth century, the Supreme Court had won its century-long struggle to use its powerful tool of judicial review. The Court now could act with courage and determination to review the powers exercised by the executive and legislative branches of the federal government, and determine whether they were constitutional. Judicial review had become a vital part of the Court's power, and would play a major role in the American political system.

ARTICLE I—Commerce Clause: Through the Nineteenth Century; Contracts Clause; The Necessary and Proper Clause; ARTICLE II—The Treaty Power; ARTICLE III—Establishment of Judicial Review: *Marbury* v. *Madison*; Impact of Judicial Review: *Dred Scott* v. *Sandford*; The Judiciary; ARTICLE IV—Fugitive Slave Clause; Republican Form of Government; ARTICLE VI—Supremacy Clause; THIRTEENTH AMENDMENT—Slavery and the Constitution; THIRTEENTH AMENDMENT: Enforcement; FOURTEENTH AMENDMENT—"Separate but Equal"

Impact of Judicial Review: *Dred Scott* v. *Sandford*

Christopher L. Eisgruber

In *Scott* v. *Sandford* (1857), which is often referred to as the *Dred Scott* decision, the Supreme Court denied claims brought by an African-American family seeking freedom from slavery. Some of the justices hoped that their decision in this case would settle the national debate over slavery. Instead, the Court's decision pushed the nation closer to the Civil War.

Origins of the Case

Dred Scott began life as an enslaved African. Scott and his owner, John Emerson, lived in Missouri, where slavery was permitted. Between 1834 and 1838, Emerson took Scott with him to several places north of Missouri, including Minnesota. Minnesota had not yet become a state. It was part of a federal territory governed by the United States Congress. Slavery was illegal in Minnesota because Congress, in 1820, had passed a law that soon became famous as the Missouri Compromise. The Missouri Compromise prohibited slavery in Minnesota and all the territories north of what is now the southern boundary of Missouri.

Dred Scott with his wife Harriet.

When Scott and Emerson made their journey, most lawyers believed that slaves became free if their owners voluntarily took them to places like Minnesota where slavery was illegal. There is evidence that Scott exercised the rights of a free man while he was in Minnesota. For example, slaves did not have the legal right to marry, but Scott married Harriet Robinson in a civil ceremony conducted by a government official.

Later, Emerson and the Scotts moved back to Missouri. No one knows why the Scotts returned. Since it was a slave state (despite the Missouri Compromise), it was a difficult place for African Americans to live. Some historians have thought that perhaps the Scotts were forced back there against their will.

In Missouri, Emerson continued to claim the Scotts as his slaves. Following Emerson's death, Dred Scott, Harriet Robinson Scott, and their two daughters were placed under the control of his brother-in-law, John Sanford. (Because the Supreme Court misspelled Sanford's name, the case became known as *Scott* v. *Sandford.*) In 1846, the Scotts sued Sanford, claiming that the Missouri Compromise had made them free people. Sanford answered by claiming, among other things, that the Missouri Compromise was unconstitutional. It took ten years for the case to reach the Supreme Court.

Slavery in the Territories

Scott was a politically explosive case, and the justices knew it. Early in the nation's history, many Americans hoped that slavery might disappear slowly and peacefully. But in the years leading to the *Scott* decision, the conflict over slavery grew more divisive and more violent. The question of whether slavery would spread to the federal territories soon became the focus. It grew in importance because the territories could apply to become new states. Slaveowners would not be able to move to territories

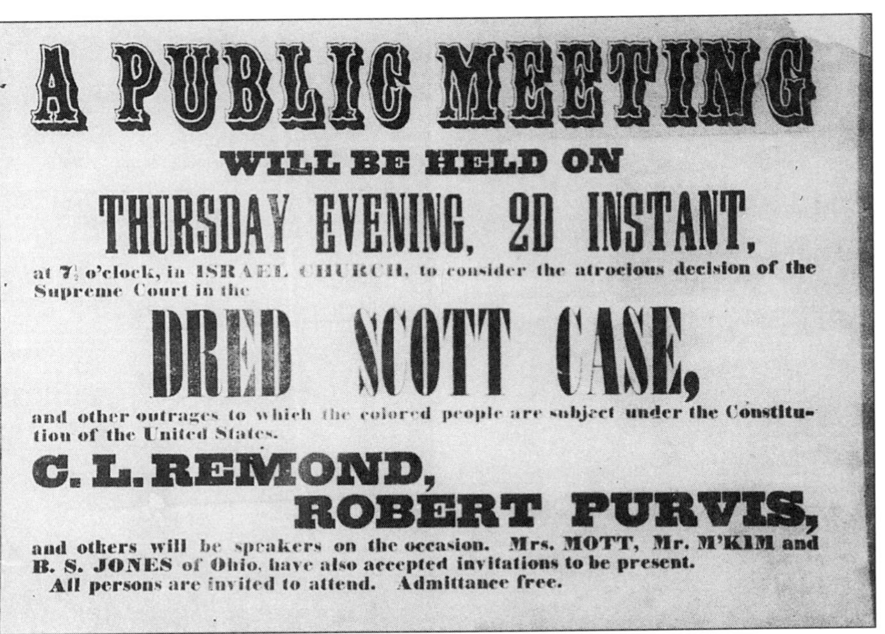

A Public Meeting flyer used to denounce the *Dred Scott* decision.

Abolitionist John Brown, invoking the power of both the rifle and the Bible, separates opposing factions in the "Bleeding Kansas" conflict.

where slavery was illegal, and therefore the territories would enter the Union as "free" states. The free states might then gain enough power to amend the Constitution to abolish slavery.

By 1857, the issue of slavery in the territories was being fought with guns as well as words. Kansas was a major battleground. Antislavery and proslavery forces fought over whether it should enter the Union as a slave state or a free state. Riots and raids led to bloodshed, earning the territory its unwanted nickname of "Bleeding Kansas."

The outcome of the *Scott* case would affect the balance of power in the Union. If the Supreme Court held that the Missouri Compromise was unconstitutional, then it would be easier for slavery to start in new territories and new states. If the Court upheld the Missouri Compromise, it would strengthen the antislavery cause.

The Court Reaches Its Decision

At first, many of the justices wanted to dispose of the Scotts' case on a minor technical point. If the Court had done so, the Scotts would have remained slaves, but the justices would have avoided the explosive political issue of the Missouri Compromise. Two antislavery justices, Benjamin Curtis and John McLean, refused to go along. They announced that they were going to write dissenting opinions upholding the Scotts' rights.

Whether because of this threat of dissents or for some other reason, the seven justices in the majority decided not to duck the fateful issue. They held that the Missouri Compromise was unconstitutional. The case was a victory for Sanford and the pro-slavery cause.

In most Supreme Court cases, one justice writes an opinion on behalf of all the justices in the majority. In *Scott*, however, each justice instead wrote his own opinion. Chief Justice Roger Taney wrote the most important one. Taney was from Maryland and had owned slaves himself, although he freed them early in his life. He also was an experienced politician who had served as secretary of the treasury under President Andrew Jackson.

In his *Scott* opinion, Taney took an extreme position. He said that "the right of property in a slave is distinctly and expressly affirmed in the Constitution." He further stated that when the Constitution referred to "people" and "citizens," it meant only white people and white citizens. Chief Justice Taney also declared that Congress lacked the power to pass the Missouri Compromise or any other law prohibiting slavery in the territories.

The Lincoln-Douglas Debates

The Supreme Court's decision in *Scott* v. *Sandford* was extremely controversial. One important response came from Abraham Lincoln, who was running for the Senate in Illinois. In the summer of 1858, Lincoln and his opponent, Senator Stephen Douglas, held a series of debates. Douglas said that he accepted the Court's decision in *Scott*, because the Supreme Court should have the last word on what the Constitution means.

Only once before the *Dred Scott* case had the Supreme Court declared an act of Congress unconstitutional. That was in *Marbury* v. *Madison* in 1803, which established the principle of judicial review. In *Marbury,* the law directly concerned the federal judiciary. But the Missouri Compromise was a general law, on the books for thirty-four years, when the Court sanctioned the doctrine advocated by the southern politician and political philosopher John C. Calhoun that slavery was national in scope. Oregon and Nebraska, as well as Kansas, were opened to it. Slavery was theoretically legal in every territory. Charles Evans Hughes, before becoming chief justice in 1930, put it best when he listed the *Dred Scott* case as the first of the Court's "self-inflicted wounds."

Lincoln disagreed. He pointed out that Taney was wrong when he said that "the right of property in a slave is distinctly and expressly affirmed in the Constitution." In fact, the word "slavery" never appeared in the Constitution. For example, Article IV, Section 2, paragraph 3, is commonly referred to as "the fugitive slave clause," but it never uses the word "slavery." According to Lincoln, the Framers avoided using that word because they knew that slavery was immoral and they did not want the Constitution to approve it.

Lincoln also challenged Taney's comments about the Declaration of Independence, which proclaims that "all men are created equal." According to Taney, the men who signed the Declaration did not really mean what they said. Many of them owned slaves, Taney observed, and they could not really have believed that those slaves were their equals. In Taney's view, when the Declaration said "all men," it meant "all white men." Lincoln said that, again, Taney was wrong, and that the Declaration applied to people of all races.

Lincoln lost the Senate race in Illinois, but his arguments captured the public's attention. Before the debates, Douglas had been considered a strong presidential candidate. After the debates, Douglas's star faded, and Lincoln's rose. Politics became even more polarized now, as the nation moved closer to the Civil War.

After the Civil War ended, the Court's opinions in *Scott* were overruled by the Thirteenth and Fourteenth Amendments to the Constitution. *Scott* lingers in the nation's legal memory as an example of the Supreme Court at its worst. Conservative and liberal lawyers sometimes accuse one another of behaving like Taney. Conservatives point out that Taney cited the due process clause, the same provision that liberal justices later used to protect abortion rights. To this, liberals respond that Taney relied heavily on the intentions of the Framers, just as conservative justices often recommend that the Court should.

These accusations produce more heat than light. Anyone interested in learning the lesson of *Scott* should turn instead to the Lincoln-Douglas debates, which are an awesome mix of argument and wit. If *Scott* is the Court's worst decision, Lincoln's response is among the nation's finest moments.

see also

ARTICLE III—Contemporary Judicial Review; ARTICLE IV—Fugitive Slave Clause; FIFTH AMENDMENT—Substantive Due Process

Extent of Judicial Review: *Lochner* v. *New York*

Roger K. Newman

The words "due process" invite judges to evaluate the process that is due. To discover what this is, judges may look to history, tradition, nature, or to what they believe the community feels is reasonable. Due process cannot be defined exactly. It implies procedure—notice and the right to be heard. But beyond that, people bring their own views to what else due process includes.

The Court and the Rise of the Industrial State

The rise of the industrial state in the United States in the late 1800s created an ever-growing class of workers who depended on factory

The number of bakeries increased greatly on New York City's Lower East Side at the turn of the twentieth century as more women worked outside the home in garment factories and had less time to bake bread. The stores were clean and the bread healthy, but conditions in the basement of the apartment buildings where the bread was prepared and baked were usually filthy and dangerous. Most of the cellars had dirt floors and were infested with roaches and rats.

Bakers at the time usually worked six days each week for a total of seventy-four hours. There were reports of bakers working as much as fifteen hours a day, six days a week, and twenty-four hours on Thursday, for a total of 114 hours weekly. Most bakers were required to take room and board in the shop. The lucky ones slept on a cot while most men slept on the boards they used for squeezing and pressing the bread. The bakers were paid by the day. They were exposed to flour dust, gas fumes, dampness, and extremes of hot and cold. Lung diseases were common. Bakers died of tuberculosis at unusually high rates. Most were weakened to the point that they were forced to "retire" by the age of forty-five. It was these facts that the Supreme Court chose to ignore in the *Lochner* case.

legislation the power and work of making laws

laissez-faire (French, "let do") a policy of making as little interference with freedom of choice and action as possible

employment to earn their living. Legislatures responded to the needs of the workers. In 1895, New York passed a law that limited the hours a baker could work to ten hours a day and sixty hours a week. An owner of a Utica, New York, bakery was convicted (and fined $50) for violating the law. His lawyer argued before the Supreme Court, in *Lochner* v. *New York*, that limiting the working hours for laborers might deprive both them and the employer of liberty without due process of law. The Supreme Court agreed.

Justice Rufus Peckham wrote the Court's opinion. He had also spoken for the Court in 1897, when it rejected a Louisiana law that regulated the content of insurance contracts. Due process of law, Peckham wrote then, guaranteed "the right of a citizen . . . to be free in the enjoyment of all his faculties; . . . and for that purpose to enter into all contracts which may be proper, necessary, and essential to his carrying out to a successful conclusion the purposes above mentioned." Freedom of contract was born.

Are We at the Mercy of the Legislature?

In *Lochner* v. *New York*, Peckham similarly wrote: "The limitation of the hours of labor does not come within the police power. . . . Common understanding" is that "the trade of a baker has never been regarded as an unhealthy one . . . It might be safely affirmed that almost all occupations more or less affect the health. But are we all, on that account, at the mercy of legislative majorities?" He noted that he did "not believe in the soundness of the views in support of such legislation."

A dissenting voice. Justice Oliver Wendell Holmes, Jr., disagreed. In a short dissent he said that the meaning of the word "liberty" changes "when used to prevent the state from limiting hours of work as a proper measure on the score of health." The Court's opinion, he wrote, was based "upon an economic theory which a large part of the country does not entertain . . ." A constitution, Holmes continued, "is not intended to embody a particular economic theory. . . ."

Economic theories in question. Holmes was referring to the economic theory of laissez-faire, a doctrine claiming that the economy functions best when there is no interference by government. Herbert Spencer was the leading proponent of "social Darwinism," a belief that, just as in biological evolution, only "the fittest" people and societies survive. In the late nineteenth century and continuing well into the twentieth, this theory exerted much influence. It fitted well with laissez-faire economics and the constitutional right to own, use, and dispose of private property with minimal governmental interference at a time when everyone wanted to "make a fortune."

A Controversial Theory

Lochner v. *New York* reflected a controversial constitutional theory based on the Fourteenth Amendment due process clause that had been gaining importance since the 1880s. The theory depended on three concepts.

Substantive due process. The first concept was substantive due process. This idea was that the substance of a law could deny a person life, liberty, or property.

Liberty of contract. The second was liberty of contract. According to this idea, the Fourteenth Amendment's guarantee of liberty includes the freedom of two or more people to make nearly any agreement they wish.

Police power. The third concept was a narrow view of the police power. The police power is the government's authority to impose restrictions on people's rights for the sake of public welfare, order, and security. Behind this concept was the idea that a state's power was limited to making laws that brought about health, safety, morals, and peace and good order.

authority the power to grant legal allowance

In the *Lochner* case, the argument of health, safety and welfare was not enough to overcome the dislike of a majority of the Supreme Court justices' for such legislation. The case raised questions about the extent to which people could look to government to solve the economic and social problems that industrialism had created. Legislatures had to draft laws with judges looking over their shoulders. Judges threatened to become like a third legislative chamber. Theodore Roosevelt complained that the Supreme Court had "created an insurmountable barrier to reform."

The Heyday of Substantive Due Process

The period from 1905 to 1937 was the heyday of substantive due process. The phrase "liberty of contract" could not be found in the Constitution, but the Supreme Court regularly used the due process clause of the Fourteenth Amendment to strike down states' regulation of business. From 1899 through 1937, the Court overturned approximately two hundred state and federal economic regulatory laws while upholding 369 state laws of all sorts. Between 1899 and 1918, it rejected fifty-three laws enacted under the state police power, but between 1920 and 1930, it threw

Little girls at work in a hosiery mill in Tennessee (1910). In spite of information suggesting that long work hours were harmful to laborers—especially women—the Supreme Court was slow to accept the constitutionality of state economic and social regulation.

out 140. Yet in the decade after *Lochner*, the Court upheld a law limiting working hours for women and a law regulating work of both men and women.

The first of these decisions was *Muller* v. *Oregon* in 1908. Louis D. Brandeis (who later joined the Court in 1916) argued the *Muller* case. The written brief that he presented to the Court was original. Brandeis largely ignored *Lochner* and relied mostly on social science data to show that long hours of work were especially harmful to women. A legislature could appropriately pass a law to protect them. The Court agreed unanimously.

brief a written document presented to a court by the lawyer arguing the case; it contains the facts and points of law

Trying to Overthrow *Lochner*

Many people thought that *Lochner* was overruled as a result of *Muller*. They especially thought so when the Supreme Court in 1917 upheld an Oregon law setting a ten-hour workday with an overtime provision for men. But *Lochner* was revived in 1923, when the Court, in *Adkins* v. *Children's Hospital,* overturned a minimum-wage law for women in the District of Columbia. (In this case, the Court noted in passing that the Nineteenth Amendment, adopted in 1920, had reduced the civil inferiority of women almost "to the vanishing point.")

The Court ruled in 1923 that, under the due process clause, a legislature could not fix the weight of loaves of bread. In the same way, in 1932, the Court invalidated a certificate that Oklahoma issued to those in the business of making ice. The pendulum swung once again in 1934, in *Nebbia* v. *New York*, when the Court upheld a New York law regulating the price of milk. But in 1936 the justices held a New York minimum-wage law unconstitutional.

"The Switch in Time That Saved Nine"

Finally, in 1937, the Court upheld a minimum-wage law for women. This case, *West Coast Hotel* v. *Parrish*, specifically overruled the *Adkins* case and implicitly overruled *Lochner*. It came as President Franklin D. Roosevelt's plan to enlarge the Supreme Court was before Congress. The Court changed direction on the constitutionality of state regulation of wages and then on the reach of the commerce clause. Though the Court-packing bill, as it was known, failed to pass either house of Congress, Roosevelt won the war for regulatory laws. Quickly, the Court's about-face was called "the switch in time that saved nine."

Alluding to President Franklin D. Roosevelt's proposed legislation to increase the number of Supreme Court justices, American jurist Robert Eugene Cushman asked—

"If the Constitution, as interpreted by the Court, prevents the proper solution of our social and economic problems, should we do something to the Constitution to meet the difficulty, or should we do something to the Supreme Court?"

Changes in Thinking

The pressing demands for the use of the state police power during the Great Depression and new attitudes on the Court brought a major change. By the 1940s the Court seemed to take the position that state economic regulation was not subject to any constitutional prohibition except specific constitutional limits on state power. And substantive due process began to be used in noneconomic cases.

Fifth Amendment—Substantive Due Process; Fourteenth Amendment—Enforcement; Nineteenth Amendment

Lochner has come to symbolize raw judicial power: judges deciding cases on the basis of their economic and political dispositions. Its fame stems from the power of Holmes's dissent. Commentators across the political spectrum regularly bring up the case to condemn decisions that they believe are wrong.

Contemporary Judicial Review

Erwin Chemerinsky

In 1937, a radical change occurred in constitutional law. Conservative justices had controlled the Supreme Court for the prior forty years. During that period, the Court had declared unconstitutional more than two hundred laws protecting workers and consumers. For example, the Court had overturned a federal law prohibiting interstate commerce in goods made by child labor, and ruled that state laws requiring employers to pay workers a minimum wage were unconstitutional. In two dramatic decisions in 1937, however, *NLRB* [National Labor Relations Board] v. *Jones & Laughlin Steel Corp.* and *West Coast Hotel* v. *Parish*, the Court clearly changed course. The Court now no longer would act forcefully to limit the government's ability to regulate the nation's economy. Instead, the Court would allow legislatures to act, and it would uphold laws regulating the workplace and economic conditions.

Pressures on the Supreme Court

This remarkable shift in the Court's approach reflected many pressures. The Great Depression of the 1930s created a widely supported need for government action. Equally important, President Franklin D. Roosevelt's proposed court-packing plan put heavy pressure on the justices. Furious at the Court for striking down his New Deal programs, President Roosevelt asked Congress to increase the size of the Court by adding one new seat for every justice over the age of seventy, up to a maximum of six new members. Since six of the nine justices were older than seventy, this plan would have created an immediate majority on the Court who would support the president's views.

Franklin D. Roosevelt approves social security legislation (1935). Republicans' challenges failed to prevent the bill from going through.

Although President Roosevelt's plan was never adopted, it may have helped persuade Justice Owen Roberts to change his mind. He cast the decisive fifth vote for the majority in the two 1937 decisions upholding New Deal measures, favoring laws he had ruled against in the past. Then, soon after these 1937 decisions, the conservative justices began to retire, and President Roosevelt was able to appoint nearly all the members of the high Court.

Thus, the contemporary era of judicial review began in 1937. Since then, two issues of judicial review have clearly stood out: first, the Court's role in economic matters and personal liberties; second, the debate on the interpretation of the Constitution.

The Distinction Between Economic and Political Rights

The Supreme Court in 1938 clearly stated the philosophy of judicial review that it has generally followed ever since. Although the Supreme Court has generally deferred to the two elected branches of government in matters involving regulation of the economy, it has been much more willing to act in reviewing laws affecting individual rights and civil rights. Oddly enough, the Court did so in a footnote to its decision in *United States* v. *Carolene Products* that upheld a federal law prohibiting the sale of "filled milk," a substance made by mixing vegetable oil with skim milk. Footnote four to this opinion said that there was a presumption in favor of upholding laws regulating commercial dealings and that such laws would be allowed as long as they are reasonable. At the same time, the Court also declared that it would not similarly defer its rulings on laws that affected fundamental rights or that discriminated against "discrete and insular minorities."

presumption an attitude or belief guided by probability, taken for granted as true

discrete and insular minorities groups such as African Americans, who had long been discriminated against and were unlikely to succeed in ending discrimination through the political process

The Supreme Court thereby created a dual standard of judicial review. Government laws regulating consumers, employment, or economic activities have almost always been upheld. The Court has continually proclaimed that economic regulation is a legislative, not a judicial, matter. Since 1937, not a single federal or state law has been ruled unconstitutional for infringing freedom of contract as protected by the liberty of the due process clause in the Fifth and Fourteenth Amendments. (The exception involves government actions in taking private property without just compensation, in violation of the Fifth Amendment.) Moreover, only a handful of the Court's rulings have invalidated laws regulating economic activity.

infringe exceed the limits of, or violate

In sharp contrast, the Court has actively moved to review laws discriminating against minorities and infringing fundamental rights. *Brown* v. *Board of Education* (1954) is perhaps the single most important decision in contemporary constitutional law. In *Brown,* the Court declared that state laws requiring segregation in education were unconstitutional. This ruling marked the beginning of an era in which the Court carefully examined laws that discriminated against racial minorities. Such laws are upheld only if they are necessary to achieve a compelling government purpose. This is a far stricter standard of judicial review than merely that the laws must be reasonable, which the Court uses in judging economic regulations.

compelling government purpose the government must show that the law is necessary for achieving its goals

Similarly, laws interfering with fundamental rights must meet this demanding standard of a compelling government purpose. Since 1937, the Court has vigorously protected enumerated rights, such as freedom of speech, which is safeguarded in the First Amendment, as well as non-enumerated rights, such as privacy and the right to travel. For instance, in *Shapiro* v. *Thompson* (1969), the Court declared unconstitutional a state law requiring that individuals live in the state for a year in order

to receive welfare benefits. The Court said that the law discouraged interstate travel and was unconstitutional because it was not necessary to achieve a compelling government interest.

Thus, contemporary judicial review is very much based on a double standard: judicial deference to economic regulations, but vigorous judicial review of laws that discriminate against minorities or interfere with fundamental rights. The Court presumes that economic regulations are constitutional, and invalidates them only if it can be proved that they are not reasonably related to a proper government purpose. Laws that discriminate or interfere with fundamental rights are presumed to be unconstitutional, and are upheld only if the government can prove that they are necessary to achieve a compelling purpose.

In *The Struggle for Judicial Supremacy* (1941), U.S. General Attorney and U.S. Supreme Court Justice Robert H. Jackson (1892–1954) stated:

"The ultimate function of the Supreme Court is nothing less than the arbitration between fundamental and ever-present rival forces or trends in our organized society."

The Debate Over Interpreting the Law

A controversial debate has been waged among the justices, legal commentators, politicians, and the American public alike over whether the Court should protect rights not enumerated in the Constitution. Decisions such as *Brown* v. *Board of Education* triggered this often heated debate about the appropriate method of judicial review, and decisions such as *Roe* v. *Wade,* which held that laws prohibiting abortions are unconstitutional, made it even more intensive.

On one side of the debate have been justices such as Antonin Scalia and Clarence Thomas. These justices have opposed strongly any judicial protection of rights not mentioned in the Constitution. For example, they believe that *Roe* v. *Wade* was wrongly decided and thus their position that there is no right to abortion is based on the fact that this right is not mentioned in the Constitution and the Framers did not intend it. Their supporters argue that it gives an unelected judiciary too much power if it is allowed to identify and protect rights that are nowhere stated in the Constitution.

On the other side of the debate have been justices such as John Paul Stevens and the late William J. Brennan, Jr. They believe it is essential for the Court to interpret the broad language of the Constitution to protect fundamental rights such as privacy and the right to travel. They argue that a Constitution written over two hundred years ago for a vastly different world must evolve by interpretation and not just by constitutional amendment. They contend that it is the role of the judiciary to identify and protect rights that are essential parts of liberty.

In the end, this struggle focuses on the proper role of judicial review in a democratic society, and it affects countless issues that come before the Supreme Court. Should there be a right to buy and use contraceptives and a right to abortion? Should there be a right to doctor-assisted suicide? Should there be a right to travel in the United States? All of these questions, and many more, depend on one's views about how the Constitution should be interpreted.

INTRODUCTION—Constitutional Concepts; ARTICLE I—Commerce Clause: The New Deal; AMENDMENTS—The Courts and the Bill of Rights; FIFTH AMENDMENT—Substantive Due Process; FOURTEENTH AMENDMENT—Abortion; *Brown* v. *Board of Education*; Privacy; School Desegregation After *Brown*

Right to a Jury Trial

Vikram David Amar

ARTICLE III, SECTION 2, CLAUSE 3, OF THE CONSTITUTION STATES

*The trial of all Crimes, except Cases of **Impeachment**, shall be by Jury; and such Trial shall be held in the States where the said Crimes shall have been committed; but when not committed within any State, the trial shall be at such Place or Places as the Congress may by Law have directed.*

impeachment method by which the House of Representatives may charge the nation's highest-ranking officials, including the president, with wrongdoing; following impeachment, if the officials are found guilty of the charges, the Senate then may try them and remove them from office

To the Framers, no idea was more central to constitutional government than the citizen jury. The Framers cherished it not only as a shield against government tyranny, but also as an essential tool for educating Americans in the duties and habits of citizenship. Accordingly, they sought to make the right to trial by jury one of the cornerstones of a free society. They carried out this plan in Article III of the Constitution, as well as in the Sixth Amendment (which calls for speedy public jury trials in criminal cases), the Fifth Amendment (which provides for grand juries as charging bodies in criminal cases), and the Seventh Amendment (which provides for jury trials in civil cases).

A Cornerstone of Democracy

The Framers of the Constitution believed that juries were absolutely necessary to prevent government officials from abusing their powers. They believed juries could accomplish this, because they would be composed of ordinary citizens under no financial or other obligation to the government. When the **Anti-Federalists** argued that the original Constitution did not go far enough in protecting juries, the **Federalists** agreed to enact the Fifth, Sixth, and Seventh Amendments to strengthen jury protection.

Anti-Federalist member of the group opposing the adoption of the U.S. Constitution; favored states' rights and argued successfully for the Bill of Rights

Federalist advocating a strong central government of separate states and the adoption of the U.S. Constitution

prosecution being charged with a crime and put on trial

The role of juries took on special importance in criminal cases. A grand jury could block any **prosecution** its members decided was unfounded; and a trial (petit) jury had the power to act to protect an innocent defendant. The key importance of the jury system had already been dramatized in the Zenger case in 1735. In that case, New York's royal governor tried to stifle criticism of his policies by John Peter Zenger, a newspaper publisher, but New York grand juries refused to indict (to bring a formal accusation against) Zenger, and the trial jury refused to convict him.

militia a part-time army made up of ordinary citizens

prejudice premature or unjustified opinion

The Framers' concept of the jury went far beyond protecting those accused of a crime. To them, the jury was a democratic body whose role was closely tied to other democratic ideas in the Bill of Rights such as the right to vote, free speech, and citizen **militias**. The jury was essential to democracy because it enabled citizens to take part in governing themselves. Nowhere else—not even in the voting booth—did Americans have to come together to weigh fundamental matters of policy and justice. As jurors, citizens have a solemn duty to put aside personal differences and **prejudices** in order to administer the law fairly.

The jury's educational mission was also very important to the Framers. They believed that citizens learn self-government by practicing it in jury service. Their ideas were reflected in the words of the celebrated

A boorish jury is caricatured to satirize the constitutional provision giving every man "the right to be tried by a jury of his peers."

nineteenth-century French political scientist Alexis de Tocqueville, who wrote, "The jury is both the most effective way of establishing the people's rule and the most effective way of teaching them how to rule." Lessons learned by serving on juries would also help Americans in other political activities.

Frank Murphy (1890–1959), governor of Michigan, U.S. Attorney General, and U.S. Supreme Court Justice, stated in *Thiel* v. *Southern Pacific Co.* (1945):

"Jury service is a duty as well as a privilege of citizenship; it is a duty that cannot be shirked on a plea of inconvenience or decreased earning power."

Criticisms of Juries

At the end of the twentieth century, the jury as a democratic institution came under attack. During the 1980s and 1990s, a series of notorious criminal trials raised many difficult questions about the value of the citizen jury. The prosecution of Lieutenant Colonel Oliver North in the Iran-Contra case, and the trials of O. J. Simpson, the Menendez brothers, and the police officers who beat up Rodney King—to name some of the most high-profile cases—allowed millions of Americans to become armchair jurors. These cases clearly brought out the failings of the jury system.

The process of selecting jurors appeared to be stacked against people who were well educated, well informed, and observant and to favor potential jurors whose thinking would be easier for skillful lawyers and judges to control. In selecting juries, prosecutors and defense attorneys have the right to dismiss possible jurors for many reasons, including race, gender, and other supposed indicators of bias. As a result, the jurors who were finally seated to try these high-profile cases did not represent a cross section of the United States population.

Other weaknesses, too, came to the surface. After they have been subjected to repeated summonses and probing personal questions, jurors often must endure trials that are poorly run and dragged out for lengthy periods. To make matters worse, during these trials jurors have little to do. Such a passive role makes it nearly impossible for them to weigh their findings in a meaningful way. It is no wonder, then, that many citizens try

The jury was well established in English law by the thirteenth century. Early juries consisted of persons with personal knowledge of a dispute. Gradually, however, formally produced evidence became the basis of decisions made by an objective jury. By the eighteenth century, the jury had become an important protection against judicial and administrative tyranny in both England and the American colonies. Contemporary federal law requires twelve-person juries, although the Constitution provides only that juries must consist of at least six persons. Furthermore, conviction in federal courts must be by unanimous vote. Although a jury verdict traditionally has had to be unanimous, some states have allowed majority verdicts, provided that the jury consists of at least six persons.

to avoid jury duty. Yet their doing so only tends to make the juries that are in the end selected even more unrepresentative than they would otherwise be.

Proposals for Reform

The weaknesses of modern jury trials are sometimes blamed on ordinary citizens' lack of ability to understand and judge matters of law and fact in an increasingly complex society. It is true that jurors do not always decide a case correctly. But the real problem may be not that the jury process relies too much on men and women of ordinary intelligence and common sense, but rather that it cannot rely on them enough. The reason is that the jury is hampered by obstacles put up by the courtroom professionals—the trial lawyers and judges.

The highest constitutional duty of the jury is to serve the people—their fellow citizens—and not the lawyers and the parties in the case. The best way jurors can fulfill that duty is to become involved in the administration of justice and democratic self-government. To restore this ideal of the Framers, reformers have suggested a variety of changes designed to make the jury more democratic, that is, more representative and more deliberative.

peremptory challenge a challenge by a lawyer without any reason needed for refusing to seat a potential juror

Some of the reforms that have been proposed seem simple enough, such as allowing jurors to take notes during trials and to question witnesses by passing their questions to the judge. Other suggested reforms are more controversial. These include eliminating peremptory challenges of jurors by lawyers. Other ideas for change are to enforce jury duty so that citizens cannot escape this key civic duty, and even to increase pay for jury service so that people do not avoid becoming jurors because doing so could cause financial hardship. While many disagree with these proposed reforms, the very purpose of the Constitution itself, when it was adopted, was far more controversial—the idea of government of the people, by the people, and for the people.

ARTICLE I—Congress

Treason

Daniel R. Ernst

ARTICLE III, SECTION 3, OF THE CONSTITUTION STATES

Treason against the United States, shall consist only in levying War against them, or in adhering to their Enemies, giving them Aid and Comfort. No Person shall be convicted of Treason unless on the Testimony of two Witnesses to the same overt Act, or on Confession in open Court.

The Congress shall have power to declare the Punishment of Treason, but no Attainder of Treason shall work Corruption of Blood, or Forfeiture except during the Life of the Person attained.

Treason is an attempt to overthrow the government by a person, usually a citizen, who owes allegiance to that government. It is the only crime defined in the Constitution. The Framers of the

Constitution wanted to protect the new nation from subversion, or being undermined or destroyed from within. At the same time, they also wanted to safeguard the individual's right to criticize the government and to prevent public officials from punishing lawful dissent, as they believed royal officials in England had done. Yet the Framers did not wish to make the definition of treason too vague. As one of the Framers, James Wilson of Pennsylvania, warned, doing this would allow government to "degenerate into arbitrary power."

How the Framers Defined Treason

To help them spell out the meaning of treason, the Framers turned to an English statute of 1350 that named several kinds of treasonous acts, including plotting the death of the king. Under this doctrine of "constructive treason," English judges had punished several well-known persons for protesting a monarch's actions. The Framers were determined to prevent American judges from acting in this way. Thus, the Framers included a provision in Article III of the Constitution, which establishes the judicial branch, that defines just two actions that could be punished as treason: (1) "levying war" against the United States, and (2) willingly supporting a foreign nation at war with the United States. They also rejected the English punishment of "corruption of blood," which prevented the children of anyone convicted of treason from inheriting property from their parent. In addition, the Framers made it very hard for the government to prove a person guilty of treason by requiring that two witnesses must testify that such an act was committed. Neither testimony by only one witness nor circumstantial evidence alone is enough to convict a suspected traitor.

judicial having to do with judgments in courts of justice or with the administration of justice

Iva Ikuko Toguri d'Aquino was the woman American authorities charged as being "Tokyo Rose," the Japanese American woman who broadcast propaganda for the Japanese during World War II. At her 1949 treason trial, she insisted that she was forced to make the broadcasts. She was found guilty of a lesser charge. President Ford pardoned her in 1977.

Levying War Against the United States

To commit an act of treason by "levying war," a person must plot with others to undertake an "overt act" for the purpose of overthrowing the government or its laws. Raising an armed force is such an act, even if the troops never attack. However, just plotting a rebellion is not enough. The rebels might not intend to overthrow the entire government; they might simply unite to prevent the government from enforcing some federal law or policy.

Prosecutions for Treason

Federal officials in the 1790s prosecuted persons for treason who acted to violently oppose the collection of federal taxes. In 1808, they prosecuted as traitors persons who violently opposed a ban on trade with England. In 1851, violent opponents protesting the enforcement of the Fugitive Slave Act also were charged with treason. In all of these cases, the charge of treason changed ill-considered acts of political dissent into a betrayal of the nation, the very thing the Framers had feared. Fortunately, most of the persons accused in these cases were found innocent or pardoned.

Moreover, many times when persons might have been charged with treason, they were brought to trial for rioting or committing less politically explosive offenses.

English-speaking radio listeners in the Pacific during World War II called Iva Toguri D'Aquino "Tokyo Rose," because of her broadcasts from the Japanese capital. She was a college graduate from Los Angeles who was visiting Japan when the war broke out. The Japanese secret police forced her to make the broadcasts even though she refused to renounce her American citizenship. After the war in 1949, she stood trial for treason. The government bribed one of the witnesses in her defense to give false testimony and threatened and tried to bribe other witnesses. The judge made it hard for the jury to acquit her and she was found guilty of trying to undermine American morale during the war and sentenced to prison.

Aiding the Enemy

To commit treason by giving aid and comfort to the enemy means that a person commits an act supporting a nation at war with the United States. That act must be observed by witnesses and be intended to betray the nation. Indirectly supporting an enemy nation is not enough. For example, a strike in an American weapons factory might help an enemy, but the union leaders who ordered it would not be guilty of treason if they called the strike to help their workers, and not to undermine the war effort.

Is Treason Free Speech?

Treasonous acts that give aid and comfort to the enemy have sometimes been spoken words. Several sensational treason cases were brought to trial after World War II. These involved American citizens who had broadcast radio propaganda over German, Italian, and Japanese stations to demoralize American troops. Others were tried for acts of treason such as aiding enemy spies and saboteurs, supplying enemy troops, helping enemy prisoners of war to escape, joining an enemy army, and mistreating American troops held as prisoners of war overseas.

Before he became president, Thomas Jefferson once complained that in European nations, the law of treason did not properly "distinguish between acts against *government* and acts against the *oppressions* [unlawful or harsh actions] *of the government*." In the United States, the treason law has not always clearly separated them either. For instance, although the Constitution carefully defines the crime of treason, this has not prevented Congress from punishing as sedition the use of spoken or written words contemptuous of the government or of public officials. The First Amendment's guarantee of free speech and the treason clause must be balanced to safeguard political dissent.

sedition incitement of resistance to or insurrection against lawful authority

In the final analysis, the treason clause has served as the Framers intended, punishing wartime disloyalty without allowing the government to crush lawful protest. In all the years before 1942, fewer than forty treason cases were tried in federal courts. Not one of the persons accused was ever executed—not even Jefferson Davis, the president of the Confederacy during the Civil War. As Supreme Court Justice Robert Jackson observed, only a nation "singularly confident of external security and internal stability" could have such a proud record.

ARTICLE IV—Fugitive Slave Clause

Article IV

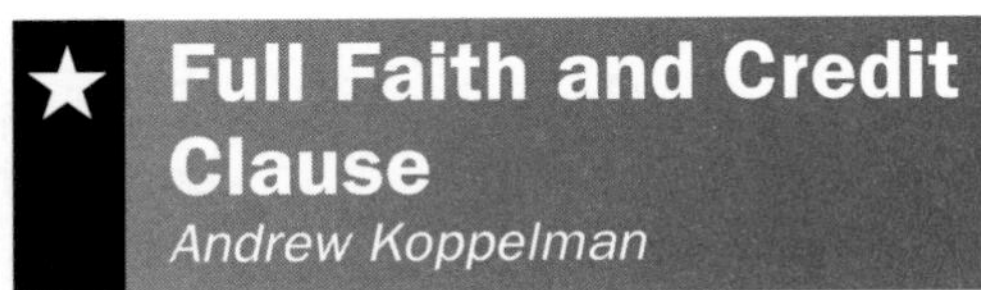

Full Faith and Credit Clause

Andrew Koppelman

ARTICLE IV, SECTION 1, OF THE CONSTITUTION STATES

Full Faith and Credit shall be given in each State to the public Acts, Records, and judicial Proceedings of every other State. And the Congress may by general Laws prescribe the Manner in which such Acts, Records and Proceedings shall be proved, and the Effect thereof.

The full faith and credit clause requires states to recognize each others' laws, public records, and court rulings. The Framers included the clause as part of their effort to unite the thirteen former colonies into a single nation. Although the first part of the clause was adapted from the Articles of Confederation of 1781, the Constitution's granting Congress the power to carry out the provision was new.

Articles of Confederation the first constitution of the thirteen original United States; in effect 1781–1789

Impact on Court Judgments

In its decision in *Magnolia Petroleum* v. *Hunt* (1943), the Supreme Court held that the purpose of the clause was to establish "throughout the federal system the salutary principle of the common law that a litigation once pursued to judgment shall be conclusive of the rights of the parties in every other court as in that where the judgment was rendered."

salutary promoting a beneficial effect

litigation a lawsuit

The full faith and credit clause has its greatest impact in court judgments. Courts usually enforce each others' judgments—even when the courts are in different countries. But sometimes a state court will decide that another's judgment goes against its own state's policies and therefore refuse to enforce it. The full faith and credit clause means that courts may not refuse to enforce the decisions of other states' courts.

judgment a decree issued by a court at the end of a lawsuit that determines the rights and the liabilities of the parties involved

***Fauntleroy* v. *Lum*.** Yet, parties to a lawsuit sometimes have tried to get around a state law they do not like by getting a judgment in another state. For example, Mississippi once outlawed contracts in cotton futures, or the right to buy or sell cotton at certain prices at a future date. To take advantage of this law, one defendant in a lawsuit signed a cotton futures contract in Mississippi, and then refused to pay as agreed. He did this relying on Mississippi courts not to enforce the contract, because it was illegal under that state's law. When the defendant traveled to Missouri, however, the other party to the contract lawsuit, the plaintiff, sued him (the defendant) in a Missouri court and won the case. But when the plaintiff tried to have the judgment enforced in Mississippi, that state's courts again rejected his efforts.

defendant a person against whom a legal action is brought

plaintiff a person who brings a legal action against another

The Supreme Court heard the case, *Fauntleroy* v. *Lum* (1908), and ruled that the Mississippi courts must enforce the judgment, because it had been legally obtained in another state. Even though the contract violated Mississippi law, that state was obliged to help the plaintiff collect the money he was owed for the cotton futures contract.

jurisdiction the territory or area within which authority may be exerted

ARTICLE I—The Necessary and Proper Clause; ARTICLE III—The Judiciary; ARTICLE VI—Supremacy Clause

Supreme Court Judge Robert H. Jackson called the full faith and credit clause "the lawyers' clause" of the Constitution. It raises tricky questions of interpretation, and the Framers' intent is unclear at best. The clause is especially important in the area of divorce law, where states must recognize other states' divorce decrees. For example, Nevada's easy divorce laws long made it a haven for people seeking a divorce. They went there for the necessary six weeks in order to become a resident under Nevada law, were granted a divorce, and then returned to their original state. Under this clause, that original state had to recognize the divorce. Starting in the 1960s, however, no-fault divorce laws made such a trip no longer necessary.

***Allstate Insurance Co.* v. *Hague*.** Although the full faith and credit clause refers to state actions as well as judgments, it has not had much effect on "conflict of laws" questions. In conflict of laws questions, a court must decide how a legal question will be affected by the fact that the dispute concerns more than one legal jurisdiction. Suppose a person in Minnesota files a lawsuit there arising from an automobile accident that happened in Wisconsin. The Constitution does not forbid the Minnesota court from deciding the case and basing its decision on Minnesota's laws, not Wisconsin's laws. The Supreme Court ruled, in *Allstate Insurance Co.* v. *Hague* (1985), that a state may apply its own law as long as the case involves "a significant contact" so that the state's choice to apply its own law is "neither arbitrary nor fundamentally unfair." Only in very rare cases does the full faith and credit clause restrict the choice of which jurisdiction's law to apply.

Congress used its power to pass laws to help carry out the clause soon after the Constitution was adopted. In 1790, it passed a law providing that state judgments were to have the same effect everywhere as they had in the state where they were issued. This law remains valid today.

In 1996, when it seemed that Hawaii was about to recognize same-sex marriage, Congress passed the Defense of Marriage Act to avert the result that all states would have to recognize such marriages as legal. The law stated that no "public act, record, or judicial proceeding" recognizing same-sex marriage is entitled to full faith and credit. This action partly repeals the full faith and credit clause even with respect to court judgments. Scholars disagree about whether Congress has the power to do this. The courts will ultimately have to resolve this question.

Privileges and Immunities of State Citizenship

Sheldon Goldman

immunity protection from legal action

Articles of Confederation the first constitution of the thirteen original United States; in effect 1781–1789

ARTICLE IV, SECTION 2, OF THE CONSTITUTION STATES

The Citizens of each State shall be entitled to all Privileges and Immunities of Citizens in the several States.

The privileges and immunities clause of the Constitution is intended to prevent unreasonable acts of discrimination by a state or its governmental subdivisions against citizens of another state. This protection is a carryover from Article IV of the Articles of Confederation of 1781.

Article IV in the Articles of Confederation read, in part: "The better to secure and perpetuate [continue] mutual friendship and intercourse among the people of the different States in this Union, the free inhabitants of each of these states, paupers [the poor], vagabonds [homeless persons], and fugitives from justice excepted [not included], shall be entitled to all privileges and immunities [protections] of free citizens in the several States; and the people of each State shall have free ingress [entry into] and egress [departure from] to and from any other State, and shall enjoy therein all the privileges of trade and commerce, subject to the

Cartoon on equal rights for all citizens. A figure representing the United States stirs a stewpot mixture of American society.

same duties, impositions [taxes] and restrictions as the inhabitants thereof respectively, provided that such restrictions shall not extend so far as to prevent the removal of property imported into any State, or to any other State of which the owner is an inhabitant. . . ."

In the Constitution, Article IV guarantees the same rights to citizens of all the states as Article IV of the Articles of Confederation. But the Constitution greatly simplifies the guarantee and makes it more liberal by not excluding paupers and vagabonds from enjoying the privileges and immunities of citizenship. Under the Constitution, poverty is not a reason to deny people their rights.

Supreme Court Rulings

In 1869, in *Paul* v. *Virginia*, the Supreme Court held that the privileges and immunities guarantee in Article IV was intended "to place the citizens of each State upon the same footing with citizens of other States, so far as the advantages resulting from citizenship of those States are concerned." More than a century later, the Court noted in *Supreme Court of New Hampshire* v. *Piper* (1985), that strengthening the nation's economy was an important purpose of this guarantee. The Court found that the clause was intended "to create a national economic union" in order to "fuse into one Nation a collection of independent, sovereign states."

The absence of any definition of privileges and immunities in the clause meant that much or little could be read into what this guarantee meant. In 1823, for example, Supreme Court Justice Bushrod Washington took a very broad view of the privileges and immunities protected by the clause. He declared that it included privileges and immunities "which are fundamental; which belong, of right, to the citizens of all free governments." Among the rights he listed were the right to travel, the right to sue in state and local courts, and the right of out-of-state residents to be treated equally in taxation. These rights, Justice Washington suggested, "have at all times been enjoyed by citizens of the several States which compose this Union, from the time of their becoming free, independent, and sovereign."

But the Supreme Court later suggested, in the *Slaughterhouse Cases* (1873), that the guarantee was more limited in its scope. In that case, the Court ruled that the privileges and immunities clause created no new rights for citizens in relation to their own states but was intended to protect out-of-state residents.

The Right to Travel

free ingress and egress freedom to enter and leave a state

The right to travel was protected in the Articles of Confederation, which declared that "the people of each State shall have free ingress and egress to and from any other State." Although the Supreme Court's rulings on the privileges and immunities clause have largely viewed it as a guarantee of equal treatment of the citizens of all states, this clause as well as other provisions of the Constitution have protected the right to travel.

Alexander Hamilton in *The Federalist*, No. 78 viewed the idea that states could not discriminate against citizens of other states as no less than "the basis of the Union." The Constitution and court rulings have confirmed Hamilton's belief. A citizen of the United States who travels or moves to another state is entitled to be treated the same way as a permanent resident of that state. The privileges and immunities clause uses the term "citizen," but the Supreme Court has said that for analytical purposes the terms "citizenship" and "residency" mean essentially the same thing.

Residents and Nonresidents

Several Supreme Court rulings have treated out-of-state residents differently than in-state residents. When an out-of-state business has suffered a commercial disadvantage as a result, however, the commerce clause, not the privileges and immunities clause, usually has been applied. This is especially true for corporations, because they are not considered "citizens" entitled to privileges and immunities.

Does the privileges and immunities guarantee mean that each state must treat residents and nonresidents exactly the same? The rulings by the Supreme Court have been mixed on this question. In *Baldwin* v. *Fish and Game Commission of Montana* (1978), the Court upheld a Montana law that imposed a license fee on out-of-state elk hunters that was twenty-five times larger than the fee for Montana residents. The justices ruled that the law did not violate Article IV, when they declared, "Whatever rights or activities may be fundamental under the Privileges and Immunities Clause, we are persuaded, and hold, that elk hunting by nonresidents in Montana is not one of them." Similarly, the Court has permitted **residency requirements** for public office and for voting if they are reasonable.

residency requirement requirement that persons must live in the state, and usually, must have been living there for a specific time period

The Court has ruled, however, that residency requirements must be shown as necessary for a compelling state reason, because they appear to interfere with the right to travel. Thus, the Court struck down a one-year residency requirement for a person to be eligible for welfare in a state. It also overturned an Alaska law that required that all jobs in the oil and gas industry must be given to qualified Alaska residents before out-of-staters could be hired. The Court also has ruled that requirements for practicing law must be the same for residents and nonresidents alike.

Yet the Supreme Court approved a one-year residency requirement for an out-of-state student attending a public state university before that student may claim state citizenship and, with it, the lower tuition rates that in-state students are charged.

The Court's decision in the student residency case was based on the due process clause of the Fourteenth Amendment rather than the privileges and immunities clause. That the Court based its ruling on the Fourteenth Amendment highlights how the privileges and immunities guarantee became much less important once the Fourteenth Amendment was added to the Constitution in 1868. At the close of the twentieth century, this constitutional provision was seldom raised in cases.

ARTICLE IV—Right to Travel; FOURTEENTH AMENDMENT—Introduction

Right to Travel

Sheldon Goldman

ARTICLE IV, SECTION 2, CLAUSE 1, OF THE CONSTITUTION STATES

The Citizens of each State shall be entitled to all Privileges and ***Immunities*** *of Citizens in the several States.*

immunity protection from legal action

The right to travel is an idea with a long history. It can be traced as far back as biblical sources. When Moses asked the pharaoh to "let my people go" the prophet was invoking the right to travel, in

Throughout most of American history, a passport was not a legal requirement for leaving or entering the United States. Before 1856 various federal, state, and local officials, as well as notaries public, issued either certificates of citizenship or documents such as letters of introduction to foreign officials. Congress in 1856 passed a law granting only to the Secretary of State the power to issue passports under rules the President prescribes. Restrictions otherwise were few. These took place almost exclusively during wartime. In 1952, however, Congress made it illegal for an American citizen to leave or enter the country without a passport. For several years thereafter passports were often denied on ideological grounds.

that case, the right to leave the country. And again, in 1215, when the English barons met King John at Runnymede to hammer out the Magna Carta, they insisted on a provision, which became Article 42, that recognized a right to travel abroad.

The right to travel also means the right to travel freely within one's country, including the right to resettle in another part of the nation. In the American colonies, settlers took full advantage of that right. Although the Framers of the Constitution did not specifically recognize a right to travel in that document, they assumed it to be one of the privileges and immunities guaranteed in Article IV, Section 2, Clause 1. That the Framers intended to recognize the right to travel is suggested by other clauses that restrict travel under certain conditions. Moreover, Clause 2, which restricts the right to travel of persons accused of a crime by providing for their extradition, or return, if they flee to another state, supports the Framers' intent. In addition, Clause 3 also restricts travel, providing that persons "held to Service or Labour"—that is, slaves or indentured servants—who escape to another state must be returned to their owners or those "to whom such Service or Labour may be due."

The Issue of Slavery and Race

Because northern states prohibited slavery, the right of slaveowners to travel to those states with their slaves became a major political issue in the years leading to the Civil War. Opponents of slavery recognized that slaveowners could travel in the free states of the North. However, if they brought their slaves there, these opponents argued, once those slaves set foot on free soil, the law set them free. Slaveowners had a very different view. They argued that slaves were property, and that their property could not constitutionally be taken from them. In the *Dred Scott* decision of 1857, the Supreme Court agreed with the slaveowners' interpretation of their rights.

Removal of a segregated seating sign from a Dallas, Texas bus in compliance with a 1954 Supreme Court ruling banning segregation in public transportation.

Actor and singer Paul Robeson (right) arriving at the State Department with his attorney in 1955. Robeson was seeking permission to travel abroad, a right he said the State Department had been denying him for five years.

After the Civil War, Congress passed laws prohibiting discrimination based on race in public transportation and other public facilities. In 1883, however, the Supreme Court declared this legislation unconstitutional. The southern states and border states then enacted new laws requiring the segregation, or separation of races, in most public facilities, including transportation. In 1896, the Court upheld such racial segregation in a case involving railroad travel. Not until sixty-eight years later, in its decision upholding the Civil Rights Act of 1964, did the Court officially recognize that segregation in public facilities and transportation greatly restricted African Americans in exercising their right to travel.

Travel Abroad

The right to travel to foreign countries is derived from the Fifth Amendment. To travel abroad, Americans must first obtain a passport from the federal government. Usually, this restriction on travel causes few problems. Individuals can obtain a passport by applying for it, submitting proof of citizenship and a passport photo, and paying the fee required. However, in 1948, the Department of State denied passports to members of the American Communist party and others whose political beliefs and associations were considered a threat to the nation's security. In 1958, in *Kent* v. *Dulles*, the Supreme Court struck down this restriction on travel. The Court declared that the ability to travel is "a natural right" protected from being interfered with by the federal government by the due process clause of the Fifth Amendment. Later, the Court modified this ruling, allowing the government to forbid American citizens (even those with valid passports) from traveling to certain nations with which the United States had foreign policy disputes.

Travel Within the Nation

The right to travel within the United States is the most important travel right for most Americans. In 1868, the Supreme Court recognized this right in *Crandall* v. *Nevada.* In that decision, the Court struck down a tax that Nevada levied on any person leaving the state on public transportation. The right to travel from state to state, the Court affirmed, is a right of national citizenship. Later rulings by the Court strengthened this right. One notable decision was in *Edwards* v. *California* (1941), in which the Court struck down a California law barring poor people coming from other states to enter California.

Requirements that persons must reside in a state in order to receive benefits from the state or to exercise certain rights such as voting can also act to discourage travel. Although the Supreme Court has found some of these requirements to be reasonable, it has rejected others as unreasonable interferences with the right to travel. A notable example was the ruling by the Court in *Shapiro* v. *Thompson* (1969), which struck down Connecticut's one-year residency requirement for receiving welfare benefits.

residency requirement requirement that persons must live in the state, and usually, must have been living there for a specific time period

The *Thompson* case involved a single parent, Vivian M. Thompson, who, traveling with one child and pregnant with another, moved from

Massachusetts to Connecticut to be with her mother. She applied for welfare benefits, but Connecticut officials denied them because she had not lived in the state for one year. Thompson then sued the Connecticut Commissioner of Welfare, Bernard Shapiro, in federal district court. The judges decided in favor of Thompson. When the Supreme Court heard the case, it struck down the state residency requirement as an unconstitutional burden on the right to travel. The Court declared that the freedom to travel "throughout the length and breadth of our land uninhibited by statutes, rules, or regulations which unreasonably burden or restrict this movement" is a fundamental personal liberty.

In short, the basic concept of a right to travel clearly exists. Although this right is not spelled out in the Constitution, it nevertheless is a right that all Americans enjoy, derived from Article IV, Section 2, Clause 1, as well as other provisions of that document.

ARTICLE I—Commerce Clause: After the New Deal; ARTICLE III—Impact of Judicial Review: *Dred Scott* v. *Sanford*; FOURTEENTH AMENDMENT —"Separate but Equal"

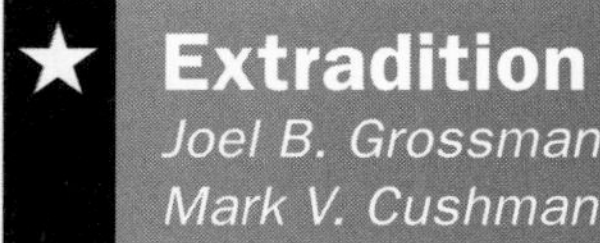

Extradition

Joel B. Grossman
Mark V. Cushman

ARTICLE IV, SECTION 2, CLAUSE 2, OF THE CONSTITUTION STATES

*A person charged in any State with **Treason**, **Felony**, or other Crime, who shall flee from justice, and be found in another State, shall on Demand of the executive authority of the State from which he fled, be delivered up, to be removed to the State having **Jurisdiction**.*

treason the offense of attempting to overthrow the government of a state

felony a crime usually punished by death or a lengthy prison sentence

jurisdiction the territory or area within which authority may be exercised

treaty binding international agreement

A person who has fled from justice is surrendered and returned through the legal process of extradition. The Constitution provides for extradition of fugitives by the states. Yet it does not mention extradition between the United States and other nations. The Supreme Court, however, has ruled that the government does have authority over international extraditions. That authority is derived from the treaty-making powers of the president and the Senate. The Court has further held that international extradition is strictly a federal matter in which the states play no role.

Extradition Treaties

Congress has enacted laws requiring that extradition of persons to or from another country must be based on a treaty with that country. By the late 1990s, the United States had signed extradition treaties with one hundred three countries. Without such a treaty, international extradition is legally impossible. For example, countries such as Libya, Indonesia, and Morocco, which do not have extradition treaties with the United States, are safe havens for people fleeing from American courts or avoiding them.

Extradition Between the States

Article IV, Section 2, Clause 2, of the Constitution provides for extradition between the states of fugitives from justice. This provision sets forth

Governors occasionally refuse to honor extradition requests even though the Supreme Court has made it clear that federal courts have the power to order governors to fulfill a state's obligation under the extradition clause. In 1990, New York Governor Mario Cuomo denied such a request from Alabama Governor Guy Hunt. The four persons involved were officials of a New York company who faced charges of transmitting obscene films by satellite. The officials had never been in Alabama, and it was very questionable that the films would have been declared obscene in either New York or Alabama. In any event, Alabama never followed up on its request.

two important principles. The first is the principle of comity. Comity means that each state must respect requests by other states to return those fleeing from justice. The second principle is that only those persons who meet the Constitution's definition of being a "fugitive from justice," a person charged with "treason, felony, or other crime," can be extradited. Not all people fleeing from a state meet this definition. Persons charged with civil violations or sought as witnesses in either criminal or civil trials usually cannot be extradited.

The extradition clause seems to focus on the recapture and return of persons who have not yet been found guilty or innocent in a court of law. But in practice, extradition proceedings are used to secure the return of those already convicted of a crime, such as escaped prisoners.

Fugitive Slaves

When the Framers wrote the extradition clause, one main concern was dealing with the problem of fugitive slaves. Clause 3 in Article IV, Section 2, often referred to as the "fugitive slave clause," applies the extradition principle specifically to "persons held to service or labour in one state, under the laws thereof, escaping into another." Such persons must be "delivered up on the claim of the party to whom such service or labor may be due." The word slave is not used, but everyone understood that the main reason for the clause was to protect the interests of the slave states.

The Fugitive Slave Act of 1793 allowed a master or his agent to "seize and arrest" enslaved Africans and bring them before a federal judge or local magistrate. The Supreme Court upheld this law in *Prigg* v. *Pennsylvania* (1842). But northern **abolitionists** resisted the return of fugitive slaves so fiercely that their extradition became a major political issue before the Civil War. Abolitionists set up the "underground railroad," a system by which they used private homes and churches to provide food and

abolitionist person favoring principles or measures fostering the end of slavery

The extradition of fugitive slave Thomas Sims to Georgia (1851).

> "Let every man and woman, without distinction of sect or party . . . bear testimony against the system which fills the prisons of a free republic with men whose only crime is a love of freedom—which strikes down the habeas corpus and trial by jury, and converts the free soil of Massachusetts into hunting ground for the Southern kidnappers."
>
> —Henry Wilson (1812–1875), U.S. Senator from Massachusetts and Vice President of the United States under Ulysses S. Grant, in a handbill calling for a political rally in opposition to the Fugitive Slave Law of 1850.

shelter to help escaping slaves reach freedom, largely in the north but sometimes in Canada, beyond the reach of state or federal officials.

The Fugitive Slave Law of 1850 modified the original fugitive slave law. Under it, United States commissioners were appointed to enforce the law nationwide. The new act also set harsher penalties for refusing to aid the commissioners or for assisting escaping slaves. Northern states argued that the law interfered with a state's right to determine the status of persons within its borders. The Supreme Court of Wisconsin ruled it unconstitutional, but the U.S. Supreme Court reversed that decision and upheld the Fugitive Slave Law of 1850 in *Ableman* v. *Booth* (1856).

State and Federal Extradition Laws

The Supreme Court ruled, in 1861, that state governors have a legal duty to extradite a fugitive sought by another state. It was not until 1987 that the Court overturned this precedent and declared that state governors were not allowed any power to act in extradition cases. Nor can an extradition hearing be turned into a retrial or an appeal of the original conviction, at least not as a formal part of the hearing. In fact, in most cases extraditions are routine matters that are not contested in court. States also may make extradition agreements with one another, without any need of Congress's approval.

Modern state extradition laws have generally been based on federal law, particularly on the Uniform Criminal Extradition Act. Another federal law, popularly called the "Fleeing Felon Act," makes it also a federal crime to cross state borders, or help a fugitive do so, in order to avoid state prosecution. In such cases, the Federal Bureau of Investigation (FBI) and other federal law-enforcement officials have legal authority to help capture fugitives who have committed only state crimes and thus would not be subject to federal law.

ARTICLE III—Impact of Judicial Review: *Dred Scott* v. *Sandford*;
ARTICLE IV—Fugitive Slave Clause

Bail, Bounty Hunters, and Bondsmen

The extradition clause of Article IV, Section 2, is like nearly all provisions of the Constitution in that it applies only to government actions, not actions of private citizens. However, English common law for centuries has recognized that citizens who post **bail** on behalf of a person accused or convicted of a crime can use force to seize that person if he or she "jumps bail." That is, those who post bail may take such action if the person does not appear before a court or judge as required by the terms of bail.

bail money or property pledged to guarantee that the accused person will appear in court for trial

In the United States, during the nineteenth century, **bounty hunters** were often used in capturing fugitives. In addition, **bondsmen** became part of the justice system. The Supreme Court ruled that bounty hunters and bondsmen had common law rights that are valid across state lines. Bondsmen are not required to respect the constitutional rights of fugitives, and they may capture them wherever they find them.

bounty hunters people who hunt and seize for payment those who have jumped bail

bondsmen people who make money by posting bail for the accused

★ Fugitive Slave Clause

Earl M. Maltz

ARTICLE IV, SECTION 2, CLAUSE 3, OF THE CONSTITUTION STATES

No Person held to Service or Labour in one State, under the Laws thereof, escaping into another, shall, in Consequence of any Law or Regulation therein, be discharged from such Service or Labour, but shall be delivered up on Claim of the Party to whom such Service or Labour may be due.

The Framers of the Constitution made a conscious decision not to refer either to slaves or slavery in the fugitive slave clause. But as the Framers intended, the clause was generally understood to be aimed at slaves who might escape from their owners and then make their way to states where slavery was illegal. Slave owners regarded this clause as an important new protection for their interests. Even so, unlike other provisions of the Constitution relating to slavery, the fugitive slave clause caused little controversy at the Constitutional Convention itself or during the ratification process.

ratification process of making a document legal by giving it formal approval

The Fugitive Slave Issue

The question of how to deal with fugitive slaves caused serious friction between the slave states and the free states in the years leading up to the Civil War. The legal issues involved in the interpretation of the fugitive slave clause created political controversy. The clause clearly prohibited the courts in the states without slaves from freeing slaves who had escaped and entered their borders. Still, the clause left a number of important questions unanswered. First, it did not deal directly with the practice of recaption. Second, unlike other provisions of the Constitution, the fugitive slave clause did not specifically give Congress the authority to pass laws to enforce it. Finally, the clause was silent on the question of whether states could pass laws regulating the recapture of escaped slaves. Many free states passed such laws, known as "personal liberty" or "anti-kidnapping" laws.

recaption the action by slave owners and their agents of seizing persons whom they claimed were fugitives and returning them to slavery, without a court ruling that they were in fact slaves

An impassioned condemnation of the law passed by Congress in 1850.

A Divided Supreme Court

The Supreme Court was faced with all these issues in *Prigg* v. *Pennsylvania* (1842). In this case, the justices wrote seven separate opinions that expressed at least six different positions on the proper interpretation of the fugitive slave clause. Justice John McLean of Pennsylvania took the strongest anti-slavery stand. He conceded that the federal government had authority to pass laws to enforce the clause. But, he argued, the clause did not allow the states to enact legislation to strengthen the federal laws that helped slave owners reclaim slaves. Justice McLean concluded, however, that the states could pass laws requiring that slave owners claiming the right of recaption needed to follow legal procedures nearly impossible to meet. At the other extreme, Chief Justice Roger B. Taney held that the states not only had the right to enact laws that aided slaveowners to reclaim slaves, but they were required to do so. Taney declared further that the states had no power to interfere with the right of recaption.

see also

ARTICLE IV—Extradition; THIRTEENTH AMENDMENT—Slavery and the Constitution; Thirteenth Amendment: Enforcement

The Supreme Court's Ruling

Justice Joseph Story wrote the Court's prevailing opinion. He took a middle position, ruling that the fugitive slave clause made the right of recaption constitutional. The federal government had the authority to pass laws to enforce this practice, Story declared, but it could not force state officials to help enforce those laws. Nor could states pass any laws that added strength to the federal laws or pass any laws of their own regulating the right of recaption. Several years later, in *Jones* v. *Van Zandt* (1847), the Supreme Court again upheld Congress's power to enforce the fugitive slave clause.

The adoption of the Thirteenth Amendment in 1865, outlawing slavery, effectively invalidated the fugitive slave clause. Nonetheless, the broad view of the federal government's power to enforce laws, set forth by Justice Story in *Prigg*, had lasting significance, and those who took a broad view of congressional power to enforce the Thirteenth, Fourteenth, and Fifteenth Amendments often cited his ruling. Ironically, the Supreme Court opinion that was at first widely regarded as pro-slavery in time became a tool in the hands of those who urged strong measures to protect the rights of newly freed African Americans.

> The Underground Railroad was a secret and loosely organized network of hiding places and routes for helping fugitive slaves escape to the North or Canada. The name comes from the Kentucky master of a slave who unsuccessfully pursued him across the Ohio River and said he "must have gone off an underground road." It flourished in northeast Ohio after the War of 1812 and spread to fourteen northern states after 1830, helping an estimated thirty thousand slaves escape to freedom by the time of the Civil War. It seldom worked in an organized manner. Individual persons gave most help to fugitives.

★ Admission of New States and Territories

Peter Onuf

ARTICLE IV, SECTION 3, OF THE CONSTITUTION STATES

New States may be admitted by the Congress into this Union, but no new State will be formed or erected within the ***Jurisdiction*** *of any other State; nor any State be formed by the Junction of two or more States, or Parts of States, without the Consent of the Legislatures concerned as well as of the Congress.*

The Congress shall have the Power to dispose of and make all needful Rules and Regulations respecting the Territory or other property

jurisdiction the territory or area within which authority may be exercised

belonging to the United States; and nothing in this Constitution shall be construed as to Prejudice any Claims of the United States, or of any particular State.

This provision gives Congress the authority to govern land that is not part of any state and to form new states in this territory or out of land claimed by existing states, with their approval. Article IV, Section 3, Clause 1, of the Constitution addressed circumstances that did not exist when the Continental Congress drafted the **Articles of Confederation** in 1777.

Articles of Confederation the first constitution of the thirteen original United States; in effect 1781–1789

ratification process of making a document legal by giving it formal approval

Under the Articles of Confederation, Canada could join the Union whenever it chose, and other (presumably British) colonies could do so with the approval of nine states. When Congress sent the Articles to the states for **ratification**, there was no territory for Congress to administer. This situation soon changed when several states, including New York in 1782, Virginia in 1784, Massachusetts in 1785, and Connecticut in 1786, gave up their claims to western land. When the Constitution was written, these former land claims were national territory. So Article IV, Section 3, represented the Framers' effort to deal with this fundamental change in the Union. Henceforth, the United States would be more than a simple Union of states.

These first land cessions by the states to the Confederation made up the Northwest Territory, the vast region north and west of the Ohio River that Native Americans still largely controlled. Congress was granted the authority to administer this territory. When Virginia ceded the most important of these overlapping claims, it specifically called for the eventual creation of new states there. Responding to these grants of western land, and eager to establish its authority in the Northwest, Congress passed the Land Ordinance of 1785. The Ordinance provided a system for surveying this land and for its sale, which resulted in a rectangular grid land pattern throughout the territory.

Signing of the Louisiana Purchase agreement. Seated is President Thomas Jefferson. Signing are special envoy to Paris James Monroe and U.S. minister to France Robert Livingston. Louisiana was bought from France in 1803.

The Northwest Ordinance

A law was passed in April 1784, as a companion measure to the Land Ordinance, providing for territorial government and the formation of new states. The Northwest Ordinance of July 1787 replaced it before legal settlement of the territory began. This famous ordinance was passed by the Confederation Congress meeting in New York (while the Constitutional Convention met in Philadelphia). It set forth the broad framework for governing the nation's original territories as well as the regions the United States might later acquire.

The Northwest Ordinance has no formal constitutional standing beyond the provision in Article VI that recognizes "Engagements entered into, before the Adoption of this Constitution." Even so, the Ordinance worked as a kind of constitution for frontier regions before they became part of the Union. Later Congresses, however, did not hesitate to tinker with the specific provisions of the Northwest Ordinance.

> The Northwest Ordinance paralleled the Bill of Rights. It stated: "No person demeaning himself in a peaceable and orderly manner, shall ever be molested on account of his mode of worship or religious sentiments in the said territory. The inhabitants . . . shall always be entitled to the benefits of the **writ of habeas corpus**, and of the trial by jury; of a proportionate representation . . . in the legislature; and of judicial proceedings according to the course of the common law," or due process of law. In addition, "no cruel or unusual punishments shall be inflicted." Involuntary servitude except in punishment of crime was prohibited.

writ of habeas corpus (Latin, "produce the body") a court command to produce the person being held in order to determine whether the person's detention is lawful; a way of making sure that a criminal trial has been fair

Expanding the Union

The language of Article IV, Section 3 ("New States may be admitted") was important because it enabled Congress to fulfill the Confederation government's pledge to the states that had ceded their western claims and to the settlers on this federal land. Congress no longer would have to amend the Articles, which required the approval of all the states, in order to admit a new state. And as long as the promise of statehood was considered binding, Article IV, Section 3, would be regarded as a farsighted provision that promoted republican government and the expansion of the Union.

Disputes among the states had nearly destroyed the Confederation government and all but halted the possibility of admitting new states. The new provisions in the Constitution solved these problems. By making careful provisions about the creation of new states, the Constitution reduced the fears of the small states that they might be swallowed up by their large neighbors. Section 3 also reassured the states that had not completed ceding their western land that Congress would continue to rely on their claims to establish its authority in frontier regions. The new Congress, therefore, would not gain control over land in the Southwest until North Carolina and Georgia ceded their disputed claims there. North Carolina did so in 1790, and Georgia in 1802.

Slavery in the Territories

discretionary authority power that may or may not be used

Jurisdictional disputes resulting from Article IV, Section 3, sorely tested the strength of the Union. But when the issue of expanding slavery divided Congress along sectional lines, Congress's **discretionary authority** over admitting new states allowed it to postpone granting statehood. At the same time, Congress's power to make "all needful Rules and Regulations" for territorial government began to be widely attacked. Could Congress indefinitely deny self-government to citizens living in the territories? Could Congress prohibit citizens of slave states from taking slaves as their "property" with them into the territories? These questions were not finally answered until the Civil War resolved another crisis of the Union.

★ Republican Form of Government

Gordon B. Baldwin

ARTICLE IV, SECTION 4, OF THE CONSTITUTION STATES

The United States shall guarantee to every State in this Union a Republican Form of Government, and shall protect each of them against Invasion; and on the Application of the Legislature, or of the Executive Office (when the Legislature cannot be convened) against domestic Violence.

This provision stands for basic political values for which Americans shed their blood in the Revolutionary War. The Framers deeply believed in representative state governments and in the national government's

obligation to defend the states against both domestic and foreign threats. This provision—the guarantee clause—also remedied a glaring weakness of the Confederation scheme.

Articles of Confederation the first constitution of the thirteen original United States; in effect 1781–1789

Under the Articles of Confederation of 1781, the new nation was made up of thirteen state governments and a loose central structure. Nearly all of the national government's power was placed in a weak Congress, which proved unable to prevent trade wars and disputes between the states. Nor could this weak central government protect the states from foreign dangers or domestic unrest.

Americans hearing the news of their newly declared independence from the British crown in 1776.

The Meaning of the Clause

The Framers of the Constitution met at Philadelphia in 1787 to create a new and stronger government. They agreed that all levels of government in the United States must have a republican form, but they did not define what the term "republican" meant. Yet they agreed that the thirteen states had that quality, despite the clear flaws in their governmental structures.

The Framers debated the meaning of "republican" but were unable to agree. Some argued that "republican" meant rule by the majority in which the minority must comply. Others said that it meant a government in which representatives were regularly elected. The Framers did agree that a republican form of government required a separation of legislative and executive powers. The guarantee clause provides that the national government can assist a state if the state's legislature requests its aid, or if the state's chief executive makes this request when the legislature is not in session. The preference for a request from the legislature shows that the Framers thought that a republican form of government needed a strong legislative authority.

Madison's Views

The Framers also agreed that a republican form of government must not be monarchical, aristocratic, or despotic. They also concurred that states must be free to change their forms of government, within the limits of a republican form. That is, they did not want the guarantee clause to restrict the states to the systems of government they had in 1787.

James Madison reflected this view in 1788, when he wrote in *The Federalist,* No. 43: "As long . . . as existing republican forms are continued by the States, they are guaranteed by the Federal Constitution. Whenever the States may choose to substitute other republican forms, they have a right to do so, and to claim the federal guaranty . . . . The only restriction imposed on them is, that they shall not exchange republican for anti-republican Constitution . . . ."

The Scope of the Clause

Other parts of the Constitution describe national powers in terms of which branch of the government may exercise them. In contrast, the guarantee clause imposes a duty on the United States as a whole. It does

When Benjamin Franklin was leaving the last session of the Constitutional Convention in 1787, a woman asked him, "What kind of government have you given us, Dr. Franklin? A Republic or a Monarchy?" Franklin replied, "A Republic, Madam, if you can keep it."

not specify which branch of government is responsible for enforcing the guarantee of a republican form of government. Does this clause require action by Congress, or can the president alone decide to act?

It would seem almost certain that the clause applies to the president, because only the president can command the armed forces to resist invasion. Under Article II, the president is obliged to support the Constitution, and as commander in chief he has the power to defend the country against invasion and to supply military aid to the states when they request it.

The guarantee clause reflects two fears held by many Americans in 1787: the threats of foreign invasions and of mob violence at home, both of which might endanger republican forms of government in the United States and had to be resisted. The guarantee clause thus reflects a key purpose of the Framers—to form a national government powerful enough to resist foreign threats and, as the Preamble states, a central government competent to ensure "domestic tranquility."

The Clause Applied

abolitionist person favoring principles or measures fostering the end of slavery

Opponents of slavery invoked the guarantee clause many times in debates from 1840 to 1860. **Abolitionists** insisted that slavery offended republican principles. Slavery supporters responded that the guarantee clause was intended only to protect against foreign invasion and domestic violence, and that the states remained free to decide who could vote or hold property, and what property rights meant.

In 1849, the Supreme Court ruling in *Luther* v. *Borden* interpreted the guarantee clause narrowly and refused to apply it to a dispute in Rhode Island about the state's form of government. A charter granted to Rhode Island by the British Crown is 1633 formed its original government. The charter, which included no provision for amendment, gave the colonists very limited voting rights. By the mid-nineteenth century, many people in Rhode Island, probably a majority of them, wanted a more modern government, and by popular vote (men only), they created a new government and elected a new governor. This led to armed clashes between supporters of the old and the new governments. The supporters of the new government were defeated, and agents of the old government broke into buildings claimed by the new government.

Entering the buildings was lawful if done by the lawful government, but which government had the right to this property? The two sides asked the federal courts to decide which was Rhode Island's lawful government. The guarantee clause appeared relevant because the old government clearly was in the hands of an aristocratic minority.

In *Luther* v. *Borden*, the Supreme Court ruled that federal courts lacked the power to decide the issue. The Court held that this case raised a political question, not a legal one, because it was the president who had the authority under the guarantee clause to protect Rhode Island. Since President Zachary Taylor had recognized the old governor, the justices ruled that "no courts of the United States . . . would be justified in recognizing the opposing party as the lawful government."

Roger Brooke Taney, chief justice from 1836 to 1864. The ruling in *Luther* v. *Borden* was made under his watch.

> Every major nation in the world had a king when the United States won its independence, and monarchy had been the accepted form of government throughout history. Yet George Washington, who everyone assumed would head the new government, strongly opposed monarchy. "I must view with abhorrence and reprehend with severity a conception that was big with the greatest mischiefs that can befall my country," he wrote in 1782. The American experiment in self-government was unprecedented. Even so, it was inconceivable that a new King George I (Washington) would replace King George III, whose army Washington had defeated.

The Court's ruling went beyond deciding the particular issue before it. The Court declared that Congress had the authority to decide whether a state government was republican, because Congress had the power to seat the senators and representatives selected by Rhode Island and "must necessarily decide what government . . . is republican. . . ." The Court also said that it could not identify the qualities that necessarily made a government "republican."

The *Luther* v. *Borden* ruling is still cited to support the claim that courts have no role in deciding whether a change in state government violates the guarantee clause. Other parts of the Constitution, including the Fourteenth Amendment and Article I, Section 10, expressly limit state government decisions. In most cases, then, people's claims that a state has violated their rights rest on the Fourteenth Amendment, not the guarantee clause.

Individual justices have suggested at times in separate opinions that the courts should enforce the guarantee clause. For example, in the case of *Plessy* v. *Ferguson* (1896), which upheld racial segregation on public railroad trains, Justice John M. Harlan wrote a dissenting opinion. He insisted that segregation violated the guarantee clause as well as other provisions of the Constitution. But he failed to persuade the other justices.

Current Status of the Clause

In 1992, Justice Sandra Day O'Connor, writing the majority opinion of the Court in *New York* v. *United States,* reviewed the history of the guarantee clause in the courts. "In most of the cases in which the Court has been asked to apply the Clause," she wrote, "the Court has found the claims presented to be nonjusticiable under the 'political question' doctrine."

nonjusticiable not liable for trial in court; not subject to court judgment

In the *New York* case, the Court decided that Congress had violated the authority of the states by attempting to force states to take title to low-level radioactive waste. The Court struck down the law without relying on the guarantee clause, but noted that in some unknown circumstances the clause might require judicial review. Justice O'Connor noted that in a 1964 case, the Court had ruled only that "some questions raised under the guarantee clause" were not matters for courts to decide. Her words suggest that situations might arise that would require courts to protect a "republican form of government."

INTRODUCTION—Constitutional Origins;
ARTICLE II—Commander in Chief;
FOURTEENTH AMENDMENT—
"Separate but Equal"

The guarantee clause remains important because it embodies a major political principle: The United States supports responsible, elected state governments, and the system allows the states a wide choice of forms of government within this broad mandate. The clause calls upon the president, and perhaps the Congress, to protect states from invasion and, upon their request, from domestic threats. However, the guarantee clause does not appear to give courts additional authority to protect constitutional values. Yet Justice O'Connor's cautious words suggest that it is possible that there may be a use for the guarantee clause in the future.

mandate command, order, or requirement

Article V

ARTICLE V OF THE CONSTITUTION STATES

The Congress, whenever two-thirds of both Houses shall deem it necessary, shall propose amendments to the Constitution, or, on application of the legislatures of two-thirds of the several States, shall call a convention for proposing amendments, which, in either case, shall be valid, to all intents and purposes, as part of this Constitution, when ***ratified*** *by the legislatures of three-fourths of the several States, or by conventions in three-fourths thereof, as the one or the other mode of ratification may be proposed by Congress; provided that no amendment which may be made prior to the year 1808 shall in any manner affect the first and fourth clauses of the Ninth Section of the First Amendment of the First Article; and that no State, without its consent, shall be deprived of its equal* ***suffrage*** *in the Senate.*

ratify give official approval or confirmation to

suffrage the right to vote

Great Britain has no formal, written constitution. Parliament, Britain's national legislature, is sovereign. It is the supreme law of the land. However, the Framers of the American Constitution believed a written document, one that could not be changed by enacting laws, was a better guarantee of liberty.

sovereign having complete independence in its relations with other nations or units of government

supreme having the highest authority

After the Framers completed the Constitution in 1787, they recognized that it was not perfect. They believed that the Constitution would serve the nation's needs in their own time. They also knew that events in the future might require that changes be made in it. However, if the Constitution were too flexible, then its guarantees would not mean much. Likewise, if the Constitution were too rigid, Americans later might have to resort to revolution, just as the founders of the nation had. Therefore, the Framers kept both these crucial needs in mind when they designed a method of amending, or changing, the Constitution. Article V of the Constitution sets forth this amendment process.

Important Precedents

During the colonial period and in the early years of the nation, Americans had grown used to written charters and constitutions. Many of these documents specified how they could be amended. For example, William Penn's charters for his colonies in the 1680s included amending clauses. Some state constitutions allowed the state legislatures to make constitutional changes, usually requiring a very large majority vote. Other state constitutions relied on state constitutional conventions called to make specific amendments, or provided for periodic reviews by special Councils of Censors.

The Framers of the Constitution also remembered their own unsuccessful efforts to amend the Articles of Confederation. Based on the principle of state sovereignty, the Articles provided that Congress could

Articles of Confederation the first constitution of the thirteen original United States; in effect 1781–1789

propose amendments, but those changes had to be ratified by all the states. Because of this consensus requirement, it was too difficult to make needed changes in the Articles of Confederation. As a result, the delegates sent by the states to the Constitutional Convention in Philadelphia in 1787 drafted a new plan of government, the Constitution of the United States. The Constitution that went into effect in 1788 was ratified by three-fourths of the states, as required in Article VII.

consensus general or unanimous agreement

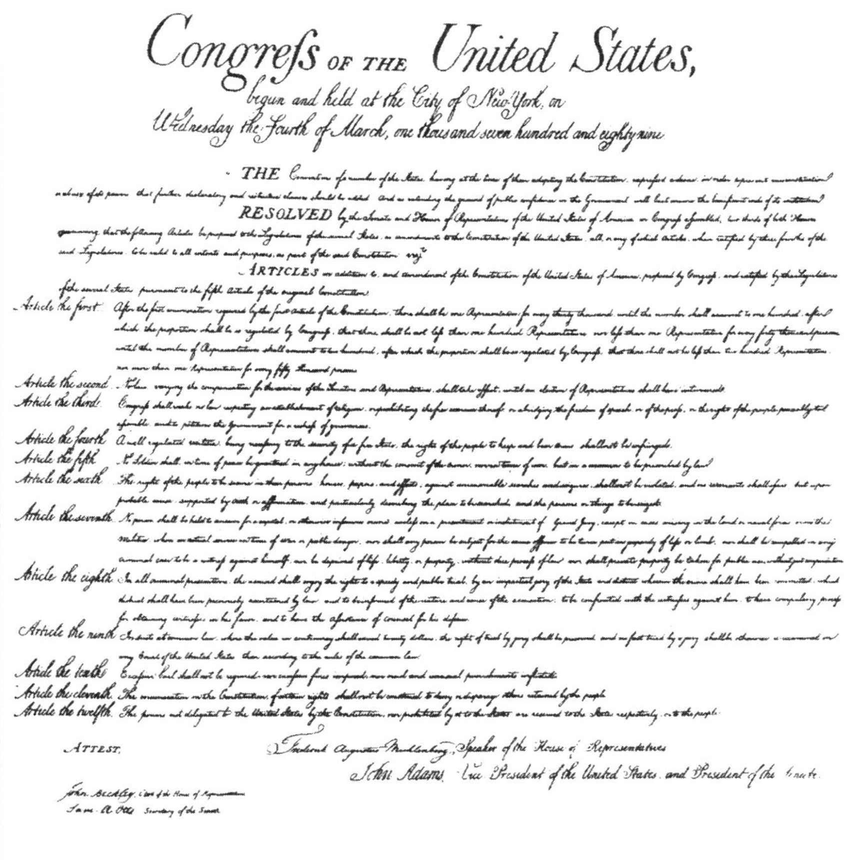

Congress of the United States,
begun and held at the City of New-York, on
Wednesday the Fourth of March, one thousand seven hundred and eighty nine

THE ...

RESOLVED ...

ARTICLES ...

Article the first ...

Article the second ...

Article the third ...

Article the fourth ...

Article the fifth ...

Article the sixth ...

Article the seventh ...

Article the eighth ...

Article the ninth ...

Article the tenth ...

Article the eleventh ...

Article the twelfth ...

ATTEST,

Frederick Augustus Muhlenberg, Speaker of the House of Representatives

John Adams, Vice President of the United States, and President of the Senate

John Beckley, Clerk of the House of Representatives

Sam. A. Otis Secretary of the Senate

The first page of the Bill of Rights as sent to the states by the first Congress of the United States (1789).

The Amendment Process

The delegates to the Constitutional Convention in Philadelphia were split over whether Congress or the states should have greater power in amending the Constitution. They wisely reached a compromise that divided this responsibility, giving both Congress and the states important powers.

Article V provides two methods for proposing amendments to the Constitution and two methods for ratifying them. Only one form of each method has been used, in nearly every case. Congress has proposed all twenty-seven amendments to the Constitution, and the state legislatures have ratified all except the Twenty-first Amendment.

Conventions called by three-fourths of the states ratified the Twenty-first Amendment. The other method of proposing amendments—having

When the Constitution was completed, Thomas Jefferson, who was to be the nation's third president, argued that each generation of Americans should change its Constitution and "set it to rights" if it wished. James Madison, often called "the father of the Constitution," who was to be the fourth president, opposed this idea. He feared that if each generation tried to rewrite to the Constitution, this practice might undermine America's respect for the document. Amendments, he said, should be reserved for "great and extraordinary occasions." He was unwilling to "see a door opened for a reconsideration of the whole structure of the Government." Madison's view prevailed. Article V does not require any periodic review.

Congress considered 1,736 proposed constitutional amendments during its first century (1789-1889). From 1890 to 1926, 1,316 amendments were introduced. From 1926 to 1963, 2,340 more proposals were submitted. Nearly 6,000 were introduced from 1963 until the end of the twentieth century alone. These proposals cover not only matters of national importance such as school prayer and term limits, but also, for example, allowing citizens to recall elected officials, and enact and repeal laws at the ballot box.

two-thirds of the states petition Congress to call a convention to propose an amendment—has never been used. Debate has persisted over how such a convention called by the states to propose a change in the Constitution might work. Congress has never adopted legislation defining what procedures state conventions should follow or even for how long the states' petition to hold a convention remains in effect.

If a state convention proposed any amendment, states would have to ratify it. Congress would have to specify whether it required ratification by three-fourths of the state legislatures or, as in the case of the Twenty-first Amendment, by conventions called by three-fourths of the states.

federalism a system of political organization; a union is formed of separate states or groups that are ruled by a central authority on some matters but are otherwise permitted to independently govern themselves

referenda (singular: **referendum**) voting by the people; done usually to overrule the lawmaking body

Although more than 11,000 amendments have been introduced by Congress, only 33 have received the necessary two-thirds majority vote. The states have ratified twenty-seven of these proposed amendments. Unlike the practice of many other countries, the Constitution's emphasis on federalism kept the Framers from providing a method that allowed amendments to be ratified by national referenda. In 1920, the Supreme Court refused to allow state legislatures to delegate their ratification power in this way.

Unanswered Questions

The Constitution does not specify the time period in which an amendment may be ratified. Some amendments, however, have included a provision that limited the ratification time to seven years. Even so, in 1992 Congress accepted final state ratification of the Twenty-seventh Amendment, which related to increasing congressional salaries, that was first proposed, without a time limit, in 1789.

Scholars have debated whether the Twenty-seventh Amendment was validly ratified. Those who argued that it was validly ratified point out that neither the amendment itself nor Article V specifies any time limit for ratifying an amendment. Those who argue that it was not validly ratified point to the Supreme Court's 1921 decision in *Dillon* v. *Gloss*. In that case, the Court ruled that amendments should reflect a contemporary consensus, that is, an agreement reflecting the view in its own time. Since the states had ratified this amendment more than a century after it was proposed, the scholars argued, the ratification was not valid.

Limits on Amendments

import bring in goods from another country

Article V contains two clauses designed to safeguard certain provisions of the Constitution against amendment. The first of these "entrenchment" clauses set a twenty-year limit for any amendment relating to importing slaves. This clause was added because some Southern states demanded it before they would ratify the Constitution. The second clause provided that no state would be denied equal representation in the Senate without its consent. This clause, which presumably is still in force, highlights the importance of the compromise over representation in Congress, which was agreed to in order to muster support from both small and large states for the Constitution.

RATIFICATION OF THE EQUAL RIGHTS AMENDMENT

States Ratifying

1972
Hawaii, Delaware, Nebraska, New Hampshire, Idaho, Kansas, Texas, Maryland, Tennessee, Alaska, Rhode Island, New Jersey, Wisconsin, West Virginia, Colorado, New York, Kentucky, Massachusetts, Pennsylvania, California

1973
Wyoming, South Dakota, Minnesota, Oregon, New Mexico, Vermont, Connecticut, Washington

1974
Maine, Montana, Ohio

1975
North Dakota

States Rescinding

1973
Indiana

1974
Tennessee

1977
Idaho

1978
Kentucky (rescission bill vetoed by acting governor)

States Not Ratifying

Alabama, Arizona, Arkansas, Florida, Georgia, Illinois, Louisiana, Mississippi, Missouri, Nevada, North Carolina, Oklahoma, South Carolina, Utah, Virginia

Scholars still debate the question of whether there are any unwritten limits to the content of amendments that can be proposed and ratified. Could an amendment be so contrary to the rest of the Constitution that the Supreme Court might declare it unconstitutional? This question remains unanswered, since the Court has never ruled on this issue.

Other Methods of Change

The formal amendment process has not been used often in American history. The most active periods for amendments occurred shortly after the adoption of the Constitution, immediately after the Civil War, and in the early years of the twentieth century. In other periods of great change in America, for example, during the New Deal, almost no revisions were made in the written Constitution.

Because relatively few amendments have been added to the Constitution, some scholars argue that it has been changed more by other means. Most agree that changes in the customs and practices of Congress, the actions of presidents, and court rulings often alter understanding of the Constitution. Amendments can be passed to reverse such interpretations. The Eleventh, Fourteenth, Sixteenth, and Twenty-sixth Amendments have overturned constitutional interpretations by the courts.

Article V in Practice

Persuaded by the arguments of Roger Sherman, a Connecticut delegate, the Framers of the Constitution tacked the first ten amendments on at the end of the document rather than incorporating them within the text.

The adoption of amendments to the Constitution reflected important developments and events in America's history. The first ten amendments, the Bill of Rights, were adopted to ease the fears of Anti-Federalists that the new national government would restrict individual liberties. The Thirteenth through Fifteenth Amendments outlawed slavery and guaranteed the rights of formerly enslaved African Americans. The Sixteenth through Nineteenth Amendments further incorporated elements of direct democracy into the federal system—including granting women the right to vote and providing for the direct election of senators. Several later amendments also further extended the right to vote and remedied minor flaws or omissions in the original document.

Some scholars and politicians have expressed concern over the number of amendments that have been suggested. Yet, since the Twenty-sixth Amendment lowered the voting age to eighteen in 1971, only one amendment has been ratified (the Twenty-seventh Amendment relating to increasing congressional salaries, first proposed in 1789). Moreover, the states have failed to ratify the last two amendments that Congress proposed. In 1982, the Equal Rights Amendment was not ratified by enough states. Nor was another amendment, proposed in 1978 to give voting representation in Congress to the District of Columbia. It seems fair to say that the Framers invented a complicated method of making formal changes in the Constitution that was difficult but not impossible.

Anti-Federalist member of the group opposing the adoption of the U.S. Constitution; favored states' rights and argued successfully for the Bill of Rights

Article VI

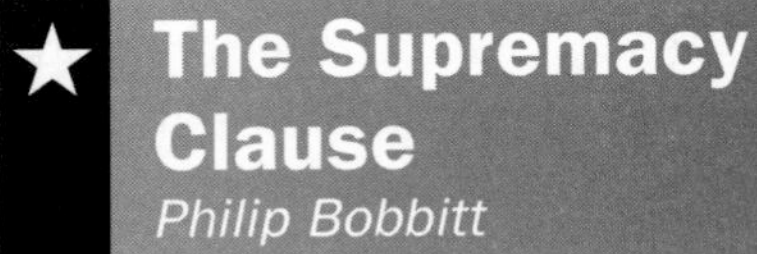

The Supremacy Clause

Philip Bobbitt

ARTICLE VI, CLAUSE 2, OF THE CONSTITUTION STATES

*This Constitution, and the Laws of the United States which shall be made in the Pursuance thereof; and all **Treaties** made, or which shall be made, under the Authority of the United States, shall be the **supreme** Law of the Land; and the Judges in every State shall be bound thereby, any Thing in the Constitution or Laws of any State to the Contrary notwithstanding.*

treaty binding international agreement

supreme having the highest authority

Clause 2 of Article VI of the Constitution has become known as the supremacy clause. The wording of this clause has been used to establish the supremacy of the federal government in the United States. This supremacy clause also provides the foundation of several fundamental doctrines in the nation's system of government. Among these key doctrines are **federalism**, **sovereignty**, **judicial review**, and **constitutional interpretation**.

federalism a system of political organization; a union is formed of separate states or groups that are ruled by a central authority on some matters but are otherwise permitted to independently govern themselves

sovereignty the state of having supreme and independent power

judicial review a court's authority to evaluate laws for their constitutionality

constitutional interpretation figuring out what the provisions of the Constitution mean

Federalism

Federalism defines the relationship between the national government and the states. The **Articles of Confederation**, the nation's first constitution adopted in 1781, established the first system of government for the thirteen American states. But the Articles proved unworkable as a framework for government. Under them, the central government had sole powers in foreign affairs as well as over western lands and Indian affairs. State governments had no power in these matters. But the central government had no executive branch or judicial branch. Instead, Congress exercised the legislative powers, and committees of Congress carried out the laws as well. Even so, the central government was weak, because it lacked the power to tax or regulate citizens directly and had to depend on the state governments to do so.

Articles of Confederation the first constitution of the thirteen original United States; in effect 1781–1789

In 1789, the Constitution of the United States was adopted, replacing the Articles of Confederation. The Constitution strengthened the power of the central government, dividing its power among three separate branches. Congress headed the legislative, or lawmaking, branch; the president was the head of the executive branch, which enforced the laws; and the Supreme Court and lower federal courts made up the judicial branch. The Constitution granted the national government important powers, but it also reserved many other powers to state governments.

The Constitution also provided for concurrent powers, or powers that both the national government and the state governments could exercise, such as legislation regulating the economy. As a result, states might pass laws on the same subject covered by laws enacted by Congress. In such cases, the question arose: Which law should citizens obey? The supremacy clause provided the answer. When state laws conflict with federal legislation, the federal law is supreme.

Sovereignty

The Constitution recognized the existence of a sovereign country called the United States, with power to enter into relationships with other countries, including the power to make treaties and even use armed forces. All sovereign countries have these powers, but the United States was different in a very important way. The U.S. Constitution established a system of government based on popular sovereignty, that is, government based on the will of the people. The people, not the government, are the source of power, and government exercises its power only to the extent that the people wish. This idea was a very radical one in 1789, but became one of the foundations of American government.

popular sovereignty government created by and subject to the will of the people

Sovereignty poses a problem, however. As the Constitution provides, Congress enacts laws for the United States based on the will of the people. At the same time, the president arranges treaties, or agreements with other nations that are not controlled by the American people. What, then, is the relationship between a law and a treaty? Is one superior to the other? Do treaties apply only in an international court, such as the International Court of Justice at The Hague, and laws apply only in courts in the United States? The supremacy clause solves this problem by putting laws and treaties on the same basis. This means that a treaty is superior to any state law that conflicts with it. The supremacy clause created sovereignty in the United States that is different from that in most countries. In the United States, sovereignty comes from the people, not the government.

The supremacy clause has been called the linchpin of the Constitution, the sticky glue that makes federalism work. It makes the Constitution the supreme law of the land, as the Court said in *Cooper* v. *Aaron* in 1958, when it ordered immediate compliance with a federal court's order integrating Central High School in Little Rock, Arkansas. "The federal judiciary is supreme in the exposition of the law of the Constitution," the Court wrote. This is "a permanent and indispensable feature of our constitutional system." The principle of integration that the Court had announced in the school segregation cases is the supreme law of the land, and "every state legislative and executive and judicial officer is solemnly committed by oath pursuant" to Article VI, Section 3, "to support this Constitution." To make its point even more strongly, the Court issued its opinion in the name of all the justices, not merely in the name of one justice as spokesman as it usually does. This made clear that the Court intended to forbid resistance to the principle of integration. The supremacy clause made the modern civil rights movement possible.

Judicial Review

A court may examine a law or an act of government to decide if it is constitutional and should be applied. Or, after such an examination, the court may judge that this law or government act is not in keeping with the Constitution and, therefore, should not be applied. This process by which the courts determine the constitutionality of laws is known as judicial review. The supremacy clause carefully defines "the law of the land" as laws that are made "in pursuance of" the Constitution. Judges must always determine whether the law they are to enforce is in keeping with the Constitution.

The supremacy clause requires state judges to undertake judicial review by declaring that "judges in every state" must recognize the supremacy of the Constitution and federal laws despite state laws to the contrary. State judges also must examine all state laws to see that they are based on the Constitution, because it is supreme. They also must determine whether a federal law that conflicts with a state law is constitutional before they recognize the federal law as overriding state law.

Constitutional Interpretation

It is through constitutional interpretation that the meaning of the words, the purposes, the structure and the ethical content of the Constitution

have been defined, as well as how these concepts have been applied and should be applied. The supremacy clause commands all citizens of the United States to recognize the Constitution as the supreme law of the land. This means that every person called upon to perform an official act—whether to arrest someone, to veto a bill, or filibuster in a session of Congress—must also decide whether this act carries out or violates the intent of the Constitution.

veto refuse to sign a bill into law

filibuster prolonged floor debate aimed at defeating measures by preventing a final vote

Some legal scholars have argued that the United States could survive if the Constitution did not include Article II, providing for the presidency, or Article III, establishing the federal courts, or even if it lacked the Bill of Rights. They hold this belief because they think that these institutions and the rules they follow can be determined by reading the rest of the Constitution. But this view could not hold true of Article I, which establishes Congress and its powers. Nor is it true of the supremacy clause, which ranks with just a very few provisions of the Constitution as indispensable to the American system of government. Indeed, the supremacy clause reflects the judgment of the Framers about the kind of government the United States should have: a government that is by the People, of the People, and for the People.

INTRODUCTION—Constitutional Concepts; Constitutional Origins; ARTICLE III—Establishment of Judicial Review: *Marbury v. Madison*; Origins of Judicial Review; ARTICLE VI—States' Rights and Federalism; AMENDMENTS—The Courts and the Bill of Rights

States' Rights and Federalism

Paul A. Sracic

Federalism is a system of government in which power is shared by the national and state governments. A federal system is different from a confederation, where the states have most of the power, and it is different from a unitary system, where the central government is in charge.

federalism a system of political organization; a union is formed of separate states or groups that are ruled by a central authority on some matters but are otherwise permitted to independently govern themselves

Federalism is also a political principle which is sometimes put forth as a limit on national power. This was, in fact, the intention of the Framers of the Constitution and the Bill of Rights. But the principle of federalism is also viewed as the continually changing and developing relationship between the national government and state governments. Defining federalism in this way raises many difficult questions and issues, because federalism refers to no precise plan or agreed-on formula of government. In the United States, federalism may be best understood as an evolving set of compromises between rival authorities.

Government in the American Colonies

Before the American Revolution, the only central authority that ruled the thirteen colonies was the British government. The colonies had equal power and privileges in their relations to each other. After the Revolution, the colonists were not eager to establish immediately another powerful central government to govern their newly independent states.

Oddly enough, the actions of the British government during the colonial period had shown the colonies and their leaders how much they shared and how dependent they were on one another. The colonists saw

Alexander Hamilton, the Father of Federalism

Articles of Confederation the first constitution of the thirteen original United States; in effect 1781–1789

sovereignty the state of having supreme and independent power

ratify to formally approve a document, thereby making it legal

that if only a few of the colonies resisted the harsh measures the British government had imposed, their efforts would surely fail—and all the colonies would have to share the costs of that failure. The colonists realized that they needed to speak to Great Britain in a single voice, so they formed one centralized committee to represent them. This committee became the Continental Congress, which guided the colonies through the American Revolution. After the nation won its independence, the Continental Congress became the model for the "federal" government of the new United States of America.

The States and the Federal Government

The relationship between the states and the new national government had hardly been considered by the leaders of the new American nation. The first formal plan of government for the newly independent states began to take shape in the Articles of Confederation. The Articles granted extensive powers to the national government, while recognizing only a "league of friendship" in which each state retained "its sovereignty, freedom and independence."

Congress was the only branch of government that the Articles of Confederation created. Although they gave Congress power to govern, Congress was in fact nearly powerless and depended completely on the states for both raising money and enforcing the laws. The economic crisis that followed on the heels of the Revolution made clear this contradiction.

Strengthening the central goverment. The Constitutional Convention of 1787 attempted to resolve the problems in the Articles of Confederation by strengthening the central government. But the Framers, who were political realists, did not expect that the state legislatures would willingly hand over their power to a new national government. They decided to bypass the state legislatures when it came time to ratify the Constitution; and at the same time, they continued to argue that the new federal form of government established by the Constitution was a mixture of unitary and confederate forms.

Questions about federalism continued to be raised even after the Constitution was ratified in 1788. The concerns of those who favored states' rights led to the inclusion of the Tenth Amendment in the Bill of Rights, ratified in 1791. The Tenth Amendment reserves to the states, or to the people, all powers not expressly granted to the national government. But the Tenth Amendment did not settle the debate, since it seems to have merely reaffirmed the federal relationship between the states and the national government already set forth in the Constitution.

The power to interpret the Constitution. Two key questions about federalism were still left unanswered. First, precisely what powers does the Constitution grant to the national government? Second, who has the authority to interpret the meaning of these grants of power? James Madison attempted to answer the first question in 1798 when he, along with Thomas Jefferson, stated that the doctrine of nullification was a limit on the power of the national government. Under this doctrine, states were able to nullify—declare unlawful—an act of Congress which, in their

sedition incitement of resistance to or insurrection against lawful authority

In 1995 the Supreme Court decided a case, *U.S. Term Limits Inc.* v. *Thornton*, that challenged a state's right to add qualifications for serving in Congress. Justice John Paul Stevens' majority opinion was based on the concept of the federal union as a compact among the people with "a single National Government" serving as their agent. "Allowing individual States to adopt their own qualifications for congressional service," he wrote, "would be inconsistent with the Framers' vision of a uniform National Legislature representing the people of the United States." Justice Clarence Thomas dissented for the minority of four. He advanced a view of federalism that no justice had advocated in over sixty years, since before the New Deal. "The ultimate source of the Constitution's authority," he wrote, "is the consent of the people of each individual State, not the consent of the undifferentiated people of the Nation as a whole." This position would make the nation nothing more than an agent of the states and all of its powers would be narrowly defined.

secession formal departure or withdrawal from an organization

dual federalism doctrine that holds that both the state and the federal government are supreme and autonomous within their respective areas

supreme having the highest authority

opinion, was unconstitutional. Although Madison and Jefferson used this doctrine in an attempt to nullify the Sedition Act passed by Congress in 1798, that law expired before the doctrine could be fully evaluated.

Supreme Court decisions answered the question of who has the authority to interpret the meaning of the Constitution. In *Marbury* v. *Madison* (1803) and *McCulloch* v. *Maryland* (1819), the justices held that the Supreme Court itself had the final word and then used this authority to increase the power of the national government. Specifically, the Court ruled that the national government could use the necessary and proper clause in Article I, Section 8, of the Constitution to exercise powers not expressly granted elsewhere in the document.

But the doctrine of nullification, though buried, was not dead. By 1828, John C. Calhoun of South Carolina again began the process of nullification. According to Calhoun, the Constitution was created by agreement not of the people but of the states. Because the states had established the national government, they were sovereign and superior to that government. This same idea, sometimes known as the compact theory, was used to justify secession by the Confederate states from the Union more than thirty years later, leading to the Civil War.

Federalism in Modern America

The victory of the Union in the Civil War finally put to rest the compact theory of government and its related doctrine of nullification. By the end of the nineteenth century, a new theory known as dual federalism gained popularity. This theory was based on the Tenth Amendment, and held that both the national and the state governments have authority within their separate spheres. In other words, a use of Congress's authority that would otherwise be legal was unconstitutional if it involved a subject over which the states, rather than the federal government, were sovereign. The dual federalism doctrine holds that both the state and the federal government are supreme and autonomous within their respective spheres.

The New Deal. The Great Depression of the 1930s and the programs of the New Deal eventually brought the dual federalism theory to an end. The states were helpless to solve the terrible economic crisis facing the American people as a whole. Since the theory of dual federalism acted to limit national power, either it or the New Deal would have to go. In the end, President Franklin D. Roosevelt ensured that his New Deal's policies would triumph.

President Roosevelt's victory in the 1932 election, and especially his landslide reelection in 1936, sharply changed the character of federalism in the United States. The national government began to act in ways that the Framers could never have imagined. The New Deal began a trend toward increasing the power of the national government and reducing the authority of state governments. That trend continued until the 1980s, when Ronald Reagan was elected president.

The "Reagan Revolution." Historians and political scientists are still attempting to evaluate the impact of the "Reagan revolution," which began when Ronald Reagan defeated President Jimmy Carter in the 1980

election. One of the major themes of Reagan's presidency was termed "the New Federalism." By this, President Reagan meant returning power to the states by allowing them to take over matters that had long been accepted as responsibilities of the national government. This concept of federalism also guided the Republican-controlled Congresses of the 1980s and 1990s, and also, to some extent, the policies of the Democratic Clinton administration in the 1990s. In what came to be called devolution federalism, Congress, in 1996, changed the Aid to Families with Dependent Children (AFDC) program into a block grant program, giving the states almost total control over the nation's welfare policies.

devolution federalism federalism where powers are transferred from the central government to local authorities

Emergence of judicial federalism. Supreme Court decisions during this period, too, followed along this line. In 1980, in *PruneYard Shopping Center* v. *Robins*, the Court allowed state courts to base their decisions solely on state constitutional guarantees, thereby granting their residents rights not contained in the Constitution. Then, in *Prinz* v. *United States* (1997), the Court ruled that Congress cannot order state officials to conduct background checks on persons who want to purchase handguns. Some legal scholars have argued that the Court's narrow interpretations support its efforts at encouraging the development of judicial federalism.

judicial federalism federalism in which the courts determine how powers are shared between the national and state governments

Given the nation's history, the struggle over the limits that federalism places on the national government's powers and the rights reserved to the states probably is far from over. It is important to understand that while these disputes can divide the nation, they also symbolize America's flexible national character. As times and circumstances change, so do the ideas about how the powers of government should be shared. Devolution federalism is probably just another stage in the continuing evolution of federalism itself.

INTRODUCTION—Constitutional Concepts; Constitutional Origins; ARTICLE VI—The Supremacy Clause; TENTH AMENDMENT

No Religious Test for Public Office

Richard E. Morgan

ARTICLE VI, SECTION 3, OF THE CONSTITUTION STATES

The Senators and Representatives before mentioned, and the Members of the several State Legislatures, and all executive and judicial Officers, both of the United States and of the several States, shall be bound by Oath or ***Affirmation*** *to support this Constitution, but no religious Test shall ever be required as a qualification to any Office or public Trust under the United States.*

affirmation declaration under the penalty of perjury

When the Constitutional Convention was held in 1787, all thirteen states in the Confederation except New York and Virginia had religious tests for public office. That meant that only persons who declared their belief in certain religious truths could hold public office, such as serving in legislatures or as governors or judges.

In Massachusetts, persons seeking public office had to declare, "I believe in the Christian religion, and have a firm possession [knowledge] of its truth." New Hampshire's constitution required state officials

This is the oath U.S. representatives and senators have to take. The language of the oath is set by statute and has changed several times since 1789. In 1994, it read:

> I do solemnly swear that I will support and defend the Constitution of the United States against all enemies, foreign and domestic; that I will bear true faith and allegiance to the same; that I take this obligation freely, without any mental reservation or purpose of evasion, and that I will well and faithfully discharge the duties of the office on which I am about to enter. So help me God.

to announce openly that they practiced "the Protestant religion." In Pennsylvania, those elected to the legislature were required to state: "I do believe in one God, the Creator and Governor of the universe, the Rewarder of the good and the Punisher of the wicked. And I do acknowledge [believe] the Scriptures of the Old and New Testaments to be given by Divine inspiration." North Carolina barred from office any person "who shall deny the being of God or the truth of the Protestant religion, or the Divine Authority either of the Old or New Testaments."

Reasons Behind Religious Tests

From a twentieth-century viewpoint, it is easy to reject such requirements for public office as narrow-minded efforts by the dominant religious groups in these states to restrict government power to people like themselves. But the reasons behind these religious tests for office were more complex. In eighteenth-century America, many people accepted on faith that someone could not be upright and virtuous unless that person believed in a life after death, when those who had led good lives would be rewarded and the wicked punished. One Massachusetts orator declared, "A person could not be a good man without being a good Christian."

Protestant Christianity was viewed as the moving force for republican government and one of its main foundations in society. Roman Catholicism, by contrast, was regarded as the natural ally of monarchy and tyrannical government. Most people believed that only Christians could be counted on to be honest, and that only Protestants could be expected to support freedom and republican institutions.

tyrannical cruelly oppressive

The Views of the Framers

By the late eighteenth century, a different view of religion was beginning to emerge among leading spokesmen and politicians. Thomas Jefferson, in the preamble to the Virginia Statute for Establishing Religious Freedom, enacted in January 1786, wrote, "Our civil rights have no dependence on our religious opinions, any more than our opinions in physics or geometry." To keep a person from a position of public trust "unless he profess or renounce this or that religious opinion," Jefferson continued, "is a violation of that person's natural rights." Of course, most Americans in those years probably would have rejected Jefferson's views on religion, but in later years they became generally accepted as the standard for public office.

The Framers, after only brief debate, included these words as part of Article VI, Clause 3, of the Constitution: "no religious test shall ever be required as a qualification to any office or public trust under the United States." Yet scholars still disagree about the reasons that the Framers banned religious tests for holding office in the new central government. Some scholars think that the Framers took this action because they sided with Jefferson and Virginia's delegates against the traditional view that such tests were necessary. Others have argued that the Framers recognized that Americans held different religious beliefs and that the oaths in state constitutions requiring religious tests for office were worded in various ways.

The Framers realized that they could not draft a religious test acceptable to every state and finally decided it was better to have no test at all.

ratify to formally approve a document, thereby making it legal

Whatever the Framers intended, many people viewed Article VI as a bold change from the past. A number of state ratifying conventions, especially those in New England, bitterly criticized it. Nevertheless, the final ratification of the Constitution seems to have strengthened the public's growing feeling that religious qualifications for office had no place in republican governments. The Tennessee constitution of 1796 is one example. Its Declaration of Rights included a ban on religious tests in words identical to those in the Constitution itself. Yet another provision of the document (Article VIII) included more traditional words, providing that "[no] person who denies the being of God, or a future state of rewards and punishments, shall hold any office in the civil department of this State." By 1820, both Maine and Missouri renounced religious tests for office upon admission to the Union.

FIRST AMENDMENT—No "Establishment of Religion"

Ending Religious Tests

In one sense, ending religious qualifications for office, first by Virginia, then in Article VI of the Constitution, and finally by all the states, represents the triumph of an idea. The idea is that to keep from office qualified persons who hold no religious beliefs or unpopular ones violates the individual's natural right to freedom of conscience. In another sense, ending religious qualifications was part of broader developments in American politics that led to the ending of various restrictions on holding office and voting. In the early nineteenth century, as the country became more democratic, property ownership was no longer required. In the twentieth century, women gained the right to vote as a result of the Nineteenth Amendment (1920), and citizens eighteen years of age were granted voting rights by the Twenty-sixth Amendment (1971).

On a more fundamental level, the ending of religious tests for public office came in response to the increasing religious diversity among Americans. The nineteenth and early twentieth centuries witnessed successive large waves of European immigrants who were Roman Catholics or Jews entering an almost completely Protestant nation. This religious diversity continued throughout the twentieth century, when other immigrants to the United States added large numbers of Muslims, Buddhists, and Hindus to the population.

In 1961, the Supreme Court's ruling in *Torasco* v. *Watkins* struck down a provision in Maryland's constitution requiring that all persons holding office in that state must declare their belief in the existence of God. Justice Hugo Black declared that this requirement violated both the free exercise and establishment clauses of the First Amendment as well as Article VI of the Constitution. In a footnote to this opinion, Justice Black wrote, "Among religions in this country which do not teach what would generally be considered a belief in the existence of God are Buddhism, Taoism, Ethical Culture, Secular Humanism and others." This was one of the first times that secular humanism was mentioned in any judicial opinion.

Test Oaths

Robert A. Sedler

ARTICLE VI, CLAUSE 3, OF THE CONSTITUTION STATES

The Senators and Representatives before mentioned, and the Members of the several State Legislatures, and all executive and judicial Officers, both of the United States and of the several States, shall be bound by Oath or ***Affirmation***, *to support this Constitution; but no religious Tests shall ever be required as a qualification to any Office or public Trust under the United States.*

affirmation declaration under the penalty of perjury

In Article VI, Clause 3, of the Constitution, the Framers required all federal and state officials to take an oath—make a solemn promise—to support the Constitution of the United States. But at the same time, the Framers wanted to protect religious liberty. They wanted to ensure that no one would be prevented from taking an oath because he or she could not, or would not, invoke the name of God to do so. They also wanted to make sure that no one would be disqualified from holding public office because of his or her religious beliefs.

The Framers provided that an official could swear to support the Constitution by making an affirmation instead of an oath. They also permitted the president to make an affirmation instead of an oath, as prescribed in Article II, Section 1, Clause 8, when taking office.

George Washington takes the presidential oath of office at the first inauguration (April 30, 1789). The Framers allowed an affirmation instead of an oath, thereby recognizing America's growing religious diversity.

> "Christianity is part of the law of England."
>
> —William Blackstone (1723–1780), British jurist. *Commentaries on the Laws of England* (1769)

The provision for making an affirmation instead of an oath protected members of such groups as the Quakers, who had religious principles against taking oaths. The Framers also wanted to make certain that nonreligious persons, as well as members of the many different religious groups in the United States, would also be able to hold federal office. So they clearly stated that no religious test should ever be required as a condition for holding federal office.

English History and the Test Oath Clause

The Framers included the test oath provision in the Constitution because in England, and in at least nine of the states after independence, religious tests were required for serving in public office. In England, holders of public office had to belong to the Church of England. In the American states that required religious tests, public officials had to be Christians, and in some states had to be members of particular Christian denominations. Many Americans strongly believed that only members of the Christian faith should be able to hold public office.

> "When I signed the Declaration of Independence I had in view not only our independence from England but the toleration of all sects."
>
> —Charles Carroll (1737–1832), member, Continental Congress, and U.S. senator

The Framers were determined that no one should be excluded from public office because of their religious beliefs. They wanted the Constitution to avoid even the appearance of any alliance between church and state in the nation's new government, no matter what the states did under their own constitutions. A large majority of the Constitutional Convention passed Article VI, Clause 3, without much debate.

This provision, by allowing affirmations instead of oaths and prohibiting religious tests for holding federal office, may be seen as a forerunner of the religious clauses of the First Amendment. These clauses have operated together to protect religious freedom in American society. The establishment clause requires the government to be completely neutral toward religion, both regarding different religions and having religious or nonreligious beliefs. The free exercise clause guarantees freedom of belief and freedom of worship to every individual. The Fourteenth Amendment made these clauses binding on the states as well. In this way, the Constitution protects religious freedom from actions by both the federal government and the states.

Supreme Court Rulings

Because of the test oath clause in the Constitution, Congress has never imposed a religious test for holding federal office. Any federal law requiring the taking of oaths, such as by witnesses in federal court cases, has allowed an affirmation instead. The Supreme Court has never had to rule that an act of Congress violated the test oath clause. Yet the test oath clause has influenced the Court's interpretation of the establishment and free exercise clauses of the First Amendment.

The Supreme Court ruled in *Girouard* v. *United States* (1946) that a religious pacifist who refuses to take an oath to bear arms in defense of the Constitution cannot be denied the right to become a naturalized American citizen. It said that such a requirement for someone seeking

pacifist a person who opposes all wars on moral or religious grounds

AMENDMENTS—The Courts and the Bill of Rights; FIRST AMENDMENT—"Free Exercise" of Religion; No "Establishment of Religion"

The idea of a Roman Catholic as president of the United States was one of the great American taboos when John F. Kennedy ran in 1960. That September 12 he spoke to the Greater Houston Ministerial Association in Texas: "I believe in an America where the separation of church and state is absolute—where no Catholic prelate would tell the president (should he be a Catholic) how to act and no Protestant minister would tell his parishioners for whom to vote. . . . This is the kind of America I fought for in the South Pacific" during World War II. Kennedy said that if he found any conflict between his conscience and the responsibility of the presidency, he would resign the office.

John F. Kennedy delivers a speech in New York City during the 1960 presidential campaign.

U.S. citizenship would be like requiring a religious test for public office and so would violate the free exercise clause. Since Congress cannot require a religious test for public office, it cannot require a religious test for becoming a citizen of the United States. Similarly, in *Tarasco* v. *Watkins* (1961), the Court ruled unconstitutional a Maryland law requiring a belief in the existence of God as a condition for holding public office—again as violating the free exercise clause. In *McDaniel* v. *Paty* (1978), the justices overturned a Tennessee law barring members of the clergy from serving as state legislators.

Other Effects of the Test Oath Clause

The ban against religious tests explains why government officials who have promised to support the Constitution are expected to be able to separate their own religious beliefs from their constitutional duty to govern fairly and to act in keeping with the law. John F. Kennedy gave a famous speech in the 1960 presidential election campaign in which he explained that his being a Roman Catholic would not affect his ability to serve as president. Since then, a candidate's religious beliefs have not been an issue in presidential campaigns.

In the same way, a federal judge cannot be disqualified from hearing a case on the grounds that it involves an issue on which the judge's religious denomination has taken a position. To do so would result, in effect, in imposing a religious test on federal judges, in violation of the test oath clause. It must be assumed that the judge will decide the case based on the law and on his or her oath or affirmation to support the Constitution.

When the Constitution was written, the test oath clause represented a commitment to religious freedom by the new federal government. A few years later, this commitment was clearly stated in the establishment clause and the free exercise clause of the First Amendment. The test oath clause remains the first listed expression of religious liberty in the Constitution.

Article VII

Ratification of the Constitution

Roger K. Newman

ARTICLE VII OF THE CONSTITUTION STATES

The ***ratification*** *of the Conventions of nine States, shall be sufficient for the establishment of this Constitution between the States so ratifying the same.*

ratification process of making a document legal by giving it formal approval

Even before the Constitutional Convention met in 1787, some delegates believed that a new Constitution could never be ratified except by state conventions in the thirteen states. Belief in this method of ratification gradually grew as James Madison defended it at the Convention. He pointed out that since the delegates had already agreed to give some of the power that the states had under the **Articles of Confederation** to the newly formed central government, conventions made up of other men would be more likely to ratify the Constitution. "The people were in fact the foundation of all power," Madison told the delegates, "and by resorting to them, all difficulties were got over."

Articles of Confederation the first constitution of the thirteen original United States; in effect 1781–1789

The Ratifying States Issue

The Framers debated the number of states necessary to ratify the Constitution. Some delegates proposed seven states, a simple majority. Other delegates argued that since the Articles of Confederation had required all thirteen states to ratify or even amend it, all thirteen states must agree to dissolve it. The Convention finally reached a compromise that nine states were to be required, the "number made familiar by the Constitution of the existing Congress," as Edmund Randolph of Virginia reminded the delegates. The Convention also agreed that the new government under the Constitution should operate only in the states that ratified it.

electoral college a body of people chosen by the voters in each state to elect the president and vice president

The conventions of the states that ratified the Constitution passed a resolution setting March 4, 1789 as the day that the new government would begin its operations under the Constitution. On February 4, 1789 the **electoral college** unanimously chose George Washington to be president. But the vote could not be made official until the electors' ballots were counted in front of both houses of Congress. It took over a month for the necessary number of senators and representatives to arrive in New York, then the temporary capital. The counting was finally completed, and on April 14 Washington received formal notice of his election. He left on horseback from his home in Mount Vernon, Virginia, outside what is now Washington, D.C., for New York, but the trip took nearly two weeks because he was greeted so enthusiastically along the way that he frequently had to stop. The Articles of Confederation continued in effect until he was inaugurated on April 30, 1789.

The Role of the Confederation Congress

The role that the Confederation Congress should play presented a thorny question. An early draft of the Constitution provided that the existing Congress must approve the new Constitution before it was submitted to the states for ratification. Nationalists, who wanted to shift power from the states to the national government, immediately objected. The proposal was rejected, but it started a heated debate. One delegate, George Mason of Virginia, swore that he "would sooner chop off his right hand than put it to [sign] the Constitution as it now stands." The delegates finally agreed that congressional approval should not be required. But Alexander Hamilton then argued, surprisingly, that it was wrong to allow nine states to "institute a new government on the ruins of the existing one." The Convention delegates voted to reconsider their position. Finally, after more debate, they decided not to ask Congress to approve the new Constitution.

George Washington presiding over the Constitutional Convention, 1787. Painting by Howard Chandler Christie.

Much of this hotly contested issue was omitted from the Constitution. The delegates resolved that the Constitution should be presented to Congress, and that it was the opinion of the Convention that the Constitution should be presented to state ratifying conventions.

How Many States Must Ratify?

Federalist set of 85 essays published 1787–1788 that analyzed the Constitution and urged its adoption; essays were written by John Jay, Alexander Hamilton, and James Madison

Some questions still remained unanswered. In **The Federalist**, No. 43, James Madison asked, "What relation is to subsist between the nine or more remaining states ratifying the Constitution, and the remaining few who do not become parties to it?" He answered his own question: "It is one of those cases which must be left to provide for itself." In short, experience would supply the final answer.

When it called the Constitutional Convention to meet, Congress had stated that the convention's recommendations would become effective only when it approved them, in keeping with the terms of the Articles of Confederation, which required unanimous approval. Instead, the delegates to the Constitutional Convention proposed a new government almost from the ground up. Ratification by specially chosen conventions of nine of the thirteen states would achieve their goal.

The Constitutional Convention adopted the Constitution on September 17, 1787, and on September 28, 1787, it was sent to the states for ratification. Delaware was the first state to ratify it, on December 9, 1787. New Hampshire became the ninth state to ratify it, on June 21, 1788. The Constitution went into effect on March 4, 1789.

Introduction—Constitutional Origins

Amendments

★ The Birth of the Bill of Rights

Robert Allen Rutland

Built in 1679, The Province House in Boston was the residence of the royal governors of Massachusetts during the colonial period.

When the colonists living on the Atlantic seaboard created thirteen separate governments between 1619 and 1732, they attempted to follow English practice. From Massachusetts to Georgia, each colony had a royal governor (or a substitute) and a legislature elected by the voters. These legislatures usually met once a year, for a brief period, and took care of local concerns such as roads, shipping laws, and defense measures for the frontier that separated them from the Indians.

In time, the colonial lawmakers left to the English Parliament the important matters of war and peace. But they were jealous of Parliament's right to pass local tax laws. English officials approved of this arrangement, so long as the colonies supplied the mother country with raw materials (lumber, naval supplies, indigo, rice, and tobacco) and bought English goods.

The Stamp Act

The colonies carried on a brisk trade with England and the British West Indies, and prospered. Colonial capitals such as Williamsburg and Philadelphia flourished with a lifestyle that imitated British customs and manners. But a change in English policy in 1765 resulted in Parliament's passing the Stamp Act, which placed a tax on American newspapers, legal documents, and playing cards. The tax was small, but the idea that Parliament could tax the colonists directly had disastrous effects on colonial relations. Led by dissenters in Boston, Philadelphia, and Williamsburg, Americans called for a colonial congress to meet and protest the Stamp Act in the strongest terms. In 1765, this Stamp Act Congress proposed a boycott of British goods unless the Stamp Act was repealed. There was much talk at this congress about "the rights of British-Americans," and the first rumblings of "No Taxation without Representation" were heard.

Parliament repealed the Stamp Act, but in backing down it reminded the colonists that its jurisdiction over the thirteen colonies was supreme and warned that its rule over the colonies was to prevail in the future "in all cases whatsoever."

jurisdiction the territory or area within which authority may be exercised

supreme having the highest authority

For the next eight years Americans continued to prosper, and seemed to enjoy their membership in the growing British empire (which included Canada and India). Then Parliament passed another bill placing a small tax on some specific items consumed in the colonies, including tea. A band of angry Bostonians boarded a ship loaded with tea and dumped it into Boston harbor (it became known as the Boston Tea Party). Parliament reacted by closing the port of Boston, imposing a fine to pay for the destroyed tea, and sending British troops to occupy the town. The colonists reacted, too, by sending aid to Boston and calling another congress to plan a counterblow.

redress making right what is wrong

obnoxious something that brings forth or deserves strong dislike or distaste or disgust

The Continental Congress met in 1774 to petition King George III for a redress of their grievances. It also favored a boycott on British goods until the obnoxious tax bills were repealed. But neither the king nor Parliament had any intention of backing down this time. Some high-handed arrests and search parties only reinforced the Americans' view that they were entitled to the same rights as English subjects. The English Bill of Rights of 1689, which mentioned the right to a trial by jury and protection from arbitrary arrests and illegal searches, was hailed in the colonies as applying as much in Boston as in London.

American colonists cheer as demonstrators throw tea from British ships.

Americans Write a Bill of Rights

The argument across the Atlantic was still at high pitch when the American Revolution began in April 1775. The Continental Congress, still hoping to avoid outright separation from England, issued a bill of rights proclaiming what Americans have come to call "civil liberties." These included freedom of the press, the right to petition the legislature, and the right to bear arms. Congress was so enthusiastic about these proposals that it sent a copy to Canada and invited the Canadians to join the Americans in resisting "parliamentary oppression." The Canadians had other ideas, and so the effort to enlist them in the American confederation was not pursued.

As the colonies moved toward declaring their independence, a new view of statehood emerged. Virginia, the largest colony, took the lead in May of 1776 by proposing that the colonies cut all connection with Great Britain and become the United States of America.

Virginia Writes a Constitution

Moving swiftly, the colonial legislature in Virginia dissolved its allegiance to George III and called a convention to create a state government. In May and June of 1776, two men dominated the Virginia convention. George Mason, a tobacco planter of recognized abilities, was in Williamsburg, Virginia, while Thomas Jefferson, also a planter, was away in Philadelphia, serving in the Continental Congress. Both men wrote constitutions for the newly created state, but Mason was at the Virginia convention and pushed his ideas through.

inherent relating to the essential nature of something

Events in Williamsburg. The delegates named a committee to prepare a bill of rights and a constitution, and Mason took charge. Within days he presented the delegates with a bill of rights that began: "That all men are by nature equally free and independent, and have certain inherent rights . . . namely, the enjoyment of life and liberty, with the means of acquiring and possessing property, and pursuing and obtaining happiness and safety." Fifteen other "rights," such as freedom of the press and "the free exercise of religion," followed.

Jefferson's draft. George Mason's bill of rights swept through the Virginia convention, as did his constitution a short time later. In June of 1776, newspapers up and down the Atlantic coast carried full accounts of these revolutionary documents that, in effect, broke the ties binding

The Virginia Bill of Rights drawn by George Mason and adopted by the Convention of Delegates, June 12, 1776.

The Motto on Thomas Jefferson's seal read—REBELLION TO TYRANTS IS OBEDIENCE TO GOD.

VIRGINIA BILL *of* RIGHTS

DRAWN ORIGINALLY BY GEORGE MASON AND ADOPTED BY THE CONVENTION OF DELEGATES

June 12, 1776.

A Declaration of Rights made by the Repreſentatives of the good People of Virginia, aſſembled in full and free Convention; which Rights do pertain to them, and their Poſterity, as the Baſis and Foundation of Government.

I.

That all Men are by Nature equally free and independent, and have certain inherent Rights, of which, when they enter into a State of Society, they cannot, by any Compact, deprive or diveſt their Poſterity; namely, the Enjoyment of Life and Liberty, with the Means of acquiring and poſſeſſing Property, and purſuing and obtaining Happineſs and Safety.

II.

That all Power is veſted in, and conſequently derived from, the People; that Magiſtrates are their Truſtees and Servants, and at all Times amenable to them.

III.

That Government is, or ought to be, inſtituted for the common Benefit, Protection, and Security, of the People, Nation, or Community; of all the various Modes and Forms of Government that is beſt, which is capable of producing the greateſt Degree of Happineſs and Safety, and is moſt effectually ſecured againſt the Danger of Mal-adminiſtration; and that, whenever any Government ſhall be found inadequate or contrary to theſe Purpoſes, a Majority of the Community hath an indubitable, unalienable, and indefeaſible Right, to reform, alter, or aboliſh it, in ſuch Manner as ſhall be judged moſt conducive to the public Weal.

IV.

That no Man, or Set of Men, are entitled to excluſive or ſeparate Emoluments or Privileges from the Community, but in Conſideration of public Services; which, not being deſcendible, neither ought the Offices of Magiſtrate, Legiſlator, or Judge, to be hereditary.

V.

That the legiſlative and executive Powers of the State ſhould be ſeparate and diſtinct from the Judicative; and, that the Members of the two firſt may be reſtrained from Oppreſſion, by feeling and participating the Burthens of the People, they ſhould, at fixed Periods, be reduced to a private Station, return into that Body from which they were originally taken, and the Vacancies be ſupplied by frequent, certain, and regular Elections, in which all, or any Part of the former Members, to be again eligible, or ineligible, as the Laws ſhall direct.

That

Americans to Great Britain. The constitution that Jefferson drafted was shelved; but the effect of Mason's language on Jefferson's thinking became evident a month later, when Jefferson drafted the Declaration of Independence that proclaimed the ideals of the American Revolution—life, liberty, and the pursuit of happiness. The English philosopher John Locke had written of "life, liberty, and property." But Jefferson went further and spoke of the right of all people to seek a better life.

Bills of rights throughout the colonies. In a matter of months, most other newly created states discussed a bill of rights. Americans wanted their rights spelled out and written down, unlike the English constitution, which was unwritten and thus often misquoted. By 1780, eight states had followed the Virginia model, sometimes using identical wording, and including the term "inalienable rights." This idea has existed ever since.

Articles of Confederation the first constitution of the thirteen original United States; in effect 1781–1789

Strangely, the Articles of Confederation that the new nation finally adopted in 1781 had no bill of rights, but the omission was explained away. Supporters said that there was no need for a bill of rights prefacing the Articles, because these created a government made up only of states and so had no direct effect on individual citizens. Since each state was to retain its sovereignty, freedom, and independence, it followed that all guarantees of freedom for the individual citizen would necessarily come from the state, not the Confederation.

The Constitutional Convention

> "Wherever the real power of government lies, there is the danger of oppression. In our government the real power lies with the majority of the community."
>
> —James Madison, fourth president of the United States

The United States began to come apart during the years following the 1783 peace treaty with England that recognized the new but weak nation. Faced with an enormous debt abroad and tax resistance at home, James Madison and Alexander Hamilton, delegates to the Continental Congress, worked behind the scenes on a drastic revision of the Articles of Confederation. After much delay, the Constitutional Convention was called to meet in Philadelphia in May 1787 to revise the Articles. George Washington reluctantly agreed to attend, and fifty-five delegates from twelve states were chosen. (Rhode Island refused to approve the gathering.)

The Constitutional Convention voted to conduct its business in secrecy, and there was much speculation on what kind of government might emerge. The national government was broke, the army and navy were pitiful, and around London dinner tables there was speculation that the former colonies would soon be begging to be readmitted into the British Empire.

Madison had other plans. He wanted to scrap the Articles of Confederation and start over again. After weeks of noisy and sometimes bitter debate, Madison prevailed on many points. Under the new Constitution, the federal government would have a congress, a president, and a supreme court. Only Congress could raise taxes and spend money. The president was to see that the laws were carried out. And the Supreme Court would decide what laws were constitutional.

A Call For a National Bill of Rights

Late in the debates, Virginia delegate George Mason asked Convention delegates to add a bill of rights to the Constitution. "It would give great quiet to the people," he said, and "might be prepared in a few hours." The delegates were eager to conclude their work and rejected Mason's proposal by a vote of 10 to 0, each state voting as a unit. Frustrated and angry, Mason wrote his objections on the back of a copy of the final committee report: "There is no Declaration of Rights" was his opening sentence. Nevertheless, in quick order, the Constitution was finally adopted on September 17, 1787, and sent to the states for ratification.

ratification process of making a document legal by giving it formal approval

Soon, the ardent supporters of the Constitution began to think they had acted too hastily in rejecting George Mason's last-minute demand for a bill of rights. Opponents of the proposed Constitution printed and

broadcast his objections, and "There is no bill of rights!" became a rallying cry for citizens opposing ratification. A few states ratified within months, but as the winter of 1787–1788 set in, Madison and others campaigning for ratification realized their error. In Massachusetts, friends of the Constitution were in despair and prevented defeat only by agreeing to add a bill of rights to their ratification "in full confidence" that the first Congress would redress this mistake.

Ratifying the Constitution

Madison and Hamilton were worried that New York might fail to ratify the Constitution if its governor, George Clinton, kept up his opposition. So they wrote a series of 85 essays—now known as The Federalist Papers—in which they defended the Constitution almost line by line. But the two men would not budge on the issue of a national bill of rights, and Hamilton wrote an entire essay showing why there was no need for it.

The Federalist set of 85 essays published 1787–1788 that analyzed the Constitution and urged its adoption; essays were written by John Jay, Alexander Hamilton, and James Madison

The voters in state after state thought otherwise. Rhode Island, the only state where a head-count vote was taken, decided against ratification. There and elsewhere, the failure to preface the Constitution with a bill of rights was hurting the Federalist cause.

Federalist advocating a strong central government of separate states and the adoption of the U.S. Constitution

A climax to the battle came in Richmond, Virginia, in June of 1788. Patrick Henry, a powerful orator, said he had refused to serve at the Philadelphia convention because he "smelt a rat"—he feared that the convention delegates would diminish the power of the states and make the federal government supreme, which did happen. Henry joined Mason, who had been a delegate at the Virginia ratifying convention, to form a coalition pledged to reject the Constitution.

coalition an association of people or organizations who come together for a common purpose

Henry and Mason almost succeeded. They persuaded the delegates from the western part of Virginia to vote against the plan. But Madison was also in Richmond, and was able to counter Henry's thunderous but vague warnings against federal domination. John Marshall, a rising young lawyer, joined Madison on the debate floor to give Henry one of his few setbacks. Jefferson, from his post as the American ambassador to France, urged friends back home to take the package even if it was not perfect. "Half a loaf is better than no bread," Jefferson observed, as he asserted that every nation owed its citizens a bill of rights.

The art of compromise, so important in a democratic society, was the Federalists' trump card. By promising to work for a bill of rights once the Constitution's new government was in operation, the Federalists won over a handful of votes from the areas in Virginia where slavery was weakest, and where Anti-Federalists had more strength. In the final ballot Virginia ratified the Constitution, 89 ayes to 79 nays.

Anti-Federalist member of the group opposing the adoption of the U.S. Constitution; favored states' rights and argued successfully for the Bill of Rights

Some States Delay Ratifying

Although three states were still holding out—North Carolina, Rhode Island, and New York—New Hampshire ratified at about the same time as Virginia, giving the nine votes needed to adopt the Constitution. Governor Clinton tried to keep New York in the opposition, but Hamilton

George Mason was born in 1725 in Fairfax County, Virginia, where he inherited much land. In 1766 he wrote to a committee of London merchants that the colonists claimed "nothing but the liberties and privileges of Englishmen, in the same degree, as if we had still continued among our brethren in Great Britain." In 1776, Mason wrote the Virginia Declaration of Rights, which served as the model for the first part of the Declaration of Independence, and it "set a model for governments of free men the world over." Other state constitutions copied the Virginia document. It was also the basis for the Constitution's Bill of Rights. Mason then helped to revise Virginia's legal system. He had long urged the **abolition** of slavery, since it was "such a wicked, cruel, and unnatural trade." At the Constitutional Convention, Mason opposed the compromise on slavery, which he denounced as "disgraceful to mankind."

abolition the end, especially of slavery

was serving at the New York ratifying convention and skillfully made compromises so that, on the final day, the Federalists narrowly won, 29 to 27. (A weak call for another federal convention was included to give Clinton's friends a face-saving gesture. A similar idea arose in Richmond, but it was not taken seriously.) The Constitution had been ratified without North Carolina or Rhode Island.

The North Carolina convention voted to adjourn without taking action on the ratification plan. But when the first Congress met in New York and Madison kept his campaign promise to offer a bill of rights, opposition in North Carolina dissolved. In Virginia, Henry, still upset from his defeat over ratification, pushed aside a plan to send Madison to the first session of the United States Senate. Instead, two of Henry's cronies were chosen; and in his spiteful mood, Henry talked James Monroe into running for the congressional seat in the same district where Madison lived.

Madison and the Bill of Rights

In 1789 it was unusual for two opposing candidates to go out on the campaign trail, particularly when they had been close friends. But both Virginia gentlemen spoke at courthouses and before small gatherings. Madison barely defeated Monroe in his home county by promising the powerful Baptists in Orange County that he would work tirelessly for a bill of rights guaranteeing freedom of religion.

True to his campaign promise, and despite much opposition from his fellow congressmen, Madison submitted his amendments in August of 1789. Most of them survived committee bargaining, but one amendment, which would have made the guaranteed rights apply to the states as well as to the federal government, was rejected. Madison was upset, but perhaps he remembered what Jefferson said about "half a loaf" and pressed ahead. Congress debated the fourteen amendments, cut them down to twelve, and sent them to the states for ratification.

Most state legislatures quickly ratified Madison's amendments. In Rhode Island, local political problems rather than the controversy over the bill of rights were still holding back ratification. Also an exception was Virginia, because Henry was still a powerful opponent of federal power and knew how to delay a bill until he could talk the whole proposition to death.

Yet George Mason, unlike Henry, accepted Madison's proposals and said he was almost at the point "cheerfully [to] put my Hand and Heart" behind them. Finally, in December 1791, Virginia ratified the federal Bill of Rights, completing the process in the same state where the movement to preserve a citizen's rights had begun. Thereafter, the first ten amendments protected Americans from arbitrary laws and guaranteed their rights to fair trials, to fair treatment, and to pursue "happiness and safety." The Supreme Court eventually became the protector of those rights—as Madison, who feared the power of unchecked majorities, had expected.

In a letter to Patrick Henry dated September 24, 1787, George Washington expressed the following opinion on the Constution he urged his fellow Virginian to support:

"I wish the Constitution, which is offered, had been more perfect; but I sincerely believe it is the best that could be obtained at this time."

A multitude of wrongs still remained to be righted. Slavery was not eliminated even after passage of the Fifteenth Amendment. But in 1791, the American commitment to individual freedom was beyond doubt. And it was fitting that Jefferson, as Secretary of State, had the privilege of proclaiming that the Bill of Rights was now part "of the supreme law of the land."

INTRODUCTION—Constitutional Concepts; Constitutional Origins; AMENDMENTS—The Courts and the Bill of Rights

The Courts and the Bill of Rights

Roger K. Newman

In the popular sense, a bill of rights is any document setting forth the liberties of the people. These are liberties that the people must have if the people are to have the power to govern themselves and to be citizens of a democracy. The Bill of Rights consists of the first ten amendments to the Constitution. They glorify respect for the individual and his or her conscience.

What are the Rights the Bill of Rights Protects?

The First Amendment guarantees freedom of religion, of speech and press, the right of peaceable assembly, and the right to petition the government.

The Second Amendment guarantees the right to keep and bear arms.

The Third Amendment forbids quartering of soldiers without consent.

The Fourth Amendment forbids unreasonable searches and seizures.

The Fifth Amendment establishes legal rights of life, liberty, and property. It guarantees against violations of due process in criminal proceedings, provides that no person "shall be compelled in any criminal case to be a witness against himself," and prohibits double jeopardy.

double jeopardy the act of putting a person through a second trial for an offense for which he or she has already been prosecuted or convicted

The Sixth Amendment protects rights of accused persons in criminal cases. It guarantees a speedy, fair trial, an impartial jury, and the right to counsel.

The Seventh Amendment guarantees trial by jury in all major civil, or noncriminal, cases and prohibits retrial of matters already decided.

The Eighth Amendment prohibits excessive bail or fines, and cruel and unusual punishment.

bail money or property pledged to guarantee that the accused person will appear in court for trial

imply to suggest or indicate indirectly

The Ninth Amendment states that the listing of certain rights in the Constitution does not imply that the people do not retain all other rights.

The Tenth Amendment reserves to the states, or to the people, powers that the Constitution does not give to the federal government or prohibit to the states.

James Madison (left) and Thomas Jefferson (right), two of the most important contributors to the Bill of Rights, are shown discussing affairs of state in this eighteenth-century illustration.

A New Kind of Society

These guarantees represent much of America's promise of a new kind of society. It differed from Europe. As James Madison wrote, "In Europe, charters of liberty have been granted by power." But in America, "Charters of power [are] granted by liberty." Government serves the people. The people are the rulers. They do not serve government. That is the American theory of government.

Madison Introduces the Bill of Rights in Congress

Thomas Jefferson wrote Madison that "a declaration of rights" would give judges a "legal check" to prevent taking away people's rights. When Madison introduced the Bill of Rights in the House of Representatives in the first Congress in 1789, he said that even if the constitutional guarantees would be only "paper barriers," they might instill respect for individual rights. More importantly, he said that judges would "consider themselves in a peculiar manner the guarantees of those rights," and that "they will be naturally led to resist every encroachment upon rights expressly stipulated for in the constitution by the declaration of rights."

"Every democratic nation owes its judges a bill of rights," one scholar has written. Without a formal text to follow, judges would be forced to

encroachment infringement or violation
stipulated specified
declaration formal statement

substitute their own personal judgment for that of the legislature or the executive. They would usually defer to these branches of government instead of relying on specific constitutional guarantees. This belief anticipated the practice of judicial review, under which courts review legislative or executive actions and declare invalid those they find in conflict with the Constitution.

anticipate expect or foresee

judicial review a court's authority to evaluate laws for their constitutionality

Early Feelings Toward the Bill of Rights

The reaction of most Americans to the passage of the Bill of Rights in 1791 was lukewarm at best. It had little effect on their lives. The Bill of Rights was intended to limit the powers of the federal government in order to protect the rights of the people and the states. It did not protect the rights of individuals from state or local governments.

Madison, in his original Bill of Rights proposal, had included an amendment to guarantee individual rights against the states. It read: "No State shall infringe the right of trial by Jury in criminal cases, nor the rights of conscience, nor the freedom of speech, or of the press." He thought it "the most valuable amendment in the whole list," and saw "more danger of abuse by the State Governments than by the Government of the United States." But the Senate rejected his proposal.

infringe exceed the limits of, or violate

In 1833, in the case of *Barron* v. *Baltimore*, Chief Justice John Marshall wrote the common understanding into law when he ruled that the Bill of Rights did not cover the states. It applied only to the federal government. Most Americans at this time were confident that they could control their state officials but feared the new and distant federal government. That fear had been the reason why the Bill of Rights was adopted. People still remembered that some states had even refused to ratify the Constitution until they were assured that a Bill of Rights would limit the power of the federal government.

ratify to formally approve a document, thereby making it legal

The Fourteenth Amendment

The Fourteenth Amendment changed this entirely. If the Civil War amounted to a Second American Revolution, then the passage of the Fourteenth Amendment added up to a Second Constitutional Convention. It became law in 1868 in the aftermath of the Civil War. The Fourteenth Amendment was specifically designed to prevent abuse of individuals by state governments. It prohibited the states from violating a person's right to life, liberty, and property without due process of law. It also gave the federal government the authority to enforce this provision against the states.

authority the power to grant legal allowance

But for several decades after the ratification of the Fourteenth Amendment, the courts interpreted it so that states still remained the main protectors of individual rights. In the *Slaughterhouse Cases* in 1873, the Supreme Court rejected the idea that the privileges and immunities clause of the Fourteenth Amendment protected the rights listed in the Bill of Rights from violation by state governments. The justices ruled the same way in *Hurtado* v. *California* (1884), which involved the right to be

privilege a right common to all citizens under a modern constitutional government; a right granted as a benefit or advantage

immunity protection from legal action

In *The Federalist*, No. 28, dated December 26, 1787, Alexander Hamilton further explained the new system of government proposed in the Constitution that states were called upon to ratify:

"It may be received as an axiom in our political system that the state governments will in all possible contingencies afford complete security against invasions of the public liberty by the national authority."

indicted by a grand jury, but they did not completely eliminate the possibility. In both a 1900 case involving the right to trial by a jury of twelve persons and a 1908 case concerning the right against self-incrimination, the Court concluded that these claims were not sufficiently "fundamental" to be applied to the states via the Fourteenth Amendment.

The Court did not make explicit in any of these cases what makes a right fundamental under the Constitution. It simply defined fundamental rights as those without which liberty and justice could not exist. Such interpretations of the Constitution left the states with the power to pass laws that violated the Bill of Rights, and many of them did. Most judges at the time did not want to change the balance of power in the federal system of government. They did not want to expand federal control over the criminal justice system of the states or other fields that had been under local control since colonial times.

Applying the Bill of Rights to the States

The first provision of the Bill of Rights to be "incorporated" through the Fourteenth Amendment and applied to the states was the takings clause of the Fifth Amendment. This came in 1897, in *Chicago, Burlington & Quincy Railroad* v. *Chicago*. In a 1908 case, *Twining* v. *New Jersey*, the Court stated that the Fourteenth Amendment's due process clause "might protect against state action some rights similar to those contained in the Bill of Rights," but it did not uphold the claim of self-incrimination in this case.

Then, in 1925, in *Gitlow* v. *New York*, the justices announced: "For present purposes we may and do assume that freedom of speech and of the press—which are protected by the First Amendment from abridgment by Congress—are among the fundamental personal rights and 'liberties' protected by the due process clause of the Fourteenth Amendment from impairment by the States." In a series of cases over the next two decades, the Court ruled that the due process clause protected all the rights in the First Amendment from state action. These included the rights of religion, assembly, and petition as well as speech and press.

abridgment decreasing, restricting or condensing

impairment lessen or diminish

Applying Criminal Procedure Rights to the States

But the Court hesitated to apply those provisions in the Fourth through Eighth amendments that concerned criminal procedure. State governments had been much more active in this area than the federal government. In addition, procedural rights varied greatly from state to state. The justices thought it was unreasonable for the federal government to apply the special procedural guarantees of the Bill of Rights as a "straitjacket" on the states.

Most justices thought that the rights guaranteed by the First Amendment were more important than these specific procedural guarantees. First Amendment rights were widely considered to be "preferred freedoms," without which a free society could not exist.

The Court, during the 1930s, recognized certain rights of criminal

procedure as being fundamental to protect liberty under the due process clause. For example, in *Powell* v. *Alabama* (1932), it ruled that the clause required the right to counsel in death penalty cases. But in *Palko* v. *Connecticut* in 1937, the justices declared that the Fifth Amendment's protection against double jeopardy was not essential to due process. Justice Benjamin Cardozo wrote for the Court that fundamental rights were "of the very essence of a scheme of ordered liberty" while non-fundamental rights were not.

Justice Black's Position

Most Supreme Court justices at that time agreed with this position. One who did not was Justice Hugo Black. He argued that choosing between essential and nonessential rights in the Bill of Rights allowed judges to write their own personal views in the Constitution. All the specific rights in the Bill of Rights should be totally incorporated into the Fourteenth Amendment, he believed. By this he meant that they should be applied to the states with exactly the same meaning and in exactly the same way as the Bill of Rights applied them to the federal government. He stated this position at length in *Adamson* v. *California* (1947) and in many other cases in the 1940s and 1950s.

A majority of justices never accepted Black's arguments for complete incorporation. States were not held accountable to most of the protections in the Bill of Rights. The Supreme Court applied instead what Justice Felix Frankfurter called a "fair trial standard." By this he meant that a state's actions had to meet those "canons of decency and fairness" considered fundamental to traditional notions of justice, but not necessarily to the specific provisions of the Bill of Rights.

Starting in the 1960s, however, the Court changed its position. It moved beyond the First Amendment to apply to the states the rights the Constitution grants to persons accused of crime. The justices rejected the fair trial standard. Instead, they adopted a selective incorporation of most of the criminal procedure guarantees in the Bill of Rights. A general right to counsel, protection against self-incrimination and double jeopardy, and other procedural guarantees were found to be essential to due process under the Fourteenth Amendment.

In a 1954 remark to the San Francisco Bar Association, U.S. Supreme Court Chief Justice Earl Warren (1891–1974) warned—

"Our system of justice will not be adequate unless every state in the Union requires a man to be given counsel if he does not have it."

Justice Black Wins the War

The Court avoided the total incorporation position that Justice Black urged. But if he lost individual battles, he won the war. At the end of the twentieth century, the only provisions the Court had not incorporated as applying to the states were: the Second Amendment right to keep and bear arms; the Third Amendment right against quartering soldiers; the Fifth Amendment right to a grand jury hearing; the Seventh Amendment right to a jury trial in civil cases; and the Eighth Amendment right against excessive bail and fines. As a result, the Constitution insures that the basic civil liberties of citizens of the United States are protected against infringement by any part of government—federal, state, or local.

> "All government and all private institutions must be designed to promote and protect and defend the integrity and the dignity of the individual. And that is the essential meaning of the Constitution and the Bill of Rights."
>
> —David E. Lilienthal (1899–1981), chairman, Tennessee Valley Authority, and chairman, U.S. Atomic Energy Commission

The Framers and the Future

At the end of the twentieth century, some people claimed that the Framers were not aware enough of threats to rights from sources other than government. They did not foresee threats arising from economic power, for example, or from religious and racial prejudice. They were concerned with the problems of their times. They set up a framework to protect the rights of Americans and left it to future generations to enforce those rights and to expand them if they wished.

In the twentieth century, the Bill of Rights became something it never was in the eighteenth century. It remains the most important single document in the United States protecting individual rights. The struggle to extend its protections has taken more than two hundred years, and the struggle continues.

The Nationalization of the Bill of Rights

1897	No taking of property without just compensation (Fifth Amendment): *Chicago, Burlington & Quincy Railroad* v. *Chicago*
1925	Freedom of speech (First Amendment): *Gitlow* v. *New York*
1931	Freedom of the press (First Amendment): *Near* v. *Minnesota*
1932	Fair trial (Sixth Amendment): *Powell* v. *Alabama*
1937	Freedom of assembly (First Amendment): *DeJonge* v. *Oregon*
1939	Freedom of petition (First Amendment): *Hague* v. *CIO*
1940	Free exercise of religion (First Amendment): *Cantwell* v. *Connecticut*
1942	Right to counsel in capital cases (Sixth Amendment): *Betts* v. *Brady*
1947	Establishment of religion (separation of church and state; First Amendment): *Everson* v. *Board of Education*
1948	Right to a public trial (Sixth Amendment): *In re Oliver*
1948	Due notice (Sixth Amendment): *Cole* v. *Arkansas*
1949	Right against unreasonable searches and seizures (Fourth Amendment): *Wolf* v. *Colorado*
1958	Freedom of association (First Amendment): *NAACP* v. *Alabama*
1961	Exclusionary rule (Fourth Amendment): *Mapp* v. *Ohio*
1962	Right against cruel and unusual punishments (Eighth Amendment): *Robinson* v. *California*
1963	Right to counsel for all serious crimes (Sixth Amendment): *Gideon* v. *Wainwright*
1964	Right against self-incrimination (Fifth Amendment): *Mallory* v. *Hogan*
1965	Right to confront and cross-examine witnesses (Sixth Amendment): *Pointer* v. *Texas*
1965	Right of privacy (Ninth Amendment): *Griswold* v. *Connecticut*
1966	Right to an impartial jury (Sixth Amendment): *Klopfer* v. *North Carolina*
1967	Right to compulsory process for obtaining witnesses (Sixth Amendment): *Washington* v. *Texas*
1968	Right to a jury trial for all serious crimes (Sixth Amendment): *Duncan* v. *Louisiana*
1969	Right against double jeopardy (Fifth Amendment): *Benton* v. *Maryland*
1972	Right to counsel for all crimes involving a possible jail term (Sixth Amendment): *Argersinger* v. *Hamlin*

First Amendment

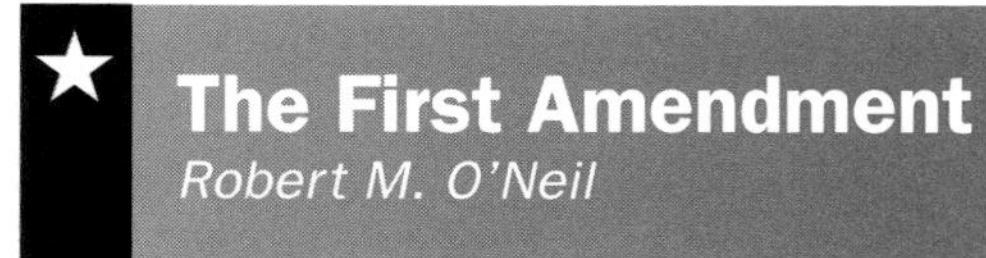

The First Amendment

Robert M. O'Neil

THE FIRST AMENDMENT TO THE CONSTITUTION STATES

Congress shall make no law respecting an establishment of religion, or prohibiting the free exercise thereof; or ***abridging*** *the freedom of speech, or of the press; or the right of the people peaceably to assemble, and to petition the Government for a* ***redress*** *of grievances.*

abridge diminish, reduce

redress making right what is wrong

The First Amendment to the Constitution of the United States is the oldest and most durable guarantee of free expression in the world. But the fundamental freedoms it protects, free speech and a free press, are not defined in the amendment. The First Amendment remains exactly as it was written in 1787 despite attempts to change its basic provisions, for example, to allow bans on burning the American flag, to permit prayer in public schools, or to include broadcasting among the protected forms of free speech.

Free Speech and the Internet

When the Bill of Rights was adopted in 1791, speech and the press involved only spoken and written words. The basic safeguards of the First Amendment have had to be adapted to the many new developments in communications technology. In 1997, the Supreme Court ruled that a law passed by Congress to restrict indecent speech on the **Internet** was unconstitutional. The Court held that electronic or digital communication was fully protected speech. The First Amendment's safeguard was applied to a medium that the Framers could not possibly have anticipated.

Internet a worldwide electronic network of communication that links computer networks and organizational computer facilities

Free Speech and Other Nonprint Media

The guarantees of the First Amendment are faring better in cyberspace than they have fared in most other media. Early in the twentieth century, when motion pictures first became a popular medium, the courts routinely upheld **censorship** of movies. The Supreme Court did not grant any First Amendment protection to motion pictures until 1952. Nor has the Court stopped communities from establishing movie censorship schemes, provided they followed certain procedural safeguards.

censorship the official restriction of any expression believed to threaten the political, social, or moral order

Licensed radio broadcasting fared even worse than motion pictures. Court rulings in early broadcasting cases established a lesser standard for broadcast speech than spoken or written speech. The Supreme Court allowed bans on the use of certain words in radio broadcasts that were considered indecent, even though these words were fully protected when they were in oral or print form.

Cable television broadcasting has received a higher level of protection in the courts, though not the full rights of free speech. In 1997, the

Supreme Court upheld requirements that cable broadcasting companies must carry certain messages, even though such requirements could not be placed on newspapers, magazines, or book publishers. The basic guarantees of free speech and free press have been applied in different and less complete ways to many new media. The Court's grant of full protection to speech on the Internet is more the exception than the rule.

Symbolic Speech

symbolic speech expression that does not use words

The courts have faced many other difficult issues in applying the First Amendment's guarantees. Much political expression has been **symbolic speech**. Nonverbal speech, to make a point, is as old as humanity itself. The Framers were familiar with such symbolic expression in politics. It is somewhat surprising, therefore, that they did not recognize symbolic speech as a right to be protected in the amendment. Not until 1969 did the Supreme Court extend the guarantees of the First Amendment to nonverbal communication, a case that involved students wearing black arm bands as a protest against the Vietnam conflict. Since then, flag burning, rock music, street art, and many other wordless messages have received protection as "speech."

Prior Restraint

prior restraint a law or court order forbidding persons to speak or write something

The Supreme Court also was slow to recognize the full meaning of other parts of the First Amendment. The text of the amendment boldly declares that "Congress shall make no law abridging" free speech or press. Yet Congress passed many laws that did exactly that, and the few challenges that got to court were not successful. As late as 1907, the Supreme Court held that a speaker or writer was protected only against **prior restraint**. But the justices declared that this same speaker or writer could be punished for the content of their communication after it was made. This ruling left authors and speakers at the mercy of courts and juries, with little grounds for defense other than proving mistaken identity. Not until 1931 did the Court rule that, except in very limited circumstances, a prior restraint against publication was unconstitutional.

The End of "Clear and Present Danger"

McCarthyism [after Senator Joseph McCarthy of Wisconsin (1908–1957)] a political attitude of the 1950s "Red Scare," characterized by indiscriminate, unsubstantiated attacks on individuals suspected of Communist sympathies, activities, or ties

In 1919, the Supreme Court recognized for the first time that punishing expression after it had been made can chill or discourage freedom of speech and press as severely as a prior restraint or a gag order can. Thus emerged the "clear and present danger" test—Justice Oliver Wendell Holmes's famous saying about a person not being allowed to shout "fire" in a theater. The Court adopted this test as its standard and applied it to various cases involving alleged threats to national security.

In the Court's early cases, as well as in many that followed in the **McCarthyism** during the 1950s and into the 1960s, the Court found the needed "clear and present danger" in pure words—usually speeches, articles, and handbills passed out by radical groups, such as the Communist

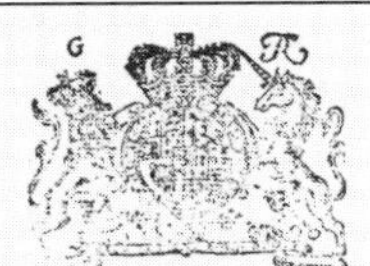

By his Excellency

William Cosby, Captain General and Governour in Chief of the Provinces of *New-York*, *New-Jerſey*, and Territories thereon depending, in America, Vice-Admiral of the ſame, and Colonel in His Majeſty's Army.

A PROCLAMATION.

WHereas by the Contrivance of ſome evil Diſpoſed and Diſaffected Perſons, divers Journals or Printed News Papers, (entitled, *The New-York Weekly Journal, containing the freſheſt Advices, Foreign and Domeſtick*) have been cauſed to be Printed and Publiſhed by *John Peter Zenger*, in many of which Journals or Printed News-Papers (but more particularly theſe Numbred 7, 47, 48, 49) are contained divers Scandalous, Virulent, Falſe and Seditious Reflections, not only upon the whole Legiſlature, in general, and upon the moſt conſiderable Perſons in the moſt diſtinguiſh'd Stations in this Province, but alſo upon His Majeſty's lawful and rightful Government, and juſt Prerogative. Which ſaid Reflections ſeem contrived by the wicked Authors of them, not only to create Jealouſies, Diſcontents and Animoſities in the Minds of his Majeſty's Leige People of this Province, to the Subverſion of the Peace & Tranquility thereof, but to alienate their Affections from the beſt of Kings, and raiſe *Factions*, *Tumults* and *Sedition* among them. *Wherefore* I have thought fit, by and with the Advice of His Majeſty's Council, to iſſue this Proclamation, hereby Promiſing a Reward of *Fifty Pounds* to ſuch Perſon or Perſons who ſhall diſcover the Author or Authors of the ſaid *Scandalous*, *Virulent* and *Seditious Reflections* contained in the ſaid *Journals* or *Printed News-Papers*, to be paid to the Perſon or Perſons diſcovering the ſame, as ſoon as ſuch Author or Authors ſhall be Convicted of having been the Author or Authors thereof.

GIVEN under My Hand and Seal at Fort-George *in* New-York *this Sixth Day of* November, *in the Eighth year of the Reign of Our Sovereign Lord* GEORGE *the Second, by the Grace of* GOD, *of* Great-Britain, France *and* Ireland, KING *Defender of the Faith, &c. and in the Year of Our* LORD 1734.

By his Excellency's Command, *Fred. Morris*, D. Cl. Conc.

W. COSBY

GOD Save the KING

The proclamation issued by the British in 1734 for the arrest of newspaper publisher John Peter Zenger. The First Amendment was enacted to protect citizens' rights from arbitrary acts of government.

party. The latter part of this period was during the Cold War—years of international tension between the United States and the Soviet Union. To the majority of the justices on the Court, the "danger" in these cases was not the possibility that these groups would actually overthrow the national government. Rather, the justices argued, the danger lay in organizing activities and teachings which the government had the right to penalize if it determined it should do so in the interests of national security.

In 1969, the Supreme Court set forth a new test that remains in effect. Subversive advocacy, the use of words urging the overthrow of the government, may be punished only "where such advocacy is directed to inciting or producing imminent lawless action and is likely to incite or produce such action." Mere apprehension that such words will cause the government's overthrow is not enough under this test. Nothing short of a clear intent and a high probability that such words will produce "imminent disorder," as the Court put it in a later case, justifies jailing a speaker.

Freedom of thought is the right of individuals to form and hold opinions whether or not those opinions are expressed or acted upon. Freedom of thought and freedom of belief are just about the same things. While the Constitution does not expressly guarantee these rights, courts have implied them from the First Amendment and have granted them great protection. "[I]f there is any principle of the Constitution that imperatively [urgently] calls for attachment more than any other," wrote Oliver Wendell Holmes, Jr., "it is the principle of free thought—not just for those who agree with us but freedom for the thought that we hate." Or as Justice Hugo Black put it, "Liberty, to be secure for any, must be secure for all—even for the most miserable merchants of hated and unpopular ideas." This freedom is total or absolute, but the freedom to act cannot be. As the Supreme Court has said, "Conduct remains subject to regulation for the protection of society."

Freedom of Association

In the late 1950s, the Supreme Court made an important addition to free expression, the freedom of association. The justices considered the right of people to associate freely—and often to keep the government from knowing what organizations they belonged to—so vital that they extended the listed liberties to include this freedom.

The First Amendment and the States

infringe exceed the limits of, or violate

The First Amendment also has another obvious gap. It mentions only what Congress may not do to infringe on the rights of the people. Thus, in theory, the states and even federal courts and agencies might have been free to abridge speech if the courts had followed only the words written in the amendment. The Supreme Court in 1925 simply assumed that the free speech and free press guarantees applied to state and local governments as well. The adoption, after the Civil War, of the Fourteenth Amendment, answered any earlier doubts. It guaranteed liberty in ways

that seemed to include the basic freedoms of the First Amendment. Other provisions of the Bill of Rights eventually applied to state and local governments. By 1925, there was no doubt that federal courts and agencies were barred from infringing speech and press, just as Congress was.

Private Property

First Amendment rights occasionally extend even beyond actions by government. In 1946, the Supreme Court ruled that a company town (a community in which a business controlled most of the jobs, housing, and stores) was so similar to a government that it could not limit the free speech of its residents any more than regular governments could. The justices, in 1968, even applied this standard to large malls and shopping centers, but withdrew this extension four years later. Some states consider handing out leaflets and picketing in malls to be protected speech. The Supreme Court has made clear that states may protect speech more fully than the federal Constitution requires. The Bill of Rights, in other words, is a floor, not a ceiling. If states want to grant speakers more freedom, they may do so—at least up to the point where such protection interferes with some other federally guaranteed interest, such as the mall-owners' right to the productive use of property.

Obscenity

obscenity material that is indecent, offensive, or disgusting, or to which the prevailing morality is strongly opposed

The courts have recognized some other exceptions to First Amendment law. While the amendment refers to Congress passing "no law," the Supreme Court has never interpreted these words literally. When the justices dealt with the issue of **obscenity** in 1957, even so staunch a champion of free speech as Justice William Brennan, Jr., held that obscenity simply never had been and was not then protected speech. Justice Brennan declared, "Implicit in the history of the First Amendment is the rejection of obscenity as utterly without redeeming social importance."

Defining obscenity became a challenge for the Court. Justice Potter Stewart, in a 1964 case, gave up hope of finding such a standard, stating, "I know it when I see it." The Court made the definition increasingly complex and added procedural safeguards to guide any seizure of allegedly obscene material.

By 1973, the justices had developed a definition of obscenity that it has continued to apply. Juries in such cases, "applying contemporary community standards, must find that the work taken as a whole, appeals to the prurient interest"; that the work "depicts or describes, in a patently offensive way, sexual conduct specifically defined by the applicable state law"; and that the work "taken as a whole, lacks serious literary, artistic, political or scientific value." In 1975, the Court ruled that a mere display of nudity or portraying normal sexual relations could not be considered obscene. Yet other restrictions might apply, as the Court made clear in 1991, when it upheld laws that forbade "public exposure" by nude dancers in nightclubs.

Child Pornography

child pornography showing a nude child for commercial or private purposes

legislation the power and work of making laws

Child pornography is related to obscenity, yet it is quite different and more strictly regulated. Although possessing such obscene pictures for private purposes may not be a criminal offense, society's interest in protecting children is so strong that in 1990 the Supreme Court refused to extend First Amendment protections to child pornography. Child pornography materials on the Internet, whether computer-generated images or actual pictures of naked children, may be made unlawful by legislation. Congress followed such a course in 1996, when it passed a law against child pornography on web sites.

Libel

libel the publication of statements that wrongfully damage a person's reputation

malice deliberate lawbreaking, or intent to cause harm without legal right or excuse

Libel is another form of expression that was long thought to be outside the protections of the First Amendment. In 1964, the Supreme Court held that public officials are not protected against libel, even if the statements about them are false. The Court argued that people who hold public offices must expect to receive harsh criticism. Protecting them from libelous charges might discourage debate on controversial issues. The justices reasoned that in a democracy "debate on public issues should be uninhibited [completely free], robust and wide-open," and this "may well include vehement [powerful], caustic [bitter] and sometimes unpleasantly sharp attacks. . . ." As a result of this decision, a public official can win libel lawsuits only by proving that the person who made the libelous false statements did so acting out of "actual malice" or with a "reckless disregard of the truth." Because proving such motives has turned out to be extremely difficult, officials seldom are successful when they sue for libel.

The Court also ruled that all public figures are outside the protection of the First Amendment when libel is the issue. Public figures are celebrities, well-known persons in entertainment, sports, and other fields. The Court came close to extending this exception even further—to cases involving issues of public importance. The Court ruled that persons who sue in such cases may not recover more than actual damages unless they can prove that "actual malice" or "reckless disregard of the truth" was involved. The Court has refused to extend the First Amendment's protection of free expression to media defendants. This standard has importance for the rapidly emerging issues of libel on the Internet.

Commercial Speech

commercial speech public expression used in advertising and for other business-related purposes

Commercial speech is a form of speech that, in the past, First Amendment guarantees did not protect, but that enjoys increasing protection. In 1976, the Supreme Court made clear that advertising deserves partial protection, though more to ensure that useful information flows to consumers than to guarantee the sellers of goods and services easier access to their markets. In 1996, the justices also reaffirmed an earlier Court standard for protecting commercial speech.

The basic test is whether the commercial speech claiming protection "concerns lawful activity and is not misleading." Courts then ask "whether the asserted government interest is substantial." If the commercial speech at

The distinction between speech and conduct lies at the heart of the First Amendment. It is an old distinction. Baron Charles de Montesquieu (1689–1755), a Frenchman, was one of the leading figures of the Enlightenment, an eighteenth-century intellectual movement in Europe and the United States in which reason and toleration were stressed. In 1748 he wrote in *The Spirit of the Laws* of the execution of Marsyas, a flute player in Greek mythology, for having dreamed of murdering Dionysus, the Greek god of fertility and wine. Dionysus's getting even at Marsyas was dictatorial, Montesquieu stated, for even though Marsyas had thought about murder, "yet he had made no attempt towards it. The laws do not take upon them to punish any other than overt (obvious) acts," or conduct. Montesquieu added, "The Thought must be joined with some sort of action." Many other Enlightenment thinkers wrote about the distinction. Thomas Jefferson was the leading American to do so, and his ideas were prominent in the minds of the Framers.

issue meets this test, the justices reasoned, "we must then determine whether the regulation directly advances the governmental interest asserted, and whether it is not more extensive than necessary to serve that interest."

Several common forms of advertising regulations failed to meet the Supreme Court's standard for protected commercial speech. A city ban on newsracks displaying commercial newspapers, a federal ban on alcohol-content labels on beer cans, and a state law prohibiting advertisements of retail liquor prices in places other than liquor stores—all were struck down by the Court as violating the First Amendment. In each case, the justices held, government had failed to prove either that the methods it used directly advanced the regulatory interest or that taking less restrictive actions would not have served the same purpose.

Many difficult cases involving protected commercial speech still remain in the courts, notably the whole controversial issues of cigarette advertising. Some critics argue that cigarettes are so inherently harmful that a different standard should apply, while others argue with equal force that commercial speech which is not misleading about a lawful product is entitled to protection. Another group of difficult cases involve questions about billboards that advertise liquor, including where they may be located and what content they may display. The issue of advertising liquor on broadcast airwaves is another challenge, one that was quiet for decades because the liquor industry itself banned advertising. In the late 1990s, however, alcoholic beverage makers indicated they wanted to advertise their products, and government predictably became concerned about this prospect and its impact on commercial speech.

Access to Information

The First Amendment has not provided access to government information, with the single exception of the right to attend criminal trials, which is a historic right of the general public rather than specifically of the news media. Even a criminal trial offers limited access. Cameras may be barred, and even print reporters may be denied coverage of certain sensitive stages of the trial. The identity of jurors may be kept unknown, and out-of-court comments by participants may be curbed in various ways to ensure the fairness of the trial.

see also

AMENDMENTS—The Courts and the Bill of Rights; FIRST AMENDMENT—Access to the Media; Computer Censorship; The Development of Standards; Freedom of Assembly and Association; Freedom of the Press: Prior Restraints; Libel and Defamation; Obscenity; Symbolic Speech

Unanswered Questions

Many fascinating First Amendment issues and questions remain unresolved. The Supreme Court has avoided the issue of media access to civil court proceedings, although state courts are beginning to consider it. Related issues concern such access to juvenile courts and to related aspects of the criminal process. The short answer to these issues is the one the Supreme Court has given repeatedly: The First Amendment is not a freedom of information law. This means that most decisions about media access to government information and activities should properly be made by the legislative branch, not the judicial branch. The growing demand for media access to a wide range of proceedings and a wide variety of information almost certainly guarantees that this issue will be near the front of the First Amendment agenda in the years ahead.

judicial having to do with judgments in courts of law or with the administration of justice

★ No "Establishment of Religion"

Jesse Choper

THE FIRST AMENDMENT TO THE CONSTITUTION STATES

Congress shall make no law respecting an establishment of religion, or prohibiting the free exercise thereof; . . .

The Supreme Court's first modern decision involving the establishment clause was *Everson* v. *Board of Education* (1947). The decision recounted that in the Old World, "with the power of government supporting them, at various times and places, Catholics had persecuted Protestants, Protestants had persecuted Baptists, Protestant sects had persecuted other Protestant sects, Catholics of one shade of belief had persecuted Catholics of another shade of belief, and all of these had from time to time persecuted Jews." Unhappily, "these practices of the Old World were transplanted to and began to thrive in the soil of the new America."

In Massachusetts, Quakers, Baptists, and other religious minorities suffered and were taxed for the established Congregational Church. In 1776, Maryland's "Declaration of Rights" stated that "only persons professing the Christian religion" were entitled to religious freedom, and Jews were not permitted to hold public office until 1826. The South Carolina Constitution of 1778 stated that "the Christian Protestant religion shall be . . . the established religion of this state."

The Framers and Separation Between Church and State

History suggests that the Framers of the First Amendment, and those whose thinking they drew upon, had many, sometimes conflicting, goals. Thomas Jefferson believed that a strict separation between church and state was necessary to protect democracy from being undermined by powerful religious groups. James Madison saw church–state separation as also benefiting religious institutions. Even more strongly, Roger Williams of Rhode Island, an earlier proponent of religious freedom, believed that it was vital to protect the church's "garden" from the "wilderness" of the state. One purpose of the establishment clause was also to protect the existing state-established churches from the new national government. (There were state-sponsored churches in Massachusetts, for example, until 1833.)

Even if the Framers' intent had been unanimous and unambiguous, it could not solve many twentieth-century problems. For example, since there was no public education then, the Framers could not have had any position on religion in public schools—a frequent establishment clause issue in modern times.

The Court Defines Separation for the First Time

The establishment clause of the First Amendment applies only to the federal government ("Congress shall make no law . . ."), but in 1947 the *Everson* case held that the Fourteenth Amendment made the clause applicable to the states. This decision, by Justice Hugo Black, attempted for the first time to define a nonestablishment principle that could apply to all situations:

> The establishment of religion clause of the First Amendment means at least this: Neither a state nor the Federal government can set up a church. Neither can pass laws which aid one religion, aid all religions, or prefer one religion over another. Neither can force nor influence a person to go to or to remain

Supreme Court Justice Hugo Black

away from church against his will or force him to profess a belief or disbelief in any religion. No person can be punished for entertaining or professing religious beliefs or disbeliefs, for church attendance or nonattendance.

Justice Black continued:

> No tax in any amount, large or small, can be levied to support any religious activities or institutions, whatever they may be called, or whatever form they may adopt to teach or practice religion. Neither a state nor the Federal Government can, openly or secretly, participate in the affairs of any religious organization or groups and vice versa. In the words of Jefferson, the clause against establishment of religion by law was intended to erect "a wall of separation between church and state."

Since this statement, however, there has been little agreement as to what practices would constitute "aid" to, or "support" of, religion.

New Tests

In 1971, in *Lemon* v. *Kurtzman*, the Court developed a three-part approach to the establishment clause and its effect on legislation: "First, the statute must have a secular legislative purpose; second, its principal or primary effect must be one that neither advances nor inhibits religion . . . ; finally, the statute must not foster 'an excessive government entanglement with religion." This test supplanted the *Everson* definition and at the end of the twentieth century had yet to be formally abandoned. By the mid-1990s, however, it had fallen out of favor with all the justices of the Supreme Court.

The endorsement test. A majority of justices has indicated (although not explicitly) that it has accepted a new approach in the endorsement test: An establishment violation occurs when government "endorses religion," that is, whenever a reasonable observer would conclude that government activity "sends a message to nonadherents that they are outsiders, not full members of the political community, and an accompanying message to adherents that they are insiders, favored members of the political community."

The neutrality approach. The interpretation of the nonestablishment principle is still debated, however, especially because a substantial minority of justices prefers a neutrality approach. Under this approach, the fact that government gives substantial assistance to religion—or that some people may conclude that government endorses religion despite its neutral stance—results in no violation as long as the government benefits for religious groups were part of a general program that include nonreligious organizations as well.

Religion in Public Schools

One of the nation's most divisive issues has been religion in public schools. In two very controversial decisions, the Court ruled (in 1962) that

levy impose or collect a tax

legislation the power and work of making laws

statute a law enacted by the legislative branch of government

secular having to do, or related to, matters that are not connected to religion

endorsement approval or sanction

nonadherent one who does not follow or support a religion, belief, or cause

adherent one who follows or supports a religion, belief, or cause

neutrality a state of not being involved on either side

state-sponsored prayer and (in 1963) that Bible reading in public schools violated the establishment clause. These cases led to serious efforts in Congress to pass a constitutional amendment in order to reverse them.

Released time. An earlier case, in 1952, involved released time—weekly classes of religious instruction during school hours by privately employed teachers for those students whose parents agreed. The Court ruled that this was unconstitutional in public school classrooms, but was permissible when "off-premises." The Court's reasoning was that if the students attended classes at their religious centers, neither public funds nor public classrooms directly supported religion.

***Stone* v. *Graham*.** The subject of religion in public schools has brought out the Court's most vigorous support of church–state separation. The case concerned a public school in Kentucky that had posted copies of the Ten Commandments (paid for privately) in all classrooms, because "the fundamental legal code of Western Civilization and the Common Law of the United States" were based on the Commandments. In 1980, the Court found that the program's purpose was religious and invalidated the law.

invalidate take away the force or value of

***Wallace* v. *Jaffree*.** This doctrine that "religious purpose equals invalidity" was reinforced in 1985. That year, the Court overturned a law that authorized a period of silence in public schools "for meditation or voluntary prayer." The Court based its ruling on the ground that the law was "entirely motivated by a purpose to advance religion." The Court indicated that a slightly different law—"protecting every student's right to engage in voluntary prayer during an appropriate moment of silence during the school day"—would be constitutional. Similarly, the Court ruled against a law that cut Darwin's theory of evolution from public school courses, because "fundamentalist sectarian conviction was and still is the law's reason for existence."

authorize grant legal allowance to

***Board of Education* v. *Mergens*.** One of the Court's few decisions upholding religious presence in public schools was handed down in 1990. It strongly illustrates the neutrality approach. The issue in the case was whether public schools that permit various student groups to meet on school premises when no classes are given could deny "equal access" to groups because of the content of the speech at their meetings. The case was brought by students who were denied permission to form a Christian club on the grounds that it would "incorporate religious activities into the school's official program" and "provide the club with an official platform to proselytize other students." The Court ruled that the schools could not deny equal access.

proselytize to convert or attempt to convert to a religion

Should Government Aid Church-Related Schools?

The Court considered a second important issue, public aid to church-related schools, in its establishment clause decision in *Everson* in 1947. The issue of whether a state may pay for sending students on public buses to schools (including Catholic parochial schools) sharply posed the difficulties in the case. The Court upheld the busing by a 5–4 vote. The majority reasoned that state funding accomplished the "public purpose" of

parochial schools schools operated by a church or a religious group

getting children "safely and expeditiously to accredited schools." The program was seen as similar to providing all schools with basic municipal services, such as fire and police protection. The majority furthermore expressed concern about excluding persons from state benefits "because of their faith, or lack of it." The dissenters protested that the program aided children "in a substantial way to get the very thing which they are sent to [parochial schools] to secure, namely, religious training and teaching."

litigated contested in court

Assistance for educational nonreligious purposes. In this most litigated area under the establishment clause, the following half century witnessed widely diverging opinions by the Supreme Court that are difficult to reconcile. For example, the Court ruled that the state could not reimburse parochial schools for the cost of administering teacher-prepared tests required by state law; but the state was allowed to compensate parochial schools for administering state-prepared tests. The government could lend textbooks to parochial school pupils because, the Court explained, the books can be checked for religious content and are "self-policing"; but the government could not lend other seemingly "self-policing" instructional items such as films, movie projectors, and laboratory equipment.

Assistance for transportation. The public could pay for transportation to religious and parochial schools; but the state was forbidden to pay for field trips "to governmental, industrial, cultural, and scientific centers designed to enrich the secular studies of students." A tax credit to cover part of tuition for parents who sent their children to private schools (or a comparable grant for those too poor to benefit from a tax credit) was forbidden; but a tax deduction for education expenses at all nonprofit schools (public, private, or church-related) was permissible, even though 96 percent of the deductions were by parents who sent their children to parochial schools.

Should Government Aid Religious Institutions?

As with religion in public schools, two important decisions on financial assistance to religious institutions have also been strongly influenced by the neutrality approach. In the first decision, in 1993, the Court upheld state payment of a sign-language interpreter for a deaf student in a Catholic school as part of a general program to aid children with disabilities. The majority wrote, "government programs that neutrally provide benefits to a broad class of citizens defined without reference to religion are not readily subject to an Establishment Clause challenge just because sectarian institutions may also receive an attenuated financial benefit." This means that even if some religious institutions receive a slight benefit, it is not enough to serve as an establishment clause challenge to a program that is neutral.

The Court has viewed aid to church-related higher education more favorably, reasoning that unlike elementary and secondary schools, church-related colleges are not "permeated" (filled through) by religion.

The second case questioned whether a state university, as part of a general program to fund student publications, was allowed to pay the printing costs of a student newspaper that offered a distinctly Christian perspective. The Court found no establishment clause violation because the program was "neutral toward religion." However, the majority

The phrase "wall of separation between church and state" comes from Thomas Jefferson. In an 1802 letter to the Baptist Association of Danbury, Connecticut, Jefferson wrote that religion belonged "solely between man and his God." Then he added: "I contemplate with sovereign reverence (deep respect) that act of the whole American people which declared that their legislature should 'make no law respecting an establishment of religion, or prohibiting the free exercise thereof,' thus building a wall of separation between church and state." Earlier, Roger Williams (1603?–1683), an advocate of religious freedom and the founder of the Rhode Island colony, had spoken of "a gap in the hedge or wall of separation between the garden of the church and the wilderness of the world."

emphasized several factors that make it doubtful that all forms of financial assistance to religion have become permissible—even if the money is spent for core religious activities rather than for secular purposes—as long as the aid is part of a neutral general program.

Should Government Acknowledge Religion?

Official acknowledgment of religion is another major area of establishment clause rulings. This consists of just a handful of decisions, all since the early 1980s. In four cases, the Court upheld the following practices: a state legislature's opening each session with a prayer by a government-paid chaplain, in 1983; a city's inclusion of a nativity scene as a part of a larger Christmas display in a city park, in 1984; a city–county display of a menorah and Christmas tree near the entrance to its office building, in 1989; and, in 1995, a state's permitting the Ku Klux Klan to erect a Latin cross in the plaza surrounding the statehouse.

These rulings make it clear that certain types of government acknowledgment of religion do not violate the establishment clause; that is, no strict separation between church and state is required. Some official recognitions of religion, however, have been successfully challenged. In 1992, the Court ruled against letting public school officials invite clergy to offer prayers of appeal or blessing at graduation ceremonies. This concept is not limited to public schools. In 1989 the Court ruled that the display of a nativity scene in a courthouse—standing alone, and not part of a larger Christmas celebration—violated the establishment clause.

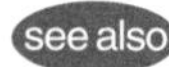

FIRST AMENDMENT—"Free Exercise" of Religion; Government and Religion in Public Places; School Prayers and Bible Reading

Freedom of Religion Against Itself

The final important establishment clause issue concerns the tension between the First Amendment's two religion clauses, one forbidding government to promote or "establish" religion, and the other prohibiting government from abridging the "free exercise" of religion. As the Court has observed, both "are cast in absolute terms, and either . . . if expanded to a logical extreme, would tend to clash with the other." In seeking not to offend either provision, the Court has favored the free-exercise clause. Government may serve religious practices by granting special religious exemptions when laws impose substantial burdens on the exercise of religion.

absolute complete, pure, free from restriction or limitation

exemption freedom or release from a requirement that others are subject to

★ School Prayers and Bible Reading

Roger K. Newman

THE FIRST AMENDMENT TO THE CONSTITUTION STATES

Congress shall make no law respecting an establishment of religion, or prohibiting the free exercise thereof; . . .

The United States is one of the most formally religious nations in the world. Church attendance has long been the highest of any Western country. For most of American history, government-sponsored prayers were a regular feature of many, perhaps most, public schools. Children whose families did not share the beliefs expressed in

those prayers had little choice in the matter. Sometimes these children, even very small children, felt that their government did not "like" them as much as those children whose religion was preferred.

The School Prayer Case

Starting after World War II, members of the Roman Catholic and Jewish faiths began to complain about Protestant prayers in the public schools. An increasing number of people began to feel that any form of government-sponsored religious exercises in public schools was inappropriate and unconstitutional. The State of New York responded by passing an official school prayer. It was short and fairly bland, and the three major religious faiths in New York at the time approved it. The prayer read: "Almighty God, we acknowledge our dependence upon Thee, and we beg Thy blessings upon us, our teachers, and our Country." No school had to use it, but if any prayer was used, the law required that it be this one.

school board a group of persons in charge of local public schools

Several local **school boards** chose to use this prayer, including the school board in New Hyde Park, a suburban Long Island town. It directed the principals of each school in the district to have all classes recite the prayer in the presence of a teacher at the beginning of each school day. Children whose parents did not wish them to participate could remain silent or leave the room. In the late 1950s, five parents of children attending a New Hyde Park, New York, public school brought a lawsuit charging that a state-composed prayer recited at the start of each school day violated the establishment clause.

Government Cannot "Compose Prayers"

The Supreme Court struck down the practice of daily praying in public schools.

The Supreme Court, in *Engel* v. *Vitale* in 1962, struck down the prayer in an 8-to-1 decision. Justice Hugo Black, who had once taught Sunday school in his hometown of Birmingham, Alabama, wrote the Court's opinion. To him, the case went to the whole purpose of why Americans have a written constitution protecting their rights. There can be "no doubt," Justice Black wrote, "that [the] daily invocation of God's blessings . . . is a religious activity. . . . In this country it is no part of the business of government to compose official prayers for any group of the American people to recite as a part of a religious program carried on by government."

Black's opinion was most unusual in that he did not mention a single case to support it. He drew instead on historical examples to show that the Framers intended to prohibit all establishment of religion, like New York State's Regents prayer program. Religion, Justice Black concluded, "is too personal, too sacred, too holy to permit its 'unhallowed perversion' [profane corruption] by a civil magistrate." When he announced the opinion from the bench, Justice Black added, with emotion in his voice, "The prayer of each man from his soul must be his and his alone."

Immediate Response

The response to the Court's decision was immediate and widespread. The practice of school prayer remained strong in parts of the South and

especially in the West despite the Court's ruling, and resentment with it was high even in many areas which complied with it. Justice Black received more than one thousand letters about the decision, and the Court more than five thousand. Most of the criticism came from the South while most of the support came from the North. Fifty-five constitutional amendments were soon introduced in reaction to the decision. As of 1998, nearly three hundred such proposals intending to overturn *Engel* had been introduced.

Congress did not pass any of them. Justice Tom Clark, who was active in the Presbyterian Church, departed from tradition to defend the Court's school prayer decision. The Constitution, he noted in a public speech in August 1962, provides "that both state and federal governments shall take no part respecting the establishment of religion or prohibiting the free exercise thereof. 'No' means 'No.' That was all the Court decided."

The Bible Reading Cases

In 1963, Edward Schempp challenged a Pennsylvania law that required that "at least ten verses from the Holy Bible shall be read without comment, at the opening of each public school on each school day." The law permitted children to be excused upon written request from their parents. In *School District of Abington Township* v. *Schempp,* the Court ruled that the required reading of The Lord's Prayer or verses from the Bible in public schools is unconstitutional.

At the same time William Murray and his mother, Madalyn O' Haire Murray, a well-known atheist (person who denies God's existence), challenged a Baltimore regulation providing for "reading, without comment, of a chapter in the Holy Bible and/or the use of the Lord's Prayer in public school daily." "Such an opening exercise is a religious ceremony and was intended by the state to be so," Justice Clark wrote for the Court. The First Amendment's establishment clause could not be avoided by making students' participation in such school exercises voluntary. Furthermore, Justice Clark stated, the free exercise clause "never meant that a majority could use the machinery of the state to practice its beliefs." The government must protect all religious liberty by neither preferring nor condemning any religious belief. The sole dissent came from Justice Potter Stewart, who had also dissented in *Engel.*

A Calmer Reaction

The reaction to the decisions in these Bible reading cases was calm compared to the reaction to the school prayer case. Some members of Congress and of the clergy (ordained religious) complained. Dozens of resolutions calling for a constitutional amendment were introduced in Congress and hearings were held in the spring of 1964. Questions were raised, such as whether a Catholic majority could insist on the Hail Mary or a reading

Hugo Black had one of the most unusual careers of any Supreme Court justice. He was born in the Alabama hill country in 1886, the son of a Confederate veteran, and practiced mainly negligence and accident law in Birmingham from 1907 until 1926; from 1914 to 1917 he was district attorney (prosecutor). Black was also an active member of the white-supremacist Ku Klux Klan, although he did not take part in any of its violence. At the same time he taught Sunday school. In 1926, with Klan support, Black was elected to the United States Senate, where he became chairman of important committees and one of the most powerful senators. President Franklin D. Roosevelt appointed him to the Court in 1937. There Black led the revolution in constitutional law. Applying the Bill of Rights to the states stands as his greatest monument. Black was also the prime mover behind the Court's hearing *Brown* v. *Board of Education*. A gentle, always courteous man who read continually, he drew lessons from history. The most important of these lessons was the absolute necessity of freedom of conscience. Above all, Black believed in almost unlimited First Amendment rights. They belong in a "high preferred place . . . in a free society," he wrote. He died in 1971, recognized by everyone as one of the handful of great judges in American history.

FIRST AMENDMENT—"Free Exercise" of Religion; No "Establishment of Religion"

from the Catholic Bible as opposed to the Protestant King James version. Congressmen admitted that they had no ready answers to such questions.

Much of the public neither understood nor accepted the Court's reasoning in the school prayer and Bible reading cases, and many of those who responded never read them. For many years, local school districts and some state legislatures continued to try to "use the machinery of the state" (referred to by Justice Clark in the Baltimore Bible reading case) to impose the practice of their own or the majority's religious beliefs on others. Many of these practices that violated religious freedom escaped inspection. But others did not.

School Prayer in Alabama

In 1985, in *Wallace* v. *Jaffree*, the Court ruled unconstitutional an Alabama law requiring all public school children to observe a daily period of silence for the explicit purpose of praying. The state could require periods of silence or quiet which children could use in any way they chose, including prayer, the justices decided. Alabama already had a law requiring a period of silence, so this new law added "prayer" as an approved activity. As a result, the Court said, the law had no valid secular purpose (justification outside religion) but was instead another attempt to impose a religious practice.

Alabama has remained a focal point of school prayer. Christianity has been the only religion promoted in some schools in the state. The state legislature has made four attempts to implement school prayer in one form or another, and federal courts struck down each attempt. In 1997, a federal judge spelled out specific guidelines on prayer and other religious activities for Alabama public schools, and threatened to hold state officials in contempt of court if they disobeyed his order.

The Court and Religion in Public Schools

The Supreme Court, however, has upheld a federal law that permitted students to form a group to read and discuss the Bible, share Christian fellowship, and pray together. But it has also ruled that the Ten Commandments cannot be posted in public school classrooms. In *Lee* v. *Weisman* (1992), the Court outlawed religious invocations at graduation ceremonies. Justice Anthony Kennedy stated in his majority opinion, "No holding by this Court suggests that a school can persuade or compel a student to participate in a religious exercise." The free exercise clause prevents a teacher from lawfully telling children to engage in religion in any form.

The First Amendment's basic premise is that people must be left to pray in their own way, and to their own God, without express or explicit coercion (force) from government. This includes public school students, and this is what the Supreme Court reaffirmed in the school prayer and Bible reading cases.

Government Financial Assistance to Religious Schools

Steven D. Smith

THE FIRST AMENDMENT TO THE CONSTITUTION STATES

Congress shall make no law respecting an establishment of religion, or prohibiting the free exercise thereof; . . .

One of the most persistent and controversial issues in church-state relations involves government aid to religious schools. The problem of the role of government in religious issues became clear in *Everson* v. *Board of Education* (1947), which was the first case in modern times that involved interpreting the establishment clause of the First Amendment. The case involved a challenge to a New Jersey law that allowed the state to pay for busing students to **parochial schools**. In a 5-to-4 decision, the Court upheld the constitutionality of the New Jersey law. But this decision left many questions about the wall of separation between state and church unanswered.

parochial schools schools operated by a church or a religious group

In *Everson*, the Supreme Court upheld two principles regarding questions of church-state relations. One was the **"no aid" principle**, the other the **neutrality principle**. Since this decision, most judges and legal scholars have accepted these ideas in some form, even though they often seem to point in opposite directions. Religious schools have been caught in the middle of this conflict.

"no aid" principle view on religious school aid that no law, tax, or other assistance may be given to support such schools or any religious activity or institution

neutrality principle view that the government may neither favor religions nor handicap them

The "No Aid" Principle

In its decision in *Everson* v. *Board of Education*, written by Justice Hugo Black, the Court declared that "[N]either a state nor the Federal Government . . . can pass laws which aid one religion, aid all religions, or prefer one religion over another." In addition, the Court said that "no aid" means that no "tax . . . can be **levied** to support any religious activities or institutions. . . ." In these words, the Court summarized its findings denying aid to religious schools. Four of the justices in the *Everson* case dissented, arguing that under this interpretation, any aid to religious schools would be ruled unconstitutional.

levy impose or collect a tax

The Neutrality Principle

The majority opinion in *Everson* declared that the First Amendment "requires the state to be neutral in its relations with groups of religious believers and non-believers." These words established the Court's finding that became known as the "neutrality" principle: The state cannot handicap or favor religions. This neutrality requirement complicates the "no aid" idea and even seems to contradict it.

The justices unanimously agreed that the state ought to provide the same kind of police and fire protection for parochial schools as it does for public schools, even though such protection is "aid" in a certain sense. Yet five of the justices, a majority, concluded that if government provides transportation for public school students, then a state program that helps pay for the transportation of parochial students is nothing more than a "neutral" policy treating all students alike, and not an unconstitutional form of aid to religion.

Principles in Conflict

It is easy to understand why this conflict between the principles of no aid and neutrality causes disagreements. If state governments provide books, busing, services, or funds for religious schools, these certainly are forms of aid to religion. So judges and legal scholars who focus mainly on the "no aid" principle have a strong argument that all government assistance to religious schools is unconstitutional.

But if government pays for public schools in which only secular, or nonreligious, subjects are taught but gives no aid to schools where religion is taught, how is government being neutral in its policy? Those who oppose aid to parochial schools usually reply in the same way as did the four justices who wrote the dissenting opinion in *Everson*. They point out that parochial school students have the choice of going to public schools. But this argument hardly proves that government is being neutral between religion and nonreligion, especially in the eyes of parents and students who regard public school education as secular and antireligious.

The conflict is still not resolved. Judges and legal scholars on both sides have had to find ways of adjusting the "no aid" or the "neutrality" principle, or both. How to accomplish this in interpreting the First Amendment's establishment clause has continued to challenge both sides.

Debate over the Establishment Clause

Judges and legal scholars have turned to history to help them understand what the Framers intended the establishment clause to mean. That clause in the First Amendment provided that "Congress shall make no law respecting an establishment of religion." Judges and legal scholars have disagreed about what this clause means. Three different views of it have developed, based on three main interpretations. These views are the **"strict separation" interpretation**, the **"no preference" interpretation**, and the **"leave it to the states" interpretation**.

"strict separation" interpretation that state and church—that is, government and religion—should be strictly separate

"no preference" interpretation that government may aid religion, but only if it does so impartially, not preferring any one religion over others

"leave it to the states" interpretation that the individual states may decide whether or not to aid religion

The "Strict Separation" Interpretation

The argument for the "strict separation" interpretation is usually made in two parts, just as it was presented in *Everson*. First, events in Virginia in 1785 and 1786 are recalled. A bill was proposed in the state legislature to use public money to support Christian ministers. Many Virginians, like James Madison, opposed the bill. He wrote a petition known as the "Memorial and Remonstrance" in which he argued that it was wrong for government to give money, in any amount, to religion. The proposed bill was defeated, and instead the Virginia legislature passed a bill drafted by Thomas Jefferson prohibiting state aid to religion. Jefferson's bill became law and was called the Virginia **Statute** for Religious Freedom.

statute a law enacted by the legislative branch of government

In the 1990s, voucher programs, which had been introduced in the mid-1980s, grew around the country because of discontent with public school systems. Under this idea, parents are provided with a voucher or check toward their child's education. Advocates claim that vouchers introduce the element of competition into the public school system and force schools to change. Opponents argue that schools are service institutions, not business markets, and they cannot respond to economic forces in the same way. The idea has been tried in a few areas with some success. In 1998, the Wisconsin Supreme Court ruled that Milwaukee could spend taxpayer money to send pupils to parochial or other religious schools. It said that the city's parental-choice program did not violate the state's existing ban on spending state funds for religious schools or the First Amendment's separation of church and state. The program "has a secular purpose," the court wrote, and "will not have the primary effect of advancing religion." The decision was the first appellate ruling that has allowed taxpayer money to go to religious schools for general education.

The second part of the "strict separation" interpretation is simpler. It asserts that, as the Court said in *Everson*, "the provisions of the First Amendment, in the drafting and adoption of which Madison and Jefferson played such leading roles, had the same objective and were intended to provide the same protection against governmental intrusion on religious liberty as the Virginia statute." Jefferson himself expressed this strict separation view when, as president, he wrote to a Baptist group in 1802, saying that the Constitution created a "wall of separation" between church and state. This phrase, "wall of separation," has been used ever since by those who support the strict separation interpretation.

Those who oppose the "strict separation" view point out that Jefferson had almost no part in drafting the establishment clause. When the First Amendment was written in 1789, Jefferson was not in Congress but was serving as the American ambassador to France. They argue that although Madison was the major sponsor of the Bill of Rights in Congress, he needed to make these ten amendments acceptable to the American people and their state legislatures. So the establishment clause was worded in a completely different way from the Virginia Statute of Religious Freedom. As a result, it is difficult to see how this clause could have the same meaning as the Virginia statute.

The "No Preference" Interpretation

Some legal scholars and a few judges, including Supreme Court Chief Justice William Rehnquist, argue that the establishment clause expressed a "no preference" view. Based on the "no preference" interpretation, government aid to religious schools is permissible as long as all religious schools are eligible for such aid.

The "Leave It to the States" Interpretation

The third interpretation of the meaning of the establishment clause is based on the fact that in the late 1700s, when the First Amendment was adopted, people's views about the proper relation of religion and government differed significantly. Some Americans, like Jefferson, believed government should not support religion. But many others (such as Timothy Dwight, president of Yale University) firmly believed that a stable society depended on religion and that religion needed the support of government. States such as Massachusetts and Connecticut continued to subsidize religion into the early 1800s. Many states also had blasphemy laws against making contemptuous remarks or acts against God, as well as laws requiring strict observance of the Sabbath (Sunday) or that permitted only Christians, and sometimes only Protestants, to hold public office.

The delegates to the Constitutional Convention in 1787 therefore found it hard to agree about the proper relationship between government and religion. No evidence exists that either those delegates or the members of the first Congress in 1789 who proposed the Bill of Rights even

> *Be it enacted by the General Assembly*, That no man shall be compelled to frequent or support any religious worship, place, or Ministry whatsoever, nor shall he be enforced, restrained, or burthened [burdened] in his body or his goods, nor shall otherwise suffer on account of his opinions or belief; but that all men shall be free to profess, and by argument to maintain, their opinions in matters of religion, and that the same shall in no wise diminish, enlarge, or affect their civil capacities.
>
> —Thomas Jefferson, *Virginia Statute for Religious Freedom*, January 16, 1786

attempted to resolve this issue by adopting some controversial principle to regulate the relations between government and religion. The Federalists, who supported the new Constitution, often said that religion would continue to be a matter for the states to deal with as they chose, without the national government interfering. This meant that states could refuse to support religion, as Virginia had done, or states could maintain an established church, as Massachusetts and Connecticut continued to do.

The Anti-Federalists, who opposed the Constitution, favored the idea of leaving religion in the hands of the states. They did not fully believe the Federalists' promises that the states would be allowed to deal with religion. They insisted that constitutional limits on the involvement of the national government in religion be put into writing. The first Congress did so by proposing the establishment clause as part of the First Amendment of the Bill of Rights. The clause explicitly prohibited the national government from making laws "respecting an establishment of religion." This provision thus prevented Congress from establishing a national church or interfering with state establishments of religion. But it did not include any general principle of religious freedom, based on either the "strict separation" or the "no preference" principles. It simply guaranteed that the states would be free to deal with religion as they chose, just as they had done before the Constitution was adopted.

The "leave it to the states" interpretation may be the most reasonable interpretation of the three, based on history. Nonetheless, it seems to be the one that is the least popular among judges and legal scholars, perhaps in part because it provides no answers to the contemporary issue of state aid to religious schools.

Modern Supreme Court Cases

Given the legal background, it is not surprising that modern judicial decisions about state aid to religious schools often seem hard to understand. The Supreme Court in *Everson* ruled that states may pay for transporting parochial school students to and from school, yet in *Wolman* v. *Walter* (1977), the justices said states could not pay for such transportation on field trips. In *Board of Education* v. *Allen* (1968), the Court held that states may provide religious schools with secular textbooks, but in *Meek* v. *Pittinger* (1975), it ruled states could not give them instructional materials, such as films, tape recorders, or overhead projectors. The Court has sometimes ruled that government may assist religious school students with some kinds of testing, teaching, and therapy—but only if these services are provided in nearby vans or buildings, not in the schools themselves. Critics of the Supreme Court often argue that these decisions and their distinctions make no sense.

The Supreme Court does seem to follow an overall pattern in its decisions. Two factors in particular help it determine how to decide a controversy. First, the Court has been much more suspicious of direct aid, that is, aid that goes directly to religious schools. It has been less suspicious of indirect aid, that is, aid that goes to students and their families. The

AMENDMENTS—The Courts and the Bill of Rights; FIRST AMENDMENT—No "Establishment of Religion"

Supreme Court has usually struck down grants of money to parochial schools, but it upheld a Minnesota program that allowed tax deductions for educational expenses, even though most of the benefits of these deductions went to parents of religious school students.

Second, the Supreme Court has paid close attention to the form of aid. Even when aid is given directly to religious schools, the Court may approve it if the aid takes a form that is secular and cannot be turned into religious use. The justices thus seem to reason that a math book can be reviewed for content, but overhead projectors might be used to present religious lessons. The Court may permit states to provide textbooks but not projectors. Money is the form of aid that is most easily used for other purposes after it is received, which is why the Court has been especially suspicious of direct monetary subsidies to parochial schools.

Many legal scholars believe that over the years the Supreme Court has become more tolerant in reviewing various programs for aiding religious schools. During the 1970s, the Court seemed very strict in its rulings on such aid. By the 1990s, the Court was more willing to allow different forms of aid to religious schools. In any case, with the growing concern about the performance of public schools and the spread of voucher systems and charter schools as alternatives, it seems certain that aid to religious schools will continue to be a controversial issue.

★ Government and Religion in Public Places

Norman Redlich

THE FIRST AMENDMENT TO THE CONSTITUTION STATES

Congress shall make no law respecting an establishment of religion, or prohibiting the free exercise thereof; . . .

The first of the two clauses regarding the relation between government and religion—called the "establishment clause"—determines the extent to which government may support religious activities. Although the First Amendment mentions only "Congress," the clause has been interpreted as applying to all elements of the federal government, as well as to the states, because the Fourteenth Amendment has been interpreted as applying most of the original Bill of Rights to the states.

Despite wide disagreement in the past over the meaning of the establishment clause, it has become generally accepted that the clause prohibits government endorsement of religion—either one religion or religions generally. Yet putting this rule into effect in specific contexts is difficult. For example, a school district may not require teachers to start the day with a prayer or a reading from the Bible; but it has been disputed whether the purpose and effect of a "moment of silent meditation" support religion or enable students to think about what they will be doing during the school day.

endorsement approval or sanction

Crèches and Menorahs

mandate command, order, or require

While mandated school prayers are an obvious form of government support for religious activities, other types of government programs are less clear. One of the most controversial of these government activities occurs during the Christmas season, when in many cities and towns local governments either pay for or allow religious displays, such as a crèche depicting the birth of Christ. In an effort to recognize the concerns of non-Christian faiths, local governments have provided similar assistance for the display of a menorah—the symbol of the Jewish holiday of Chanukah, which usually occurs around the same time. Often there is disagreement as to whether these public displays constitute government support of religion or merely the celebration of a holiday. But there is agreement that since the establishment clause prohibits government support for religion generally, governments cannot avoid the issue by arguing that it is permissible to support all religions as long as governments do not discriminate. In other words, if the crèche is unconstitutional, also allowing a menorah or another religion's symbol does not cure the problem.

Courts have established that religious displays, financed by private individuals or groups, may be set up in public areas, such as parks, where other types of activities, such as speeches, concerts, political rallies, or plays, are permitted. This means that if the Pope can conduct a mass in a city park where other types of public events occur, a religious group can set up there a symbol of the birth of Jesus or the triumph of the Maccabees. It has been argued that a permanent display might constitute more of an unconstitutional "endorsement" than, for instance, a religious service. Courts, however, have held that if governments allow other freestanding permanent displays, such as appeals for the Red Cross or United Way charities, then governments not only must also allow religious displays, but that it would probably be unconstitutional to prohibit them.

Where May a Religious Symbol Be Displayed in Public?

Difficulties with holiday displays generally arise in two contexts—(1) when the displays are financed by government and (2) when they are placed so close to a public building, such as a state house or city hall, that

A crèche on the Boston Common at Christmastime. Disagreement has been growing as to whether such a religious display on public property constitutes government support of religion.

they appear to the average person to be an official endorsement of religion. It is not surprising that court decisions have created considerable confusion in trying to answer these questions.

Conditions for financial support. Governments generally may finance religious displays such as a crèche or menorah only if the display is part of a celebration of the holiday season. That is why government-financed displays must be accompanied by reindeers, a Santa Claus, bells, bunting, or other extensive decorations that emphasize the holiday season rather than religious observance. It should not be surprising that this distinction has met with great skepticism.

Site limitations. If displays are financed by private groups and are primarily religious, they may not be placed in a location where they might appear to be an official endorsement of religion, such as on the steps or in a **rotunda** of a public building. At such locations, displays must be surrounded by holiday trappings.

rotunda large, round room

These "rules" have led to many disputes and confusing court decisions, turning on whether the display is religious or part of a holiday celebration, and whether, if religious and financed by a private group, it is so identified with a public building that it may be seen as a government endorsement of religion. It is no wonder that many observers, even including religious leaders, have concluded that the government should stop financing religious displays and that such public displays set up by private groups should be confined to facilities like parks and plazas where all forms of speech are permitted.

How Does Government Support Religious Activities?

Government support for religious activities comes in many varieties. A common example is the "Sunday closing law," which can be viewed either as a government effort to encourage people to attend church on Sundays or simply as government support for a day of rest. The Supreme Court, by a 5-4 margin, in *Braunfield* v. *Brown* (1961), held that such laws did not violate the religion clauses of the Constitution because they were construed as motivated primarily by the secular purpose of encouraging a day of rest—even though they imposed a "special burden" on businesses whose owners for religious reasons were required to stay closed on a day other than Sunday.

No endorsement of religion. Because public schools are financed and operated by governments, they have been the source of considerable controversy as courts determine the extent to which these schools may engage in religious activities. While the Constitution forbids government-prescribed prayers, individual students may say grace at lunch or pray at their desks. Teaching about religion is a permissible subject, but teaching students to follow religious beliefs or practices is the type of government support that is not permitted.

In *Lee* v. *Weisman* (1992), the Supreme Court ruled that state-sponsored prayers at public school graduation ceremonies were prohibited. But in 1995, by a narrow 5-4 margin in *Rosenberger* v. *University of Virginia*, the Court decided that providing public funds for a student-run

In a message to Congress dated December 7, 1875, Ulysses S. Grant (1822–1885), 18th President of the United States, stated:
"No sectarian tenets shall ever be taught in any school supported in whole or in part by the State, nation, or by the proceeds of any tax levied upon any community."

newspaper with a religious viewpoint did not constitute an endorsement of religion. Rather, it enabled students to exercise their free-speech rights. The sharp division on the Court showed the fine line between the endorsement of religion, which is not permitted, and the required "accommodation" of the free-speech rights of students in public institutions.

Extent of government support. Courts must also constantly decide the extent to which governments may provide financial assistance to private religious schools. Direct financial supports, like paying for teachers' salaries, are unconstitutional. It is permissible, however, for government employees to determine whether any children in religious schools have learning disabilities and to provide assistance to a disabled child in the form of a hearing aid or an interpreter. The state may pay teachers to teach remedial courses, as the Supreme Court ruled in *Agostini* v. *Felton* (1997), but such courses should be confined to rooms that are free from religious trappings and conducted by teachers who are under the control of the public school system. This means that governments are permitted to assist children in religious schools with their learning problems, but may not carry this to the point where such assistance constitutes support for the overall educational program of the religious school. In borderline cases, obviously it is easier to state the rule than to apply it.

The Voucher Movement

At the end of the twentieth century, government programs were being discussed that would almost certainly create new strains on the continuing efforts to impose constitutional limitations on government assistance to religion. These programs clearly would aid religious institutions but are defended on the grounds that they serve important governmental ends.

Vouchers for private schools. Most notable of these has been the push for educational vouchers for parents of public school students, to be used to pay in part for tuition in private (including religious) schools. Vouchers have been advanced in the interest of fairness, as a way to help parents of limited financial means give their children a private school education and so equalize the advantage enjoyed by wealthier families.

Setting a legal precedent. The voucher movement has been gaining steam in many states, with several groups supporting vouchers as a way to correct the deficiencies of the public school system. The Supreme Court, in *Mueller* v. *Allen* (1980), upheld a state law allowing a tax deduction for educational expenses incurred by parents, including the cost of sending children to private religious schools. Even though a voucher system is different from a tax deduction, which provides differing benefits depending on the taxable income and deductions of the parent, the Court could easily rely on the Mueller case to support vouchers.

Other precedents are to be found in the GI Bill of Rights, which provided tuition benefits for World War II veterans, including tuition at religious colleges. Nevertheless, a voucher plan would involve very significant and broad-based direct financial assistance to religious elementary and high schools. The Supreme Court has traditionally distinguished this from assistance at the college level, because the impact of

religious education on children is different from that on adults. But even if the Court ultimately approves a voucher system, limited government budgets, strong opposition from public school advocates and certain racial and ethnic minorities—and much debate about the actual benefits of a voucher system to students—may well limit these programs.

> The growth of religious activism has provoked court cases about the Ten Commandments. In 1995, an Alabama county judge opened court sessions with a Christian prayer. Hanging on the wall, just beside his chair on the bench, was a wooden plaque he carved of the Ten Commandments. A higher state judge ruled that these practices were unconstitutional and that the Ten Commandments could stay in the courtroom only if they were made less religious, or "secularized," by the addition of other historical documents. The county judge refused to follow this order and appealed to the Alabama Supreme Court. The governor said he would send in state troopers and call out the National Guard if necessary to defend the judge's right to display the Ten Commandments. The Alabama Supreme Court, in 1998, overturned the lower court decision on technical grounds. In 1980, the Supreme Court ruled that a Kentucky law that required that a copy of the Ten Commandments, purchased with private contributions, be placed on the wall of each public school classroom in the state had no nonreligious purpose and violated the First Amendment's establishment clause. Just as the Court ruled on the constitutionality of school prayer and Bible readings in public schools, it seems likely that the justices will have to rule on the place of the Ten Commandments in public life in America.

New Programs Present Challenges

Other programs also offer challenges to legal restrictions on aid to religious institutions. These are programs that provide government support to church groups that use religious instruction in dealing with such ills as drug abuse, domestic violence, teenage pregnancies, prisoner rehabilitation, and other types of societal problems. In the past, governments have been permitted to subsidize hospitals and day-care facilities as long as no government funds were used to teach religion. In contrast to a hospital or day-care facility operated by a church, many of the newer programs actually use religion itself as a means to achieve socially desirable ends. If religion-based programs have been shown to be more effective than other types of government-supported programs in dealing with serious social ills, it will become increasingly difficult for legislatures and courts to bar religious organizations from participating in programs that use religion as an effective means of dealing with serious social problems.

Conclusion

A challenge has been presented to those who strongly believe that the constitutional barriers against government support of religion are necessary to preserve religious liberty. The challenge is how to devise a constitutional framework that permits religious groups to run social programs without undermining the large body of constitutional law that, however imperfectly, has restricted government support of religion.

Few issues have evoked as much controversy as the application of the establishment clause to situations involving government support of religious activities. Yet it must be remembered that the United States enjoys religious freedom, religious diversity, and religious peace to a remarkable degree. The basic requirements that the religion clauses impose on governments—neutrality, noninterference, and nonsupport—have served the nation well.

FIRST AMENDMENT—The First Amendment; Government Financial Assistance to Religious Schools; School Prayers and Bible Reading

★ "Free Exercise" of Religion

Edward Gaffney

THE FIRST AMENDMENT TO THE CONSTITUTION STATES

Congress shall make no law respecting an establishment of religion, or prohibiting the free exercise thereof; . . .

Religious liberty is the first liberty listed in the Bill of Rights. Similar guarantees are found in all of the state constitutions or charters that preceded the adoption of the First Amendment. But stating with clarity either the contents or the limits of this fundamental

freedom has never been easy. Many colonies had an official state religion, called an "establishment of religion." The law conferred benefits on members of the established religion and imposed severe penalties—including banishment and death—on the practice of another faith.

banishment forcing someone to leave a country or place by decree of the government

The Founding Period

The process of securing religious liberty began with ringing provisions in the state charters and constitutions that preceded the adoption of the federal Bill of Rights. For example, the Pennsylvania Constitution of 1790 provided: "All men have a natural and indefeasible right to worship Almighty God according to the dictates of their own consciences. . . ." The founders clearly intended to protect the ability of each person and religious community to worship freely. This meant that the government would no longer have power to enact laws that punished those who practiced a religion other than the official state religion. Some colonies, notably Massachusetts, had done this before the Revolution. The purpose of not having a state religion, then, was to secure its free exercise for all people. The colonies of Carolina, Delaware, Maryland, and Rhode Island practiced this ideal.

indefeasible that which cannot be made invalid

The Framers contemplated limits to free exercise of religion, but they understood free exercise to include actions as well as opinions. For example, the New York Constitution of 1777 provides: "the liberty of conscience . . . shall not be so construed as to excuse *acts* of licentiousness, or justify *practices* inconsistent with the peace or safety of this State." Three broad conclusions flow from this text.

construed explained; interpreted

licentiousness going beyond accepted rules of behavior or moral and sexual restraints

First, religious freedom clearly does not mean that one is free to hold a religious opinion but may not do anything about it. Acts and practices are also protected. Second, the Framers intended to protect religious freedom from the law's minor or unintended effects that punish a person when he acts in keeping with his or her religious beliefs. When that occurred, the law made an exception for religiously motivated behavior. Third, the standard for setting limits on religious freedom is high. In order for the state to defeat a claim for a religious exemption, the state would have to show that the religious practice threatens a matter very important to the government such as the "peace and safety" of the community, and that there was no other way the government could reach its goal without burdening religious freedom.

burdening weighing down

The Mormon Cases

Members of the Church of Jesus Christ of Latter-day Saints, known as the Mormons, founded Salt Lake City in the then-federal territory of Utah in 1847. They claimed that polygamy was a religious duty for men. Because of this, Congress passed a series of laws from 1862 to 1874 aimed at extending direct federal control over the territory. In 1878, the Supreme Court upheld the conviction of a Mormon in Utah who had taken a second wife. This was the Court's first decision under the free exercise clause. The justices ruled that while the First Amendment protects

polygamy the practice of having more than one spouse at a time

Claims under the free exercise clause arise in any number of settings. The Court has upheld laws prohibiting business activities on Sunday, as applied to Orthodox Jews. The justices have sustained, in *Bob Jones University* v. *U.S.* (1983), an Internal Revenue Service regulation that a religious school that admits members of only one race is not entitled to a tax exemption (exception). The Court rejected the university's claim that its racially discriminatory admissions policy was based on religious doctrine, and noted that the policy would not prevent the university from practicing its religion. In this way, the IRS policy was similar to the Sunday closing laws. The justices have also allowed the Forest Service to construct a road through a portion of national forest that Native Americans hold sacred and use for religious ceremonies.

religious belief, the government may regulate religiously motivated conduct. In 1879, the Court upheld another part of the law Congress had passed that prevented Mormons from voting unless they swore that they did not believe in polygamy. The Mormon church rejected polygamy in 1890, and Utah was admitted as a state in 1896.

The Jehovah's Witnesses Cases

In the 1930s and 1940s, the Jehovah's Witnesses—another religious community that began in America in the late nineteenth century—came into conflict with the law because of their religious beliefs and practices. Every Witness is considered a minister of the gospel under a duty to spread the message of the community. The Court upheld the right of a Witness who went from door to door asking people if they would like to hear a phonograph record or accept a pamphlet. The justices ruled that a state could regulate the times, places, and manner of asking for contributions, but cannot forbid them completely.

The Witnesses also viewed the flag as a "graven image," so their children refused to salute the flag at the opening of the school day. In 1940, the Court ruled that schoolchildren must salute the flag. Three years later, the justices reversed themselves. The First Amendment does "not authorize public authorities to compel [anyone] to utter what is not in his mind . . . ," the Court wrote. "No official, high or petty, can prescribe what shall be orthodox in politics, nationalism, religion, or other matters of opinion or force citizens to confess by word or act their faith therein."

The High Point of Protecting Free Exercise

In *Sherbert* v. *Verner* (1963), the Court ruled that the states may not deny welfare benefits to persons because of their religious convictions. This

Touro Synagogue, built in 1763, is the oldest synagogue in America. It is located in Newport, in the state of Rhode Island, which even as a colony guaranteed free exercise of religion for all people.

case involved members of the Seventh-day Adventist Church, who refrain from work on Saturdays, which is their Sabbath. The Court ruled that when a claim of religious exercise is presented, "[o]nly the gravest abuses, endangering paramount interests, give occasion for permissible limitation." The Court also required the state to show that "no alternative forms of regulation would combat such abuses without infringing First Amendment rights."

paramount highest

infringe exceed the limits of, or violate

This formulation of free exercise protection came to be known as the compelling government interest test and the least restrictive alternative test. It was extended in 1972, in *Wisconsin* v. *Yoder*, to allow the Amish an exemption from compulsory school attendance laws, and in 1981, in *Thomas* v. *Indiana Review Board*, to provide unemployment benefits to a Jehovah's Witness who refused to work in a steel mill that produced military weapons.

compelling government interest the government must show that an action is necessary to gain a particular benefit

Is Free Exercise Less Protected?

In *O'Lone* v. *Estate of Shabazz* (1987), the Court refused to extend to Muslim prisoners the right of religious worship that is commonly given to members of other communities.

Starting in the 1980s, the Court has given less protection to the free exercise principle. For example, in *United States* v. *Lee* (1982), the Court refused to grant the Amish an exemption from social security taxes even though they never make any claims upon that fund. In *Goldman* v. *Weinberger* (1986), the Court refused to grant a military officer who was an observant Jew the right to wear a yarmulke beneath his military cap.

This trend came to a climax in *Employment Division* v. *Smith* in 1990. The Court ruled that a state may prohibit Native Americans from using peyote in their religious rituals without violating the free exercise clause. (Smith and others had been fired by a drug-treatment center because they used peyote and were denied unemployment compensation.) The Court abandoned the compelling interest test and contended that nothing in the First Amendment prevents states from adopting "generally applicable" laws that have the "incidental" effect of interfering with religious practices. Allowing a religious exemption from these laws, the Court said, is "a luxury" that we "cannot afford."

climax highest point

Should Government Be Neutral?

The constitutional command of protecting free exercise of religion includes a duty of the government to remain neutral in religious matters. At the very least, this neutrality must mean that the government may not target religious minorities or impose burdens on some people simply because their religious beliefs and practices seem strange to the majority of the elected representatives of the people. This bare minimum of religious freedom is known as formal neutrality. An example of this approach is found in a 1993 decision, *Church of the Lukumi Babalu Aye* v. *City of Hialeah*, that invalidated a series of municipal ordinances clearly aimed at suppressing this religion, which practices animal sacrifice.

neutral not involved on either side

FIRST AMENDMENT—Government and Religion in Public Places; No "Establishment of Religion"

Respecting Religious Differences

In response to the *Smith* decision, Congress enacted the Religious Freedom Restoration Act (RFRA) in 1993. This law sought to shift the

burden of proof in a case involving a clash between the law and a religious duty. Under *Smith*, a person bringing a religious claim could win only by showing that the law intentionally discriminated against a religious duty. Under RFRA, that person had only to show clearly that a law imposed a significant burden on free exercise. The government could win only if it showed that a compelling interest was the basis for the law and that it had no other way to do what it wanted except to pass the law. The Court was sharply split in *Smith*, however, and four justices joined in a dissent, which stated: "Our nation's founders conceived of a republic receptive to voluntary religious expression, not of a secular society in which religious expression is tolerated only when it does not conflict with a generally applicable law."

★ Conscientious Objectors

Kent Greenawalt

THE FIRST AMENDMENT TO THE CONSTITUTION STATES

Congress shall make no law respecting an establishment of religion, or prohibiting the free exercise thereof; . . .

The term "conscientious objector" is most often used for someone opposed to performing any military service or fighting in combat. Some young men and women who are conscientious objectors are willing to go to jail rather than serve in the armed forces, because they are pacifists or because they believe a particular war is highly unjust.

pacifist a person who opposes all wars on moral or religious grounds

The Question of Military Service

A society that respects individual conscience may have reasons to excuse conscientious objectors from military service. Forcing people to act against their strong moral beliefs is not usually desirable in a free, democratic society, and a genuine objector will not be forced to successfully perform acts he or she condemns. But excusing conscientious objectors from military service may be unfair to others who would prefer not to go into the armed forces but who may still end up fighting and dying. Although the most difficult questions about conscientious objectors have come up when young Americans have been drafted, similar questions are present in a volunteer army. For example, should a volunteer who becomes a conscientious objector in the middle of a term of service to which he or she agreed be allowed to leave the military?

drafted selected for compulsory military service

A person deciding whether he or she is a conscientious objector has the difficult task of examining all claims on his or her conscience: Is it absolutely wrong to kill in war? How much respect is owed to the widely held opinion that war sometimes is the right answer? The problem of whether a person should or should not become a conscientious objector involves difficult religious, moral, and political judgments.

From the government's viewpoint, the four crucial issues are these: Should an exception be made for conscientious objectors? If so, how

should conscientious objectors be defined? What procedures should be used to decide if someone falls within the group of conscientious objectors? Should those who are **exempted** from military service be required to meet some other obligation, such as civilian work in a hospital? There also are important issues about whether these choices should be left to Congress or to judges interpreting the Constitution.

exempt free from a requirement that others are subject to

Muhammad Ali was born Cassius Marcellus Clay, Jr., in 1942. He changed his name when he became a Black Muslim in 1964. After winning an Olympic gold medal in 1960, he became world heavyweight champion in 1964. Muhammad Ali was stripped of the title and banned from boxing in 1967 when he refused induction into the armed forces. He claimed exemption on the grounds that the Muslims who converted him made him a minister, and also that he was a conscientious objector. He was arrested, convicted, and sentenced to five years in prison. The Supreme Court in 1971 unanimously reversed the conviction. Ali resumed his boxing career and regained the title in 1974.

The Role of the Constitution

The Constitution says nothing about conscientious objectors, but the First Amendment, while forbidding an establishment of religion, protects the free exercise of religion. For most of America's history, it has been assumed that Congress has a free hand to decide which conscientious objectors, if any, will receive an exemption from military service. This assumption changed. The Supreme Court has not resolved whether some exemptions must be recognized, but it has indicated limits on how Congress defines the group of people who benefit from an exemption.

During the Civil War and World War I, Congress restricted exemptions from military service to members of religious denominations whose faiths forbade taking part in war. The Selective Service Act of 1940 set the basic terms of exemption that have been followed ever since. The act made a person eligible for exemption "who, by reason of religious training and belief, [was] conscientiously opposed to participation in war in any, form." In 1948, Congress defined religious belief as belief "in a relation to a Supreme Being involving duties superior to those arising from any human relation. . . ." Congress wanted to excuse only persons opposed to participation in all wars, not those opposed to particular wars, and it wanted to excuse only those persons whose opposition came from religious beliefs in a rather traditional sense.

Several important Supreme Court cases have dealt with these distinctions. In *United States* v. *Seeger* (1965), the Court ruled that a person who spoke of a "religious faith in a purely ethical creed" was entitled to the exemption because such belief occupied the same place in that person's life as did belief in God for the more traditional objector. In *Welsh* v. *United States* (1970), four justices held that even someone who made no claim to being religious could qualify for exemption. In *Gillette* v. *United States* (1971), after considering claims by both religious and nonreligious objectors to the Vietnam "war," the Supreme Court upheld Congress's determination not to exempt persons opposed to taking part in particular wars. The Court declared that the public interest in a fairly administered system supported the distinction between "general" and "selective" objectors. The justices also noted that officials would have great difficulty dealing consistently with the variety of objections persons might have to particular wars.

The Constitution allows Congress considerable choice about conscientious objection. At the same time, it protects religious liberty and requires government to be impartial toward religions. These principles are a source of value for Congress, and they limit how Congress may deal with conscientious objectors.

see also

FIRST AMENDMENT—"Free Exercise" of Religion; No "Establishment of Religion"

Freedom of Speech: The Early Years, 1791-1919

Norman L. Rosenberg

THE FIRST AMENDMENT TO THE CONSTITUTION STATES

Congress shall make no law . . . abridging the freedom of speech, or of the press; . . .

The First Amendment states that "Congress shall make no law. . . abridging the freedom of speech or of the press. . . ." What do these words mean? Alexander Hamilton, one of the Framers of the Constitution of 1789 who considered any amendments unnecessary, ridiculed this language. "What is liberty of the press? Who can give it any definition that would not leave the utmost latitude [freedom] for invasion?" Hamilton asked in *The Federalist Papers*. Most other people then disagreed. They favored the adoption of the First Amendment and tried to define the types of expression it protected.

abridge diminish, reduce

The Federalist set of 85 essays published 1787–1788 that analyzed the Constitution and urged its adoption; essays were written by John Jay, Alexander Hamilton, and James Madison

For several centuries, people in both Great Britain and colonial North America had debated the meaning of freedom of speech and of the press. During the early eighteenth century, this debate came to focus on the broad power under which government officials prosecuted acts they called seditious libel.

prosecute to begin and carry on a lawsuit; bring legal action against

Seditious Libel

common law the system of judge-made law that began in England and is based on court decisions and custom rather than on statutes passed by legislatures

What was a seditious libel? As defined by England's common law courts, it could be any political expression, spoken or printed, that tended to decrease respect for the government and the laws of the land or for the reputations of public officials. A conviction for seditious libel could result in a fine, a jail term, or both. A libel against the government or a public official, moreover, could be prosecuted whether it was true or false. Experts on the common law, such as Sir William Blackstone, insisted that if libelous criticism of public officials were true, it would be even more likely to harm their reputation than an obvious falsehood. "The greater the truth, the greater the libel," Blackstone's *Commentaries on the Laws of England* (1765–1769) argued. This approach left little space for political criticism.

The way that common law courts enforced seditious libel increased its potential threat. In a criminal prosecution, the judge determined whether or not a political statement amounted to a seditious libel. This determination decided the "law of the case." Despite a defendant's right to a jury trial, jurors only deliberated on the "facts of the case," that is, whether or not the defendant had actually said or printed what a judge already had decided was seditious libel.

Challenging Blackstone

This view was known in both Great Britain and colonial North America as the "orthodox" [conventional] and later as the "Blackstonian" position. It did not go unchallenged. The earliest dissenters included two English political writers, John Trenchard and Thomas Gordon, who wrote during

The Sedition Act of 1798 led philosophers of freedom of speech and press to develop new theories. Building on ideas earlier expressed by Jefferson and Madison, these philosophers believed that the truth of opinions could not be proved. Allowing "truth" as a defense and thinking that it was a protection for freedom made as little sense as letting a jury decide which was "the most palatable [tasty] food, agreable drink, or beautiful color." A jury cannot give an impartial verdict in political trials. These writers advocated complete freedom of political expression. Government cannot prosecute citizens for their expression of opinions. It can prosecute only for "overt [obvious] acts," or deeds. Freedom of the press was either "absolute" or it did not exist. A citizen should have the right to "say everything which his passions suggest . . . in speaking against the government . . . thus violating at once, every principle of decency and truth." This interpretation was based on the then-new theory that free government depends on freedom of political speech for its existence and freedom.

constituted amounted to

faction a party or group united by a common cause

indictment a formal written statement charging a person or persons with an offense after a grand jury has examined the evidence and found that there is a valid case

the early 1720s under the pen name "Cato." The orthodox position interfered with expression necessary for alerting citizens to a corrupt government and dishonest politicians. "Freedom of Speech is the Great Bulwark of Liberty; they prosper and die together," Cato wrote.

To better protect critical expression, Trenchard and Gordon argued against the orthodox position. They proposed that in any prosecution for seditious libel, a jury—not a judge—should decide whether or not a publication or statement constituted a libel. In other words, juries should determine both the law and the facts of the case. Cato also insisted that the truth should be a sufficient defense in a seditious libel prosecution. Unless these changes in the orthodox position were accepted, Cato concluded, the right of political dissent would be threatened. During the 1730s, Cato's ideas became central to a controversy over seditious libel in colonial New York known as "The Zenger Case."

The Case of John Peter Zenger

John Peter Zenger actually played a minor role in this case. The key participants were New York's governor, William Cosby, and an opposing group of politicians led by William Morris, who used a newspaper, the *New York Weekly Journal*, to ridicule Governor Cosby's policies and leadership. James Alexander, a lawyer and a member of the Morris faction, edited this small paper, which Zenger merely printed. Alexander dared the governor to prosecute the *Journal* for seditious libel by re-publishing Cato's earlier essays on freedom of the press. In 1735, Cosby finally accepted Alexander's challenge and secured an indictment for seditious libel—but against Zenger rather than Alexander.

The Zenger case pitted the orthodox position on seditious libel against the one Cato popularized. Governor Cosby expected Zenger's conviction because the case was to be tried before Chief Justice James de Lancey, a Cosby supporter. But the Morris faction had hired the best lawyer in the colonies, Andrew Hamilton (no relation to Alexander Hamilton), to defend Zenger.

Chief Justice de Lancey followed the orthodox position and ruled that the articles, which Hamilton conceded Zenger had printed, were libelous. de Lancey told the jury that the articles' truth could be no defense, even though Hamilton claimed he could establish it. A libel "is nevertheless a libel that it is true," the Chief Justice declared. But Andrew Hamilton, in a lengthy argument, went over de Lancey's head and appealed to the jurors.

He stressed the threat to political expression if the Chief Justice's theory of seditious libel were to prevail in colonial New York. No governmental official, he insisted, should control the people's right to voice political criticism, as the orthodox position permitted. Of what use was the "mighty privilege to resist tyranny," he asked, "if every man that suffers . . . must be taken up as a libeller for telling his suffering to his neighbor?" The jurors responded by ignoring de Lancey's instructions and returning a verdict in favor of Zenger. The court let this verdict stand.

The trial of John Peter Zenger in New York, 1734.

The Impact of the Zenger Case

The Zenger case remained controversial during the eighteenth century. Since de Lancey's ruling had technically upheld the orthodox position, lawyers and governmental leaders who favored it could insist that the Zenger case defended their view of legally protected expression. But since the jury had, in effect, overruled the judge, opponents could make the counterclaim that popular sentiment favored what became known as the "Zengerian principles"—that truth should serve as a defense and that the jury should rule on both the law and the facts of a seditious libel case.

In 1791, when the First Amendment was adopted, lawyers were still arguing over the orthodox as opposed to the Zengerian views. But this debate had lost much of its earlier importance, because during most of the eighteenth century, few politicians risked a test of popular sentiment by beginning a seditious libel case. There were only a handful of cases after the uproar over the Zenger prosecution.

The Sedition Act

Federalist advocating a strong central government of separate states and the adoption of the U.S. Constitution

All this suddenly changed in 1798. Members of the **Federalist** party, desperate to prevent the Jefferson Republicans from sweeping the national election two years later, seized on a foreign-policy crisis with France to justify passing the nation's first seditious libel law—the Sedition Act of 1798. This act, which remained in effect only until 1800, was clearly aimed at limiting Jeffersonian criticism of Federalists such as President John Adams. Federalist lawmakers, hoping to make the law more acceptable, incorporated the Zengerian principles into the Sedition Act. But in practice they proved useless to Jeffersonians.

The Federalists, who controlled the nation's legal system, packed the juries that tried Jeffersonian defendants with fellow Federalists. Jeffersonians discovered that the right to offer evidence of truth as a defense and to have a jury decide the law of the case became meaningless when **partisan** political passions were boiling over. Every Jeffersonian critic charged under the Sedition Act was convicted of seditious libel.

partisan a member of a group or participant in an event

The Impact of the Sedition Act

Jeffersonian relating to Thomas Jefferson and his political beliefs

The Sedition Act left two important legacies. First, it inspired **Jeffersonians** to rethink the meaning of the First Amendment. They now insisted that the Zengerian principles provided insufficient protection for critical expression. Jeffersonians argued that most political criticism was a matter of political opinion, not factual statements that could be proven "true" or "false." An example is the Jeffersonian claim that John Adams conducted official state dinners in a manner that suggested he was a royal monarch rather than a president. The First Amendment should protect political opinions, unless they were made or published with **malice**, these Jeffersonian theorists proposed. A few even argued that the First Amendment prevented the national government from prosecuting any political criticism, no matter how libelous or untrue.

malice deliberate lawbreaking, or intent to cause harm without legal right or excuse

The Sedition Act, in this way, produced a fierce debate over the First Amendment. Jeffersonian theory, which historians have called "the new **libertarianism**," rejected the Zengerian principles as inadequate. But in pamphlets and newspaper articles, Federalists denounced this new libertarian theory, saying that tolerating "licentious" [unrestricted] criticism that exceeded the bounds of truth recklessly endangered the authority of government and the reputation of political leaders.

libertarianism a philosophy that believes in the right to unrestricted freedom of thought and action

The second result of the Sedition Act, ironically, was to end this bitter two-year debate on an **inconclusive** note. In 1800, voters denied John Adams a second term as president and turned many other Federalists out of office. The Federalist party never recovered from this popular backlash against the Sedition Act. Many people judged the Sedition Act to conflict directly with what they understood as the First Amendment guarantee of freedom of speech and of the press. When the Sedition Act expired in 1800, few politicians dared even to talk about national prosecutions for political libels. Consequently there was simply no occasion, within the federal judicial system at least, to continue the debate.

inconclusive uncertain

The First Amendment and the Supreme Court

The Supreme Court decided few cases on any aspect of the First Amendment before 1919. The rulings it did hand down would have seemed familiar to orthodox judges and lawyers of the eighteenth century. In *Patterson* v. *Colorado* (1907), for example, the Court held that the First Amendment did not allow a defendant charged with a crime similar to seditious libel to offer evidence of the truth as a defense. In effect, this decision endorsed Blackstone's view of legally protected expression. As late as 1918, such narrow views prevailed among most judges and legal commentators.

The Development of a Counter-Tradition

But a counter-tradition championed a less restrictive theory. It emerged during more than a century of **grassroots** political struggles. Prior to the Civil War, anti-slavery forces denounced the effort by Southern states and the national government to silence them, charging that this was a violation of the First Amendment. Later, labor union activists condemned local police who arrested them simply for engaging in political demonstrations, calling this practice an **infringement** of First Amendment principles.

grassroots involving the basic elements of society, often as viewed from higher levels of power

infringement a violation or trespass on another person's rights

This counter-tradition gradually gained force in some states and among some legal theorists. Most state constitutions contained their own "little First Amendments," provisions that extended legal protection to critical expression. These provisions generally incorporated the Zengerian principles, but modified them by stating that truth could be a defense in a political libel case only when expressed with "good motives" (without malice) and for "justifiable ends." A few state courts even went beyond the Zengerian position and granted legal protection even to falsehoods if no malice was involved. Meanwhile, Thomas Cooley's *Constitutional Limitations*, an important legal treatise first published in 1868, pointedly

rejected the Blackstonian position on legally protected expression. And after 1900, members of the "Free Speech League" and other activists pressed the federal judiciary to incorporate these broader ideas into constitutional law.

By 1919, there were two conflicting lines of argument concerning the First Amendment. Many citizens and some lawyers believed that deciding political libel cases according to restrictive eighteenth-century principles, and permitting public officials, such as judges and police officers, broad authority to silence political dissenters, violated the core meaning of the First Amendment. But this view failed to persuade the Supreme Court and most constitutional experts who still followed the old Blackstonian position. Beginning in 1919, however, new cases forced the Court to begin a long process of trying to reconcile these conflicting theories of the First Amendment.

see also

AMENDMENTS—The Courts and the Bill of Rights; FIRST AMENDMENT—The Development of Standards; Libel and Defamation; *New York Times* v. *Sullivan*; Seditious Libel

★ The Development of Standards

Burt Neuborne

THE FIRST AMENDMENT TO THE CONSTITUTION STATES

*Congress shall make no law . . . **abridging** the freedom of speech, or of the press; . . .*

Freedom of speech is one of America's most cherished ideals. Why does the law treat free speech as if it were more important than other vital human needs, like housing, or health care? When the Framers put free speech at the top of the Bill of Rights, they understood that freedom to speak your mind is an essential part of living in a democracy. There are several reasons for this.

Why Free Speech Is Important

First, free speech helps us to find out the truth for ourselves. We depend on a free "marketplace of ideas" to help us separate truth from falsehood. In fact, the Framers believed that even false ideas can be helpful in seeking the truth, since the act of proving them to be false helps us to understand what is true.

Second, free speech is necessary to have real elections. In a democracy, the voters choose who should be allowed to govern. But you cannot cast an informed vote without full knowledge of the candidates and issues.

Third, the Framers believed that the freedom to express yourself is part of what it means to be human. After all, the ability to use complex language to reason and to communicate is the biological attribute that defines humanity. If we respect human dignity, we must respect the freedom to communicate.

attribute quality

Finally, speech must be free because we just cannot trust a government official to decide what can, and what cannot be said. History teaches us that whenever government gets the power to control speech, it always abuses that power. The risk of government manipulation of information is so great that the power to censor can never be placed in its hands.

censor examine in order to suppress any material considered to be objectionable

A Narrow Meaning for Free Speech?

Defending the idea of free speech in the abstract is, however, much easier than deciding exactly what freedom of speech means. It cannot mean that there are absolutely no limits on speech. So, although all Americans agree that free speech is very important, they have disagreed vigorously about exactly what it protects.

In fact, for much of American history, Congress and the Supreme Court have given freedom of speech a very narrow definition. For example, in the 1790s, when critics of George Washington and John Adams launched attacks on the policies of the Federalist party, Congress passed the Alien and Sedition Acts and critics of the government were sent to jail.

When newspaper editors friendly to the South crusaded against the Civil War, President Lincoln had their presses seized, and defended censorship in the Supreme Court. At the close of the nineteenth century, many labor organizers were jailed for peaceful picketing, and critics of America's decision to enter World War I were imprisoned for publishing "treason."

Federalist advocating a strong central government of separate states and the adoption of the U.S. Constitution

alien citizen of another country

sedition incitement of resistance to or insurrection against lawful authority

treason the offense of attempting to overthrow the government

The Idea of Free Speech Takes Root

It was not until the 1920s that modern, expansive ideas of free speech took root in the United States. The change began with a series of famous dissents by two celebrated Supreme Court Justices, Oliver Wendell Holmes, Jr., and Louis Brandeis. Their dissents argued that controversial speech could not be suppressed unless there was an overwhelming need to preserve a very important government interest. The old test had been whether speech had a "bad tendency" to bring about an evil that the government could prevent. Since most controversial speech can be said to have a "bad tendency" to lead to something unpleasant, the old "bad tendency" test did not provide real protection for dissenters.

THE GRAVE OF THE UNION.
OR MAJOR JACK DOWNING'S DREAM. DRAWN BY ZEKE.

"The Grave of the Union," a political cartoon published in 1864, shows President Lincoln and some of his supporters as undertakers about to bury the Constitution. In 1862, Lincoln had issued a proclamation "directing trial by court martial . . . of all persons who impede the draft, discouraged enlistments or committed other disloyal acts." Some 38,000 people were arrested, denied the right of habeas corpus, and held in jail until brought to trial.

Holmes and Brandeis argued for the introduction of a new test—the "clear and present danger" test—that allowed government to censor speech only if it could be shown that the speech was almost certain to cause the evil immediately, and without any opportunity for counter-speech. Clearly, the "clear and present danger" test is much more protective of speech than the "bad tendency" test. It allows prosecution for things like inciting a riot, since the incitement creates a "clear and present danger" of violence, but protects discussion of controversial ideas and publication of vigorous criticism.

prosecution being charged with a crime and put on trial

An Expansive View Emerges

Although Holmes and Brandeis originally wrote in dissent, their more expansive conception of free speech triumphed. By the 1930s, the Supreme Court was using the First Amendment to overturn convictions for displaying a red flag as a Communist symbol, for giving out controversial leaflets, and for organizing radical political organizations. The 1940s, and the advent of World War II, saw the Supreme Court expand free speech protection.

***West Virginia Board of Education* v. *Barnette*.** In this landmark case, the Court ruled in 1943 that the government could not compel a student to pledge allegiance to the flag in violation of the student's conscientious beliefs.

***Chaplinsky* v. *New Hampshire*.** In this case, also decided in 1943, the Court reaffirmed that so-called "fighting words," face-to-face insults likely to provoke a violent reaction from their target, were a category of speech that could be punished without violating freedom of speech.

McCarthyism

The *Barnette* decision's ringing endorsement of individual freedom was sorely tested in the 1950s. Driven by concerns over national security, the United States embarked on a nationwide search for Communist subversives. McCarthyism, named after Joseph McCarthy, a senator from Wisconsin who was extremely active in searching out people whom he labeled as subversive, was characterized by widespread firings of teachers, and blacklists of Hollywood figures with a left-wing past.

The security frenzy peaked with the criminal prosecution of dozens of leaders of the American Communist Party. In *Dennis* v. *United States* (1951), the Supreme Court rejected the idea that the suppression of the American Communist Party violated fundamental free speech protection. A majority of the justices invoked the Holmes-Brandeis "clear and present danger" test, arguing that the threat of Communist subversion was so great that Congress was entitled to believe that it constituted a "clear and present danger."

suppression preventing the expression of something; to restrain or prohibit

Obscenity

Another significant setback for free speech in the 1950s was the Supreme Court's recognition in a 1957 case, *Roth* v. *United States*, that a category

obscenity material that is indecent, offensive, or disgusting, or to which the prevailing morality is strongly opposed

pornography sexually explicit material that sometimes equates sex with power and violence

erotic tending to arouse sexual desire

J. Robert Kerry, U.S. Senator and former Governor of Nebraska, wrote in an article titled "The Flag Stands for the Freedom to Be Wrong" in the *Washington Post* on July 23, 1989, just after the "flag-burning case" was decided:
"We should look . . . at the two states that do not have anti–flag-burning laws. Ask yourself how it is that Alaska and Wyoming have survived without such laws. Is it because they are less patriotic than the citizens of the other forty-eight states? Is it because they simply were not aware of the great danger that exists to them without such laws? Or is it because they simply recognize that no danger exists?"

of communication about sex, called "**obscenity**," existed and did not qualify for free speech protection. The Court has experienced enormous difficulty in defining exactly what obscenity means, causing Justice Potter Stewart to remark that he could not define obscenity, but he knew it when he saw it.

The current definition, drawn from a 1973 case, *Miller* v. *California*, asks whether the speech "appeals to the prurient interest" by describing sexual conduct in a "patently offensive" way without any "serious literary, artistic, political, or scientific value." Obscenity laws continue to be enforced. The current formulation bans so-called "hard-core" **pornography**, but permits a wide depiction of **erotic** material.

Updating "Clear and Present Danger"

The failure of the "clear and present danger" test to provide effective protection to political dissenters in the 1950s led lawyers and judges in the 1960s and 1970s to explore other ways to preserve free speech.

One approach sought to rescue the original meaning of the Holmes-Brandeis formulation by arguing that judges had an obligation to force the government to prove the existence of a "clear and present danger," rather than merely to assert its existence. The Supreme Court accepted that argument in 1969 in *Brandenburg* v. *Ohio*. This case overturned the conviction of members of the Ku Klux Klan for burning a cross and making vague threats of racial violence. The Court reasoned that while the Klan's speech was repugnant in the extreme, there was no showing that it created an actual "clear and present danger" of unlawful action.

The "Strict Scrutiny" Approach

Under *Brandenburg*, efforts to censor speech must satisfy so-called strict scrutiny. Under this approach, a judge asks four skeptical questions:

1. Is the governmental interest in suppressing the speech important enough to be called "compelling"?
2. Is it clear that the speech, unless suppressed, will actually cause the feared evil to come into being?
3. Is it clear that censorship will prevent the threatened evil from occurring?
4. Are there "less drastic means" short of censorship that could be used to advance the government's interest?

In 1989, in *Texas* v. *Johnson*, a case that many believe to be the most significant free speech decision of the twentieth century, the Supreme Court used "strict scrutiny" to invalidate a Texas state that banned the burning of the American flag as an act of protest.

Protecting Speech Absolutely

A second approach was taken by persons who feared that the "clear and present danger" test gave judges too much power to "balance" free speech against competing government interests. This approach argued that while the government could regulate action, speech was absolutely protected

against government censorship. The so-called speech-action distinction provided greater protection to "speech," but ran into problems when it was applied.

"Speech" as "action." The assertion that speech was absolutely protected failed to account for the government's conceded power to punish threats, blackmail, and extortion. Adherents of the speech-action approach were forced to resort to define such speech artificially as a form of action. In addition, the assertion that action was completely unprotected failed to provide protection for so-called symbolic speech, like wearing armbands, demonstrating, or engaging in other forms of conduct designed to communicate a message.

artificially not naturally or genuinely

Symbolic activity. As the flag burning cases demonstrate, the Supreme Court ultimately provided significant protection to symbolic activity, especially when hostility to the message motivated the effort to stop it. When, however, the government's effort to punish symbolic activity is designed to advance a government interest that is "unrelated to the suppression of ideas," the Court has permitted the government to punish symbolic conduct. This may be done even though the punishment has an "incidental effect" on speech, as long as the statute is "narrowly tailored" to advance the government's non-speech interest. Thus, in *United States* v. *O'Brien* in 1969, the Court affirmed the conviction of opponents of the Vietnam War who burned their draft cards as an act of protest.

Regulating Speech Because of What It Says

A third approach sought to bar the government from regulating speech on the basis of viewpoint or content. Beginning in the 1970s, the Supreme Court imposed a strict requirement of "content neutrality" on any government effort to regulate speech. If a regulation treats one viewpoint more harshly than another viewpoint, the statute is absolutely void. That idea reached its most controversial application when, in *R.A.V.* v. *St. Paul* (1992), the Court overturned a "hate speech" conviction because the statute singled out a particular viewpoint for suppression.

neutrality a state of not being involved on either side

statute a law enacted by the legislative branch of government

Striking students at a sit-in on the University of California, Berkeley, campus. They demonstrated to protest restrictions on political activities that the university had decided to impose.

> "The Founding Fathers gave the free press the protection it must have to bare the secrets of government and inform the people."
>
> —Supreme Court Justice Hugo L. Black (1886–1971)

Using Regulations to Control Speech

Yet a fourth approach focused on the procedures used in regulating speech. It required the government to use specific and "narrowly tailored" regulations that are no broader than absolutely necessary. That idea has resulted in the invalidation of many poorly drafted, or unnecessarily intrusive speech regulations. These included *American Civil Liberties* v. *Reno*, the 1997 decision striking down the first effort to impose federal regulations on the **Internet** because they were too vague, and banned more speech than was necessary to protect children.

Internet a worldwide electronic network of communication that links computer networks and organizational computer facilities

Prior Restraints

A fifth approach focused on the timing of any attempt at censorship. Efforts to impose "**prior restraints**" on speech were viewed as particularly dangerous because prior restraints allowed the government to suppress speech without anyone knowing about it. Chief Justice Charles Evans Hughes warned about prior restraints in *Near* v. *Minnesota* in 1931. The Supreme Court heeded his warning in the Pentagon Papers' case, *New York Times* v. *United States* (1971), when it refused to permit the government to prohibit the *New York Times* and the *Washington Post* from publishing damaging information about the government's Vietnam policies.

prior restraint a law or court order forbidding persons to speak or write something

Symbolic Speech

The Supreme Court also expanded the idea of what kind of behavior counts as speech. In 1957 the Court had taken a narrow view of speech by defining obscenity as outside speech. In the 1960s and 1970s, however, the Court adopted a broad definition of what it called "symbolic speech," covering communicative behavior like wearing black armbands and engaging in mass demonstrations. The treatment of mass marches and demonstrations as protected free speech was crucial to the civil rights movement and the anti–Vietnam War movement.

The symbolic speech idea reached its broadest application in 1989, when the Supreme Court ruled that burning the American flag as a method of protest was a fully protected form of speech, in contrast to the justices' failure to protect young men who, in the 1960s, had burned their draft cards to symbolize opposition to the Vietnam War.

The American Civil Liberties Union (ACLU) is the largest public interest organization devoted to protecting individual rights in the United States. It was founded in 1920 when citizens were sitting in jail for holding antiwar views, and its special concerns remain what they were then—freedom of conscience, equality before the law, due process, and, more recently, the right of privacy. The ACLU has argued or supported nearly every major civil liberties case during this time. It appears before the Supreme Court more often than any other organization except the U.S. Department of Justice. Since the early 1980s, it has also lobbied for the passage of laws reflecting its views. The ACLU is active throughout the country, with branches in all states. It is nonprofit and nonpartisan; it has represented Communists as well as Nazis. Especially at the state and local levels, volunteer lawyers do most of the legal work. In the late 1990s the ACLU had more than 275,000 members. Its founder, Roger Baldwin, said, "So long as we have enough people in this country willing to fight for their rights, we'll be called a democracy."

Commercial Speech

Finally, the Supreme Court dramatically expanded the scope of free speech protection in the 1970s and 1980s by ruling that advertising and other forms of commercial speech are protected by the First Amendment, even though the precise legal protection is somewhat weaker.

Conclusion

It is comforting to believe that free speech is guaranteed by the text of the First Amendment forbidding Congress from making any law that

abridges freedom of speech. But history, and the extremely difficult free speech issues that arise in each generation, tell a different story. They tell us that free speech is an idea that is still being invented. They tell us that free speech is too important to be left to the so-called experts. And they tell us that each generation must fight for its free speech rights. Ultimately, the only enduring protection of free speech is the vigilance of a free people.

FIRST AMENDMENT—Computer Censorship; The First Amendment; Flag Salute Cases; Freedom of the Press: Prior Restraint; Obscenity; Offensive Speech: Fighting Words; Prior Restraints: *Near* v. *Minnesota*; Seditious Libel; Subversive Speech

First Amendment: Continuing Challenges

Burt Neuborne

THE FIRST AMENDMENT TO THE CONSTITUTION STATES

Congress shall make no law . . . abridging the freedom of speech, or of the press; . . .

The 1989 Supreme Court's flag-burning decision illustrates the extraordinary level of free speech protection that exists. But the uneven history of free speech protection makes clear that expansive protection of free speech is a relatively recent phenomenon, and that nothing about free speech is written in stone. Vigorous debate continues about exactly how much speech should be considered free from government regulation.

"Hate Speech"

For example, should victims of "hate speech" be protected against being required to endure the pain of racist or sexist insults? The Supreme Court has recognized that speech cannot be **suppressed** merely because a hearer finds the speech **offensive**. But the Court has also recognized that face-to-face insults that rise to the level of "fighting words" can be suppressed because they create a risk of violence. Is the pain experienced by the target of hate speech the **equivalent** of a risk of violence?

If we allow mere hurt feelings, even the terrible pain of enduring racist or sexist insults, to justify **censorship**, will we damage free speech protection by allowing hearers to dictate what speakers can say? Should we treat violent **pornography** as a form of hate speech aimed at women? If we ban violent pornography as a form of hate speech, are we opening the door to widespread censorship of other controversial forms of speech, like violent rap music?

suppress using force to crush or end something

offensive causing pain, displeasure, or resentment

equivalent equal in value, force, or amount

censorship the official restriction of any expression believed to threaten the political, social, or moral order

pornography sexually explicit material that sometimes equates sex with power and violence

Money and Speech

Another difficult question is how we should treat wealthy speakers who have the power to distort debate by dominating the discussion. Should wealthy persons be limited in how much they can contribute to election campaigns? If so, does not such a limitation interfere with a contributor's ability to advance political ideas? The Supreme Court, in *Buckley* v. *Valeo*

> "One man's vulgarity is another's lyric."
>
> —Supreme Court Justice John Marshall Harlan (1899–1972) in *Cohen* v. *California* (1971)

"In this nation every writer, actor, or producer . . . should be free from the censor."

—Supreme Court Justice William O. Douglas (1898–1980)

in 1976, has upheld restrictions on the amount that can be contributed to a candidate. The importance of money in the political process has increased since then, but the role of free speech in the campaign finance area remains confused.

How to Treat the Mass Media

Yet a third important free speech question is how to treat the mass media. The Supreme Court has firmly ruled, in *Miami Herald Publishing Co.* v. *Tornillo* (1974), that newspapers are entitled to full free speech protection, and cannot be forced to print responses to material appearing in the paper.

Internet a worldwide electronic network of communication that links computer networks and organizational computer facilities

Internet. The Supreme Court's first consideration of the Internet as one of the mass media treated it as an electronic newspaper entitled to maximum free speech protection. Is that the right approach to regulating the Internet?

Television and cable. Television and cable broadcasters may be subject to a greater degree of regulation. For example, when a cable broadcaster acts as a "gatekeeper," making decisions about what channels to carry, the Supreme Court ruled in *Turner Broadcasting System* v. *Federal Communications Commission* [FCC] (1994), the cable broadcaster can be regulated to assure that it does not abuse its gatekeeper authority. And in an intensely controversial ruling, *FCC* v. *Pacifica Foundation* (1978), the Court upheld a regulation banning a George Carlin monologue using seven dirty words from the radio during periods when children are likely to be listening.

The issues at hand. These opinions raise questions such as: Should the government be allowed to limit the number of television stations a single person can own? Would it be a violation of free speech to attempt to regulate the growth of huge corporate conglomerates that own newspapers, television stations, movie studios, and cable networks? Is such a concentration of media ownership wise?

"If we advert [call attention to, or refer] to the nature of republican government, we shall find that the censorial power is in the people over the government, and not in the government over the people."

—James Madison (1751–1836)

"Our First Amendment was a bold effort . . . to establish a country with no legal restrictions upon the subjects people could investigate, discuss, and deny."

—Supreme Court Justice Hugo L. Black (1886–1971)

A poster shows a book, pencil, paintbrush, and lips being destroyed by a pair of scissors, in protest of censorship of free speech and artistic expression.

see also

FIRST AMENDMENT—Access to the Media; Campaign Financing; The Development of Standards; The First Amendment; Group Libel; Hate Speech; Libel and Defamation; *New York Times* v. *Sullivan*; Regulating the Electronic Mass Media

Regulating Adult Speech—for Children

A fourth significant free speech issue is the extent to which speech directed at adults can be regulated in order to protect children. The issue arises most strongly in efforts to ban tobacco advertising in the vicinity of schools and parks.

Usually, speech to adults cannot be banned simply because children might hear it. But the Supreme Court has permitted the government to regulate the time at which certain controversial speech is broadcast on the radio to avoid periods when children would be listening. Does the same principle allow the regulation of billboards advertising cigarettes or liquor in areas where children are likely to see them?

"The incidence [or act of happening] of this enactment [law] is to reduce the adult population of Michigan to reading only what is fit for children . . . Surely, this is to burn the house to roast the pig."
—Supreme Court Justice Felix Frankfurter (1882–1965), in *Butler* v. *Michigan* (1957).

In this case, Frankurter's opinion for the Court overturned a Michigan law which made it illegal to sell a book to the general reading public which contained obscene language "tending to the corruption of the morals of youth."

Hurting Someone's Reputation

Finally, what about libel—false speech in a newspaper or on television that hurts someone's reputation? The Supreme Court has developed a complicated approach to libel. Under *New York Times* v. *Sullivan* (1964), if the target of the speech is a public figure, such as a politician, the figure must prove both that the speech is false and that the newspaper or television station either knew it was false or showed deliberate indifference to the truth before the public figure can receive damages.

That is a very high standard which many persons argue gives the media too much power to act in an irresponsible way. But, unless the media are protected against the threat of financial damages that may ruin them, they may be reluctant to print controversial material at all, leaving us without robust discussion of public affairs—which the First Amendment aims to ensure above all else.

★ The Flag Salute Cases

John P. Frank

THE FIRST AMENDMENT TO THE CONSTITUTION STATES

Congress shall make no law . . . abridging the freedom of speech, or of the press; . . .

It is common in public schools to have students begin the day by saluting the American flag. For most young people, this is an easy activity. However, for children of a religious sect called Jehovah's Witnesses, this is very difficult. Jehovah's Witnesses follow the religious teachings of Charles T. Russell, who in 1870 founded a religious sect based on his vision of the second coming of Christ and other beliefs.

Jehovah's Witnesses across the nation spread their faith by distributing books and pamphlets house to house and on street corners. One of their religious beliefs is that they should not salute the flag because doing so would be bowing down to "graven images." The Ten Commandments

Kindergarden children salute the flag.

in the Bible, in their view, forbid this practice. Because their religious views were very different from those of many other Christians, Jehovah's Witnesses often were unpopular. Some Americans also disliked their house-to-house and street-corner activities. As a result, many people became hostile to them.

Minersville School District v. *Gobitis*

Jehovah's Witnesses' children attending public schools in the late 1930s refused to salute during their class's flag salute exercise. Some of them were expelled from school for refusing to do so. In April of 1940, a case against Jehovah's Witnesses' children, *Minersville School District* v. *Gobitis*, finally reached the Supreme Court. The Court handed down its decision soon afterward, in June of 1940.

A divided court. The Supreme Court's opinion in the case was written by Justice Felix Frankfurter. In this ruling, Frankfurter reported how Lillian Gobitis, age twelve, and her brother William, age ten, had been expelled from the public schools of Minersville, Pennsylvania, for refusing to salute the American flag. The constitutional issue in the case, Frankfurter wrote, was whether "the requirement of participation in such a ceremony, exacted from a child who refuses upon sincere religious grounds, infringes without due process of law the liberty guaranteed by the Fourteenth Amendment."

infringe exceed the limits of, or violate

Frankfurter's ruling concluded that the Supreme Court upheld the children's expulsion because the flag salute laws were laws of general application, designed to teach patriotism. These laws were not aimed at any religion, and they were not intended to restrict religious beliefs. Thus, the Gobitis children could not "be excused from conduct required of all other children in the promotion of national cohesion. . . . National unity is the basis of national security."

All of the justices agreed with the decision except Justice Harlan Fiske Stone. In his dissenting opinion, Justice Stone argued that the children should not have been expelled because they refused "participation in a school ceremony contrary to their religions convictions." He pointed out that the children were ready to obey all the laws except those they sincerely believed conflicted with "the higher commandments of God." Stone concluded that liberty includes the "freedom of the individual from compulsion as to what he shall think and he shall say, at least where the compulsion is to bear false witness to his religion."

Consequences. Many Americans regarded the *Gobitis* decision as a declaration by the Supreme Court that Jehovah's Witnesses were not patriotic citizens. This ruling, together with the fact that the sect was unpopular with many Americans, soon resulted in outbreaks of violence against its followers. The events that followed the Court's ruling were horrifying. Between June 12 and June 20, 1940, hundreds of attacks against Jehovah's Witnesses were reported to the Department of Justice. These incidents occurred during dark days of World War II. France had just surrendered to Germany. The growing danger of the United States getting involved in the war alarmed many Americans.

In Kennebunk, Maine, the sect's religious hall was burned. In Rockville, Maryland, a mob broke up one of the group's Bible meetings. In Litchfield, Illinois, a mob attacked sixty Jehovah's Witnesses, and state troopers had to be called out to protect the group. In Cottonsville, Indina, a number of Jehovah's Witnesses were beaten. In Jackson, Mississippi, members of the sect living there in trailer homes were forced to leave the town. Similar attacks against the group continued for two years. Not only adults but children, too, were victims. Attempts continued to punish Jehovah's Witnesses' children who had been forced to leave school under the "salute or be expelled" regulations. Some people wanted them to go to jail as juvenile delinquents.

***Jones* v. *Opelika*.** All these incidents were described in detail by Victor Rotnem and F. G. Folsom in an article they published in the *American Political Science Review* in 1942. This article, "Recent Restrictions on Religious Liberty," had an enormous influence. Then, in June of 1942, the Supreme Court considered another case, *Jones* v. *Opelika*, also involving Jehovah's Witnesses. In that case, Justices Hugo L. Black, William O. Douglas, and Frank Murphy, who had been part of the majority opinion in the *Gobitis* case, announced that they had changed their minds. Another flag salute case came before the Court the following year. This case, *West Virginia State Board of Education* v. *Barnette*, was decided on June 14, 1943. There were now two new justices on the Court: Robert H. Jackson, appointed in 1941, and Wiley B. Rutledge, appointed in January of 1943.

The *Barnette* case. Justice Jackson wrote the majority opinion for the Supreme Court in the *Barnette* case. Jackson's ruling stated that the authority of the government would not be "impressively vindicated by our confirming power of the state to expel a handful of children from school." He made it clear that the Court favored "individual freedom of mind in preference to officially disciplined uniformity." Justice Jackson pointed to the law Congress passed about the pledge of allegiance. That law provided

authority the power to grant legal allowance to

that it should be recited "by standing with the right hand over the heart." However, he noted, that same act of Congress stated, "Civilians will always show full respect to the flag when the pledge is given by merely standing at attention," and men present taking off their hats.

Justice Jackson, in the *Barnette* case, ruled that the issue was freedom of religion. And freedom of religion could be restricted "only to prevent a grave and immediate danger to interests which the state may lawfully protect." Jackson continued that it was not the job of the government to force people all to hold the same opinions, for "compulsory unification of opinion achieves only the unanimity of the graveyard." Jackson added, "the case is made difficult not because the principles of its decision are obscure, but because the flag involved is our own." However, true patriotism would flourish only if "patriotic ceremonies are voluntary and spontaneous instead of a compulsory routine." Therefore, "The decision of this Court in *Minersville School District* v. *Gobitis*" and any decisions which followed it "are overruled."

Justices Black and Douglas agreed with Jackson's ruling. They declared, "Words uttered under coercion are proof of loyalty to nothing but self-interest. Love of country must spring from willing hearts and free minds. . . . Neither our domestic tranquility in peace nor our martial effort in war depend on compelling little children to participate in a ceremony that ends in nothing for them but a fear of spiritual condemnation." Justice Murphy, who also had been part of the *Gobitis* case majority, also strongly agreed with Jackson. However, Justice Felix Frankfurter, the author of the *Gobitis* decision, wrote a strong dissenting opinion. Justices Owen Roberts and Stanley Reed also did not change their earlier views. By a vote of 6 to 3, the *Gobitis* case was overruled.

In the early 1940s, Jehovah's Witnesses brought so many cases to the Supreme Court that Chief Justice Harlan Fiske Stone suggested that they "ought to have an endowment in view of the aid which they give in solving the legal problems of civil liberties." He thought they performed "a useful service by making [the Court] face again the issue of freedom of speech." Justice William O. Douglas wrote, "Perhaps Stone's tolerance for the religious scruples [doubts] of an unpopular minority went back to World War I, when he served on a board of inquiry to review cases of conscientious objectors who had refused to perform military service. I know from what he told me that it was for him a moving experience."

Summary. The *Barnette* decision in the second flag salute case was a landmark in the history of freedom of speech and religion. It was received peacefully across the country. By this time, the United States was deeply involved in fighting World War II. Americans had many other things to think about than whether children saluted the flag in school. The earlier violence against the Jehovah's Witnesses also died down.

★ Seditious Libel

Dwight L. Teeter, Jr.

THE FIRST AMENDMENT TO THE CONSTITUTION STATES

Congress shall make no law . . . abridging the freedom of speech, or of the press; . . .

Seditious libel makes it a crime to criticize government, government officials, courts, or laws, or to call for its overthrow. A clear measure of the amount of freedom in a society at any time or place is whether one can criticize government without being punished.

An early, notorious example of the cruelty of seditious libel in action involved English printer John Twyn, who in 1663 had printed a book, *A Treatise on the Execution of Justice*, which argued that rulers are accountable

common law the system of judge-made law that began in England and is based on court decisions and custom rather than on statutes passed by legislatures

treason the offense of trying to overthrow the government

prosecution being charged with a crime and put on trial

indictment a formal written statement charging a person or persons with an offense after a grand jury has examined the evidence and found that there is a valid case

disbar expel from the legal profession so that an attorney cannot practice his profession

arbitrary determined by chance, whim, or impulse

to the people and that the people may even take up arms against an unresponsive monarch. Twyn was charged with the common-law law of treason at London's Old Bailey Court. He had not written the book but refused to say who had. The judge pronounced John Twyn guilty, declaring that he should be drawn, quartered, and disemboweled.

The Trial of John Peter Zenger

During the colonial period in America, courts and legislative bodies assumed that they could punish criticism of government. Although there were few prosecutions for seditious libel—perhaps four—in the colonies before 1735, that year brought one of the most famous court battles: the trial of printer John Peter Zenger.

Background. Zenger's newspaper, the *New York Weekly Journal*, took the side of lawyer-politician James Alexander, an opponent of the arrogant and greedy Governor William Cosby. Anonymously, Alexander called Cosby a tyrant; Zenger's *Journal* printed those writings.

Even though the citizens on a grand jury refused to vote a sedition indictment against Zenger, the New York attorney general acted on his own to charge the printer with seditious libel. Zenger was taken into custody and held in jail eight months awaiting trial. During that time, his wife Anna Zenger continued to print the *Journal*, with more attacks on Governor Cosby. Alexander planned to serve as Zenger's attorney, but Chief Justice James De Lancey, a Cosby appointee, disbarred him.

The defense's strategy. Andrew Hamilton—who came from Philadelphia and was one of the finest lawyers in the colonies—replaced Alexander as Zenger's lawyer. Then over sixty years old (and no relation to the yet-unborn Alexander Hamilton), he faced the rigidly unfair law of seditious libel and the court rules supporting it. At the time, a defendant in a seditious libel suit was not allowed to plead truth as a defense. Although Andrew Hamilton argued his case before a jury, the jury was expected to play only a minor role in a seditious libel trial. The jury was expected to find only "the fact" of printing. The judge was to decide the "law"—to rule whether the publication was illegal criticism of the government.

Andrew Hamilton told the jury:

It is the best cause, it is the course of liberty; and I make no doubt that . . . every man who prefers freedom to a life of slavery, will bless and honor you as men who have baffled the attempts of tyranny; and by an impartial and incorrupt verdict have laid a noble foundation [giving] us a right—the liberty—both of exposing and opposing arbitrary power . . . by speaking and writing truth.

"Speaking and writing truth" were audacious words and were not the law, but the jury took them to heart. After deliberating briefly, the jury returned with a verdict of not guilty. The jury had denied the obvious, finding, in effect, that Zenger had not printed the offending words. Although this jury made no new law, the Zenger trial was the last prosecution for seditious libel in the colonies. This case still symbolizes the right of press and public to criticize government and go unpunished.

Seditious Libel in the American Revolution

Independence from Britain did not mean that free expression was guaranteed. Sir William Blackstone's *Commentaries on the Laws of England*, published from 1765 to 1769, rapidly became the most influential explanation of the common law at that time. Blackstone declared: "The liberty of the press is indeed essential to the nature of a free state; but this consists in laying no previous restraints upon publications, and not in freedom from censure for criminal matter [including criticism of government] when published."

Freedom of expression mattered little during the American Revolution. Instead of securing freedom of expression, the Revolution nearly got rid of it. If a person opposed the war, that person left the new United States or kept silent for fear of mob violence. Dissatisfaction with the Articles of Confederation led to the drafting of the Constitution in 1787, but fervent opposition from Anti-Federalists made its ratification difficult.

Articles of Confederation the first constitution of the thirteen original United States; in effect 1781–1789

Anti-Federalist member of the group opposing the adoption of the U.S. Constitution; favored states' rights and argued successfully for the Bill of Rights

ratification process of making a document legal by giving it formal approval

Federalist advocating a strong central government of separate states and the adoption of the U.S. Constitution

compromise an agreement or settlement reached when each side gives up some demands or yields on others

Federalists and Anti-Federalists argued strenuously about the Constitution's merits or demerits. Federalist arguments are remembered because of the "Publius" essays written by James Madison, Alexander Hamilton, and John Jay in *The Federalist Papers* in 1788. Anti-Federalists are less remembered because they were on the losing side of the battle over the Constitution. They responded to Federalist writings with essays such as those written under the name "Centinel."

Anti-Federalist complaints against the Constitution added up to charges of Federalist disregard for civil liberties. These complaints threatened the ratification of the Constitution. Madison crafted a compromise that promised a Bill of Rights that would protect citizens against the national government that the Constitution outlined. On the basis of this promise the Constitution was ratified, and in 1791 the Bill of Rights became part of the Constitution.

The Alien and Sedition Acts

The First Amendment's language seems clear, but arguments over its meaning continue. It says, in part: "Congress shall make no law . . . abridging the freedom of speech, or of the press. . . ." Under such language, criticism of government should have been protected. But those words did not prevent the Federalist Congress from adopting the Alien and Sedition Acts of 1798. Those measures were adopted in a time of war hysteria fanned by Federalists' fears of the anarchy of the French Revolution. They made it a crime to speak or publish false, scandalous, or malicious criticisms of the Congress, the president, or the government with intent to defame or "bring into disrepute." Excluded from the list of those who could not be criticized: the office of vice president. Thomas Jefferson, leader of the Republican opposition to the Federalist Party, was then the vice president.

abridge diminish, reduce

malicious having the intent to cause harm

Political censorship. Fourteen indictments were brought under the Sedition Act. For the most part they targeted prominent editors or

Congressman Matthew Lyon of Vermont was involved in perhaps the most famous prosecution under the Alien and Sedition Act. On the floor of Congress, he said that President John Adams had "a continual grasp for power" and "an unbounded thirst for ridiculous pomp." In 1798 he published a rehash of his remarks in a Vermont newspaper. He was prosecuted for this. He tried to base his defense on the unconstitutionality of the Sedition Act. But Supreme Court Justice William Paterson, who was presiding, refused to admit this defense. The jury convicted Lyon, and he was sentenced to four months in jail. He was reelected to Congress while serving his sentence. In 1801 he had his revenge: he cast the decisive vote that made Thomas Jefferson president—and defeated John Adams.

opposition politicians. Jefferson and Madison led opposition to the Alien and Sedition Acts with the Kentucky and Virginia Resolutions of 1798. This opposition began to define the words of the First Amendment. For example, the Virginia Resolutions—written by Madison—argued that the Alien and Sedition Acts were "leveled against the right of freely examining public characters and measures, and of free communication among the people thereon which has ever been justly deemed the only effectual guardian of every other right."

Supreme Court rulings. The Alien and Sedition Acts lapsed in 1801 during President Jefferson's first term. Outrage created by their unfairness helped Jefferson defeat the Federalists in the election of 1800. After the end of the Acts, Congress did not pass any peacetime seditious libel **statutes** for 140 years. The Supreme Court ruled in both 1812 (*United States* v. *Hudson and Goodwin*) and in 1816 (*United States* v. *Coolidge*) that, under the Constitution, federal courts had no **authority** to declare the existence of "common-law crimes," which would include seditious libel charges created by judges. Courts had to find crimes in statutes.

statute a law enacted by the legislative branch of government

authority the power to grant legal allowance to

Seditious Libel During World War I

Seditious libel statutes and prosecutions show up in times of crisis. The greater the crisis, the more severe the efforts to control expression. The onset of World War I saw numerous states passing laws to make it illegal to advocate overthrow of government. But the federal government had the greatest impact with passage of the Espionage Act of 1917 and its "sedition" amendment in 1918. These statutes outlawed comments that could be **construed** as causing disorder in the armed forces or as interfering with military enlistment or **conscription** (called "the draft" during World War II).

During World War I, **pacifist** remarks were often interpreted as interference with the war effort. Nearly two thousand persons were prosecuted under the Espionage Act, and as many as one hundred newspapers or other periodicals were banned from the mails. Victor Berger edited a well-known Socialist paper, the *Milwaukee Leader.* He had criticized the United States' getting into the war and also munitions makers who profited from death. The postmaster general banned Berger's newspaper from the mails and, when Berger was elected to Congress, the House of Representatives refused to seat him.

construed explained; interpreted

conscription enforced enrollment, particularly for military service

pacifist a person who opposes all wars on moral or religious grounds

The "Clear and Present Danger Test"

A Socialist pamphleteer, Charles Schenck, who urged young men not to submit to conscription for military service in World War I, was convicted of violating the Espionage Act. The Supreme Court in *Schenck* v. *United States* (1919) unanimously upheld his conviction, even though in ordinary times he and his codefendants had a perfect right to express their opinions. "The question," Justice Oliver Wendell Holmes wrote for a unanimous Court, ". . . is whether the words used are in such circumstances and

of such a nature as to create a clear and present danger that they will bring about the substantive evils that Congress has a right to prevent."

The famous language of the "clear and present danger test" kept few people prosecuted under the Espionage Act or similar state statutes from going to jail during the World War I period. The Supreme Court basically chose to ignore whether words created a "clear and present danger." The legal test became whether a defendant's words created a "bad tendency" of harm to government. Nevertheless, the Espionage Act of 1917 remained on the books at the end of the twentieth century.

Victories for First Amendment freedoms came in odd packages. In 1925, the Supreme Court upheld the conviction of Benjamin Gitlow, editor of *Revolutionary Age*. Gitlow, without noticeable effect, had been arguing for mass struggle and overthrow of the bourgeoisie through revolution. But in confirming his conviction by the New York courts, the Court in effect "nationalized" the free speech and free press provisions of the First Amendment. These provisions were now applicable not only to Congress but to the individual states.

A Ku Klux Klan poster showing a triumphant white man holding a naked sword aloft over the head of a vanquished black man.

Sedition in World War II and Beyond

As war threatened in 1940, Congress passed the Alien Registration Act. This law made it a crime to advocate violent overthrow of government. It was the first peacetime sedition act since the Alien and Sedition Acts of 1798 and was aimed primarily at the Communist Party. In one sense this law—often called the Smith Act after its chief sponsor, Representative Howard W. Smith of Virginia—was less repressive than the Alien and Sedition Acts of 1798. The 1798 statutes were used to punish mere criticism of Congress and government officials. The Smith Act, on the other hand, specified that prosecution could be only for advocating violent overthrow of government. Although perhaps one hundred persons were fined or imprisoned after Smith Act convictions from 1940 to 1960, it faded into disuse and ultimately was repealed in 1977.

repeal revoke or cancel

The essence of the crime of seditious libel is using the power of government to punish and silence criticism. By the 1960s, government officials did not have the weapon of seditious libel available, so some officials tried to substitute civil lawsuits for libel—court actions seeking huge financial payments by the media—by claiming that their reputations had been damaged by publications or broadcasts. In effect, seditious libel was put in new clothes when the *New York Times* was sued for carrying a full-page advertisement criticizing police for vicious attacks on the Reverend Martin Luther King, Jr., and other men and women including the "freedom marchers," struggling for equal rights in the South.

In *New York Times* v. *Sullivan* in 1964, the Supreme Court held that to collect monetary damages in a civil libel suit, a government official must meet a heavy burden of proof. Writing for the Court, Justice William J. Brennan, Jr., declared that the First Amendment requires that in order to win a lawsuit for defamatory falsehood, a public official must prove "actual malice"; that the material complained of was published with knowledge of falsity or with reckless disregard for truth. That actual malice formula

makes it difficult for public officials to sue the news media. The Court's ruling in favor of the *New York Times* means that the right to criticize government and government officials without retaliation is quite secure.

The Law at the Close of the Century

A critical test for sedition law came in 1969 in the Supreme Court's decision in *Brandenburg* v. *Ohio.* Brandenburg, a Ku Klux Klan leader, had been convicted in a state court under an Ohio statute forbidding advocacy of criminal violence or terrorism to achieve political ends. He had threatened "revengeance" against the president, Congress, and the Supreme Court for suppression of "the white, Caucasian race."

suppression preventing the expression of something; to restrain or prohibit

The Court reversed the conviction, saying that the First Amendment does "not permit a State to forbid . . . advocacy of the use of force or of law violation except where such advocacy . . . is likely to incite or produce such action."

At the end of the twentieth century, the old doctrine of seditious libel certainly could not be declared dead, but at least it is not active. But as civil libertarians have learned over the years, the fight against the concept of seditious libel—and for the right to criticize government and government officials—can never be taken for granted.

FIRST AMENDMENT—The Development of Standards; Freedom of Speech: The Early Years; Libel and Defamation; *New York Times* v. *Sullivan*; Subversive Speech

Subversive Speech

Michael R. Belknap

THE FIRST AMENDMENT TO THE CONSTITUTION STATES

Congress shall make no law . . . abridging the freedom of speech, or of the press; . . .

The First Amendment declares, "Congress shall make no law . . . abridging freedom of speech, or of the press. . . ." Although expressed in absolute terms, its prohibition is in fact an elastic one. With the exception of Justice Hugo Black—who almost always insisted that "no law" means no law—virtually all judges, legal scholars, and politicians have agreed that Congress may place some restrictions on what we say and print. The question with which they have long wrestled is how far it may go in limiting expression. The most heated debates on that issue have arisen out of governmental efforts to stifle criticism of the government itself. Supreme Court decisions in subversive speech cases have extended considerable constitutional protection to extremely unpopular words and ideas. The Court did not stretch the First Amendment far enough to do that until well into the twentieth century, however. Furthermore, during periods of great public passion, it has often read the First Amendment narrowly enough to allow authorities to abridge the speech of political dissenters.

English Prosecutions for Criticizing the Government

Colonial authorities would not have questioned the right of the government to do that. Beginning in 1476, the English king required that anyone wishing to print anything first secure a license from a royal official, who was empowered to censor out any passages he considered objectionable. Even after this system of "prior restraint" ended in 1694, Englishmen who criticized the government remained vulnerable to criminal prosecution. English judges interpreted the law of treason so broadly that until 1720 someone could be executed merely for trying to publish a book that questioned the king's authority.

censor examine in order to suppress any material considered to be objectionable

prior restraint a law or court order forbidding persons to speak or write something

prosecution being charged with a crime and put on trial

authority the power to grant legal allowance to

seditious libel the publication of material that encourages the disruption or overthrow of the government

statute a law enacted by the legislative branch of government

Even after English judges ceased punishing dissent as treason, they continued to enforce the common law of seditious libel. A 1275 statute outlawed any false news or tales that might cause discord between the king and his people or the great men of the realm. Judges expanded upon that law until even true statements that damaged the reputations of public officials became punishable. They reasoned that these did more damage than false assertions because people were more likely to believe them. Punishing those who criticized their rulers did not violate freedom of expression, Sir William Blackstone argued in his *Commentaries on the Law of England* (1765–1769) (from which most American lawyers in the late eighteenth and early nineteenth centuries learned their law). According to Blackstone, "The liberty of the press [consists] in laying no previous restraints upon publication and not in freedom from censure for criminal matter when published.

Free Speech and Press in America

Licensing of the press lasted longer in America than in England, and seditious libel was a crime in the colonies as well as in the mother country. Not many people were prosecuted for that offense, however, and in the most famous colonial seditious libel trial, a jury acquitted New York printer John Peter Zenger, who had published harsh attacks on an unpopular governor. Considerable disagreement remains among scholars about the extent to which political dissent was tolerated in colonial America.

The Framers' intent. There is also disagreement about what the First Amendment was intended to do. Some commentators contend that all the Congress that drafted it was trying to accomplish was to write Blackstone's version of freedom of the press into the Constitution. Others insist that the First Amendment was supposed to eliminate the common law of seditious libel and establish a constitutional right to criticize the government.

common law the system of judge-made law that began in England and is based on court decisions and custom rather than on statutes passed by legislatures

Federalist advocating a strong central government of separate states and the adoption

The Sedition Act. If those were its purposes, the First Amendment did not accomplish them during the 1790s. In 1798 the Federalists, who controlled Congress, enacted the Sedition Act. It was a legal weapon for use in attacking their rivals, the Jeffersonian Republicans. The Sedition

malicious having the intent to cause harm

Act made it a crime to publish with the intent to defame any false, scandalous, or malicious writings about the government, either house of Congress, or the president; to bring any of these into contempt or disrepute; to incite the public against them, or to stir up sedition or excite unlawful combinations to resist federal law or presidential action of the U.S. Constitution.

This law was actually somewhat more favorable to critics of the government than the common law of seditious libel, for it required prosecutors to prove malicious intent, made truth a defense, and allowed a jury of ordinary citizens (rather than a judge) to decide whether a given statement was defamatory. But it was administered in such a highly partisan manner that these improvements had little practical effect. Only Jeffersonians were prosecuted, and juries stacked with Federalists convicted all of them (including one member of Congress). Despite this persecution, the Republicans captured both Congress and the presidency in the 1800 elections. The Sedition Act expired, and President Thomas Jefferson pardoned all of those who had been convicted under it. Although Republicans argued passionately that this law violated the First Amendment, the Supreme Court never ruled on its constitutionality.

The First Amendment in the Supreme Court

abolitionist person favoring principles or measures fostering the end of slavery

Indeed, the Court said little about the First Amendment for more than a century. The principal reason for this was that it did not apply to the states. In 1833, the Court held that only the national government was required to comply with the provisions of the Bill of Rights. State officials often punished dissenting expression. Those in the South, for example, vigorously persecuted abolitionist speech. But they did not thereby violate the First Amendment. In 1868, the Fourteenth Amendment became part of the Constitution, and in 1925 the Supreme Court announced that the "liberty" of which it said no state could deprive any person without due process of law included freedom of speech and press. Until then, only the national government could violate the Constitution by abridging those rights. For constitutional reasons, it was comparatively inactive throughout most of the nineteenth century.

allegedly asserted to be true without or before proving

writ of habeas corpus (Latin, "produce the body") a court command to produce the person being held in order to determine whether the person's detention is lawful; a way of making sure that a criminal trial has been fair

The great exception was the Civil War, during which federal officials rounded up thousands of allegedly disloyal civilians. Some of these persons had engaged in treasonous conduct, such as guerrilla warfare, but others had done nothing more than criticize the Lincoln administration and its policies. By current legal standards, many of these arrests violated the First Amendment. Because Lincoln suspended the writ of habeas corpus, however, most of the victims had no way to get a judge to pass on the legality of their confinement. Like the Sedition Act controversy, the Civil War produced no Supreme Court decision interpreting the First Amendment.

Free Speech After World War I

The Court's first important rulings explaining what it prohibited were products of World War I. During that conflict, Congress passed two laws

insubordination failure to recognize or submit the authority of a superior officer

that appeared to abridge freedom of speech and press. The Espionage Act of 1917 made it a crime to cause or attempt to cause insubordination in the armed forces, to obstruct recruiting or enlistment, or to make or convey false statements with the intent to interfere with military operations. The Sedition Act of 1918 criminalized urging the decrease of war production and saying anything intended to obstruct the sale of war bonds. Its most repressive provision made it a crime to utter, print, write, or publish any disloyal, profane, or abusive language intended to cause contempt for the form of government, Constitution, or flag of the United States, or even the uniforms of its soldiers and sailors.

Federal judges denied that these laws violated the First Amendment. Most of them took the position that the government could constitutionally punish any speech or writing that might tend to cause someone to violate the law. This was so even if the speaker or writer did not advocate unlawful action. For example, in 1919 the Supreme Court upheld the Espionage Act conviction of Socialist party leader Eugene V. Debs for giving a speech in which he did little more than express his opposition to the war and his sympathy for those who had been convicted earlier for encouraging draft resistance.

Justice Louis Brandeis wrote in his concurring opinion in *Whitney* v. *California*, "Those who won our independence by revolution were not cowards. They did not fear political change. They did not exalt [elevate or glorify] order at the cost of liberty. To courageous, self-reliant men, with confidence in the power of free and fearless reasoning through the processes of popular government, no danger flowing from speech can be deemed clear and present, unless the incidence of the evil apprehended [caught or seized] is so imminent that it may befall [happen] before there is opportunity for full discussion. If there be time to expose through discussion the falsehood and fallacies [departure from truth], deviation to avert [avoid] the evil by the processes of education, the remedy to be applied is more speech, not enforced silence."

"Clear and Present Danger"

One member of the Court did put forward a different test for determining whether words were outside the protection of the First Amendment, and thus could be punished by the government. In *Schenck* v. *United States* (1919), Justice Oliver Wendell Holmes, Jr., declared: "The question in every case is whether the words used are used in such circumstances and are of such a nature as to create a clear and present danger that they will bring about the substantive evils that Congress has a right to prevent."

The Holmes-Brandeis rule. It is not entirely clear what Holmes meant by these words, which he included in an opinion upholding Espionage Act convictions of several Philadelphia socialists, who had urged men subject to the draft to assert their rights. He and Justice Louis Brandeis expanded upon and explained his "clear and present danger test" in a series of opinions they wrote criticizing decisions upholding convictions of radical victims of the postwar "red scare" in *Abrams* v. *United States* (1919), *Gitlow* v. *New York* (1925), and *Whitney* v. *California* (1927). Brandeis provided what came to be regarded as the classic formulation of the rule they advocated in *Whitney*, where he wrote that in order to justify suppression of free speech, there must be reasonable ground to fear that a serious evil would immediately result from the practice of this right.

suppression preventing the expression of something; to restrain or prohibit

The flag salute decision. Although Holmes and Brandeis developed the clear and present danger test in dissenting opinions, a majority of the Supreme Court had accepted it by the late 1930s. The justices used it during World War II to overturn the Espionage Act conviction of a supporter of Germany who had mailed out literature urging the occupation of the United States by foreign troops. The Court also used it in ruling, in 1943, that public school students could not be required to salute the flag. In this case Justice Robert Jackson wrote, "It is now a commonplace

that censorship or suppression of expression of opinion is tolerated by our Constitution only when the expression presents a clear and present danger of action of a kind the State is empowered to prevent and punish."

Protestors picketing anti-Communist hearings in Seattle, Washington, in 1948. The Cold War prompted the Supreme Court to support the government's efforts at prosecuting the leaders of the American Communist party.

Should Communists at Home Be Allowed Free Speech?

In *Dennis* v. *United States* (1951), a Supreme Court majority rejected the proposition that Jackson had characterized as "commonplace" only a few years earlier. The reason was the Cold War between the United States and the Soviet Union and the almost hysterical fear of Communism that it inspired. The government prosecuted the leaders of the American Communist party under a law called the Smith Act, which made it a crime to enter into an agreement to teach and advocate the violent overthrow of the government or to set up a group to do that. The Communists denied that the philosophy they taught and advocated, Marxism-Leninism, included among its principles the violent overthrow of the government. But even if it did, any revolution that might result from their agreement to teach it would not occur for years. There was, in other words, no clear and present danger.

Under the Holmes-Brandeis rule, the Communists' conviction violated the First Amendment. In order to hold that it did not and send them to jail, the Supreme Court changed the test. It announced that what determined whether a restriction on speech was justified was the gravity of the evil, discounted by the improbability of its happening. Since a revolt against the government was a very great evil, it did not matter that it was extremely unlikely to occur as a result of Communists conspiring to teach and advocate Marxism-Leninism.

Greater Tolerance

McCarthyism [after Senator Joseph McCarthy of Wisconsin (1908–1957)] a political attitude of the 1950s "red scare," characterized by indiscriminate, unsubstantiated attacks on individuals suspected of Communist sympathies, activities, or ties

The *Dennis* decision reflected the impact of McCarthyism on the United States. As this anti-Communist hysteria faded away and the political climate grew more liberal, the Supreme Court became more tolerant of subversive speech.

***Yates* v. *United States* (1957).** In this case the Court significantly modified *Dennis*, holding that in order to be constitutional, a conviction under the Smith Act required proof of "advocacy of action" (urging a course of action) rather than just advocacy of belief.

***Bond* v. *Floyd* (1966).** Here, the Court ruled that the Georgia legislature could not refuse to seat a duly elected member because he had criticized the federal government's Vietnam policy and the Selective Service system or because of his involvement with an organization that had expressed sympathy for men who resisted the draft.

***Watts* v. *United States* (1969).** With this case, the Court even overturned a conviction under a law making it a crime to threaten the life of the president. The defendant had announced at an anti-war rally that if the government ever made him carry a gun, the first man he wanted to get in his sights was Lyndon Johnson, but the Court said the First Amendment protected such "political hyperbole."

> "The defendants have as much right to publish [Bolshevik literature] as the government has to publish the Constitution."
>
> —U.S. Supreme Court Justice Oliver Wendell Holmes, Jr., in *Abrams* v. *United States* (1919)

A new test for subversive speech. The same year that it decided Watts, the Supreme Court announced a new test for determining what speech could be punished without violating the constitutional prohibition against abridging freedom of speech and press. It was even more protective of subversive expression that the clear and present danger test. In *Brandenburg* v. *Ohio* (1969), the Court reversed the conviction of a Ku Klux Klansman who had made a speech in which he declared that the Klan was going to march on Congress and included vague threats that it might someday take revenge on Congress, the president or the Supreme Court. The Court said someone could be punished for advocating the use of force or violation of the law only if he advocated doing so immediately and did this employing words "likely to incite or produce such action."

Conclusion

Since 1969, all speech and writing that attacks the government or its leaders which does not meet this "*Brandenburg* test" has been protected by the First Amendment. That does not mean that it always will be. If the United States should again be gripped by the sort of domestic political hysteria from which it suffered during World War I and the Cold War, the Supreme Court might again contract that guarantee of liberty of expression. Some words are so subversive of American values and institutions that they can be prohibited without abridging freedom of speech and freedom of the press. Which words those are changes with the mood of the country and the decisions of the Supreme Court.

see also

ARTICLE I—Writ of Habeas Corpus; FIRST AMENDMENT—The Development of Standards; Flag Salute Cases; Freedom of Speech: The Early Years; *New York Times* v. *Sullivan*; Freedom of the Press: Prior Restraint; Seditious Libel

Index to Volume 2

Note: Page numbers in **boldface** indicate main discussion of topic.

A

B

C

S

T